Being and Dwelling through Tourism

Much of the existing literature seeks to make sense of tourism based on singular approaches such as visuality, identity, mobility, performance and globalised consumption. What is missing, however, is an overarching framework within which these valuable approaches can be located. This book offers one such framework using the concept of dwelling taken from Heidegger and Ingold as the starting point from which to consider the interrelatedness of being, dwelling and tourism.

The anthropological focus at the core of the book is infused with multidisciplinary perspectives that draw on a variety of subjects including philosophy, material cultural studies and cultural geography. The main themes include sensuous, material, architectural and earthly dwelling and each chapter features a discussion of the unifying theoretical framework for each theme, followed by an illustrative focus on specific aspects of tourism.

This theoretically substantive book will be of interest to anyone involved with tourism research from a wide range of disciplines including anthropology, sociology, geography, cultural studies, leisure studies and tourist studies.

Catherine Palmer is a social anthropologist at the University of Brighton, UK. She is the joint book series editor for the Routledge Advances in Tourism Anthropology. Her publications and research interests encompass identity, heritage and materiality; post conflict/memorial landscapes; cultures of the coast/seaside; embodiment and the lived experience.

New Directions in Tourism Analysis

Series Editor: Dimitri Ioannides

E-TOUR, Mid Sweden University, Sweden

For a full list of titles in this series, please visit www.routledge.com/New-Directions-in-Tourism-Analysis/book-series/ASHSER1207

Although tourism is becoming increasingly popular both as a taught subject and an area for empirical investigation, the theoretical underpinnings of many approaches have tended to be eclectic and somewhat underdeveloped. However, recent developments indicate that the field of tourism studies is beginning to develop in a more theoretically informed manner, but this has not yet been matched by current publications.

The aim of this series is to fill this gap with high quality monographs or edited collections that seek to develop tourism analysis at both theoretical and substantive levels using approaches which are broadly derived from allied social science disciplines such as Sociology, Social Anthropology, Human and Social Geography, and Cultural Studies. As tourism studies covers a wide range of activities and sub fields, certain areas such as Hospitality Management and Business, which are already well provided for, would be excluded. The series will therefore fill a gap in the current overall pattern of publication.

Suggested themes to be covered by the series, either singly or in combination, include: consumption; cultural change; development; gender; globalisation; political economy; social theory; and sustainability.

41 Metropolitan Commuter Belt Tourism
Edited by Michał Jacenty Sznajder

42 Performing Cultural Tourism
Communities, Tourists and Creative Practices
Edited by Susan Carson and Mark Pennings

43 Advances in Social Media for Travel, Tourism and Hospitality
New Perspectives, Practice and Cases
Edited by Marianna Sigala and Ulrike Gretzel

44 Being and Dwelling through Tourism
An Anthropological Perspective
Catherine Palmer

Being and Dwelling through Tourism

An Anthropological Perspective

Catherine Palmer

LONDON AND NEW YORK

First published 2018
by Routledge
2 Park Square, Milton Park, Abingdon, Oxon OX14 4RN

and by Routledge
605 Third Avenue, New York, NY 10017

First issued in paperback 2021

Routledge is an imprint of the Taylor & Francis Group, an informa business

Publisher's Note
The publisher has gone to great lengths to ensure the quality of this reprint but points out that some imperfections in the original copies may be apparent.

British Library Cataloguing-in-Publication Data
A catalogue record for this book is available from the British Library

Library of Congress Cataloging-in-Publication Data
A catalog record for this book has been requested

Typeset in Sabon
by Apex CoVantage, LLC

ISBN 13: 978-1-03-224203-3 (pbk)
ISBN 13: 978-1-4094-2248-8 (hbk)

DOI: 10.4324/9781315568959

For Adrian

Contents

Preface and acknowledgements

This book is a conversation about the relationship between anthropology and tourism and like the best conversations it hopes to draw people in by exciting their curiosity and by offering an interesting point of view. I do not assume those of you who read this book think in the same way as me or that you will be convinced by my argument. What I do hope is that by the end of the book most readers will have been able to find something of interest because ultimately I hope to stimulate further conversations about the ideas presented here.

I was inspired to write the book after reading *The Perception of the Environment* by Tim Ingold. In this book Ingold sets out what he refers to as a dwelling perspective. This perspective was and still is particularly inspiring because at the time of reading the book I was seeking a wider, more holistic understanding of how the activity of tourism can shed light on the experience of being human. Ingold's focus on dwelling as a way of being-in-the-world is a particularly useful way of thinking through tourism because it enables tourism to be located within the totality of life and of living. Within this totality, gazing, mobility, worldmaking, identity, performance and so on, are all aspects of being and dwelling through tourism because they are part of the experience of life.

Given that a basic concern of anthropology is to understand how people who occupy the same space and time in terms of the history and geology of the earth can make very different lives, then it is surprising that anthropologists have yet to fully explore what dwelling through tourism might reveal about the experience of being human. This is what I hope to address with this book.

Although the book's heartbeat is anthropological, there is a slightly undisciplined air about my approach in that it draws from a variety of other disciplines and subject areas when doing so serves to influence my anthropological theorising of tourism. As such, my conversation includes philosophy, sociology, material cultural studies and cultural geography. This reflects the fact that a focus on being human generally and in relation to the meaning-making potential of tourism is not solely the preserve of anthropologists. Contributions from beyond the discipline are included because they contribute to anthropology's overarching mission to offer a holistic understanding of human experience.

The thinking that underpins this book draws inspiration from the work of many tourism scholars not all of whom are anthropologists, but all have in numerous ways challenged me to see and think differently. In relation to anthropology I do need to highlight the work of Tim Ingold and Michael Jackson. I am indebted to both of them for two main reasons. Firstly, because how and what they think has produced some of the most stimulating contributions to my conversation, and secondly, because their engaging and eloquent style of writing demonstrates that insight does not have to be complex. Then there is Heidegger.

Heidegger is a major part of this book because it was the discovery of *Building Dwelling Thinking*, his philosophical essay from the 1950s that inspired me to invite philosophy into my conversation. Whilst some of Heidegger's concepts have had a significant influence on my thinking the dense impenetrability of much of his writing leaves me rather cold. So, I cannot warm to him completely. In addition, my understanding of anthropology differs from that of Heidegger's (1962) who criticised anthropology (together with psychology and biology) for failing to focus on the ontological essence of being human. To my mind there is no such essence to be found through anthropology because anthropology is interested in the similarities and differences among human societies rather than in finding 'an unequivocal and ontologically adequate answer to the question about the *kind of Being* which belongs to those entities which we ourselves are' (Heidegger 1962: 75 original italic).

My use of Heidegger is, therefore, selective and contextualised within my anthropological approach to understanding human experience in all its fascinating diversity. In using Heidegger I am fully aware of the fact that he is a controversial figure because of his engagement with Nazi Germany, an engagement that has turned him into a sort of *philosopher non grata* for many academics (see Wolin 2016 for a detailed discussion of politics, philosophy and Heidegger). As a result, using Heidegger can be fraught with difficulties and Thomas (1999) provides a good discussion of the challenges and contradictions of doing so in relation to archaeology. Nonetheless, my conversation will not debate the philosophical technicalities of what Heidegger 'means' or make judgements as to the merits or otherwise of his philosophy; others are far more qualified than I to do so (see Bourdieu 1991; Dreyfus 1991; Philipse 1998; Malpas 2008). Nor will I use tourism to produce a 'reading' of Heidegger. Instead I use Heidegger as the starting point from which to fashion an anthropological interrogation of tourism in order to think through what dwelling through tourism might reveal about the experience of being human.

As indicated above, being for me is about being human in the sense of being alive, as Ingold (2011a) argues in the essays included in his book of that name. Being, for me, is not about an existential search for some form of authentic self, which in any case does not exist. What I am interested in is the experience of *being human* – in-the-world and the hyphenation here is deliberate because it highlights that human and world are as inseparable as mind and body. What humans are, what they think and what they do influences and is influenced by their engagement in (what Heidegger referred to as being absorbed in) the everyday components that make up the world. As, Heidegger argued '[t]he compound expression 'Being-in-the-world' indicates in the very way we have coined it, that it stands for a *unitary* phenomenon' (1962: 78, original emphasis).

My philosophical approach to being human-in-the-world aims to think more deeply about the components and activities that people engage with as they construct a meaningful life, activities such as tourism. In this sense, looking beneath the surface of our individual and collective engagement in the world through tourism is no different to the thinking that has opened up other aspects of life such as shopping (Miller 1998a), watching television (Scannell 2014) or hunting for food Willerslev 2007).

There is a caveat to my looking beneath the surface because the tourism that features in my conversation is necessarily one that reflects my Anglo-Western outlook. No matter how hard I try to see things through the eyes and experience of someone else I can never truly experience their past or inhabit their present. Likewise, tourism is not an activity open to everyone, and not all those who work in or are affected by tourism are able to exercise agency over their working lives. When I talk about tourism, these realities are always in my mind but they are not the primary focus of this particular conversation.

In addition, my conversation will not be unpicking the influence of politics, economics, technology, the environment and so on, or be exposing issues of power, authority and inequality in each chapter. Of course all such aspects speak of and through culture and the areas I discuss are inherently political and politicised since everything to do with tourism operates in and is conditioned by the global forces of capitalism. It is just to say that the role and implications of what Headrick (1981) refers to as *The Tools of Empire* are not what drive my thinking at this moment in time. Readers are instead pointed to the rich and extensive literature that already exists related to tourism, a few examples of which are Palmer (1994), Church and Coles (2007), Macleod and Carrier (2010), Huberman (2012) and Bianchi (2014).

I could not have started or finished this conversation without the support of my friends and colleagues at the University of Brighton, Jo-Anne Lester, Helen Atkinson and Tom Carter and of course my family, Adrian, Charlotte and Harry – all of whom have contributed ideas, challenged my thinking, given hugs and produced chocolate at appropriate times. I also need to give a huge thank you to Routledge for their patience in waiting for me to submit the manuscript. I'm afraid my thinking has more in common with the tortoise than the hare. It remains to be said that all the omissions, contradictions, mumbled speech and muddled thinking are my own.

1 Being and dwelling

Introduction

Much of the literature about tourism seeks to explore and make sense of tourism by adopting approaches that focus on particularities such as visuality, identity, mobility, myth making, tourism as a type of performance, as a networked ordering of modernity, or as a form of globalised consumption or worldmaking. Although such approaches are extremely insightful and important in relation to how we think about, create and experience the world through the activity of tourism, what is missing is a unifying framing within which they can be located. My purpose here is to set out one such framing, a framing woven out of the theoretical threads of anthropology. Threads that above all else seek a wider, more holistic understanding of how the activity of tourism enables us individually and collectively to recognise, to know and to feel that we are human, even though this may well be an unconscious recognition; in effect to shed light on the experience of being human.

In saying this I am not advocating a Grand Theory of everything, as this is neither desirable nor achievable; tourism, as a human experience, is far too complex and multi-faceted to be tied down in such a way. It is too nuanced and intricately woven in with the doing and being of life with thinking and feeling. Furthermore, there are different perspectives on how to approach and how to frame tourism depending upon the questions to be asked and the disciplinary and or ideological allegiance of the individual asking the questions; as Lowenthal once remarked 'every generation finds new facts and invents new concepts to deal with them' (1961: 245). A good example of Lowenthal's point here is the use of performance as a paradigm and a metaphor for exploring and analysing human culture, relationships and behaviour (see Goffman 1969; Turner 1974, 1982). The word and the concept of performance have been adopted by many academics (myself included) as a useful approach for exploring aspects of social life and behaviour. Indeed, the concept of performance has almost become something of a foundation metaphor for describing what tourists do and how tourism works (Edensor 1998; Haldrup and Larsen 2010; Rickley-Boyd et al. 2014). This is despite

Saldaña's (2006: 1092) poetic denunciation of the way in which *performance* has been 'overused and abused' by many academic communities. However, my view is that uncovering the complex nuances of everyday life requires a wide angled lens in order to frame the questions to be asked and performance as both paradigm and metaphor is one such lens.

I am continually fascinated by the many and varied philosophical and theoretical positions seeking to explore and to understand the contexts and the consequences of tourism on people, place and nature and the role of tourism in terms of being human (see Selwyn 1996; Franklin 2004; Sheller and Urry 2004; Hollinshead 2007; Ren 2011). The framework I am proposing is contextualised from within an anthropological perspective that views tourism as a significant human activity capable of providing insights into the experience of being human. Or more precisely, experience in the plural, as there is no singular experience but a myriad of experiences from the individual to the collective. Whilst I am not claiming that anthropology is the only discipline interested in meaning making through tourism, I am arguing that anthropology has a unique contribution to make to the study of tourism. This is because anthropologists are interested in people first and foremost, an interest encapsulated in the overarching aim to uncover what being human means and *how* we make ourselves human (Csordas 1994). Key to understanding the diversity of human experience is to focus on how people live their lives and on the differences and similarities between people, including differing notions of what a 'good life' might mean (Eriksen 2004). Tourism is for many – although by no means all people – a taken-for-granted activity capable of fleshing out what a 'good life' might look and feel like. As the writer Alain de Botton rather succinctly puts it:

> If our lives are dominated by a search for happiness, then perhaps few activities reveal as much about the dynamics of this quest – in all its ardour and paradoxes – than our travels. They express, however inarticulately, an understanding of what life might be about, outside the constraints of work and the struggle for survival.
>
> (2002: 9)

Anthropology is particularly appropriate because of the discipline's overarching aim to explore and better understanding the experience of being human in all its fascinating diversity. Within this broad aim social anthropology concerns itself with the social and cultural world of the individual, of societies, groups and communities. This concern manifests itself in the study of culture in its broadest unbounded sense, taking in what is general and specific, tangible and intangible about the lifeworld of others. The concept of lifeworld (*lebenswelt*) originates with the German philosopher Husserl (1970[1936]) and refers to a world that is familiar, a world that is *lived-in* and experienced by the individual on a daily basis and from which knowledge, meaning and understanding emerge through involvement with both human and nonhuman *others*. In effect it is the experience of *Being Alive* (Ingold 2011a) in relation to such as objects, technological systems, animals, nature, the weather and so forth (Buttimer 1976; Seamon 1979; 2000). Nature is significant here as it provides the enveloping context within which life is lived through experience, as Dewey argues:

> experience is *of* as well as *in* nature. It is not experience which is experienced, but nature – stones, plants, animals, diseases, health, temperature, electricity and so on. Things interacting in certain ways *are* experience; they are what is experienced. Linked in certain other ways with another natural object – the human organism – they are *how* things are experienced as well. Experience thus reaches down into nature; it has depth.
> (1958: 4a, original emphasis)

Involvement with others thus encompasses all that humans do across the broad spectrum of the lifeworld from hunting for food, weaving cloth and growing crops to driving a car, building a house and going on holiday. As the anthropologist Michael Jackson states 'meaning emerges not from isolated contemplation of the world but from active engagement in it' (2007: xi). Through active engagement the Cartesian-inspired dualism that separates subject and object, mind and body is dissolved in the coming together of doing and thinking, feeling and sensing as expressions of human existence. In effect to be embedded in the world, what Heidegger described as being-in-the-world. In highlighting the significance of experience I am aligning myself with an approach closely associated with Jackson, that of phenomenological anthropology. Here everyday life provides the key to thinking about and understanding the human condition, 'thought is always tied to mundane interests, material matters, cultural preoccupations and everyday situations' as such anthropology should focus on 'how thought may be anchored in rather than abstracted from human lifeworlds' (Jackson 2009: 236).

I am interested in what might emerge as a result of thinking in relation to tourism since tourism is for many people part of everyday life whether this is in terms of working in tourism or dreaming about tourism. It is worth noting at this point that references to everyday life or for that matter to the lifeworld should not ignore the fact that there are a myriad of different everyday *lives* and lifeworlds, many of which are experienced as a cold, hungry fight for survival. The everyday life of a miner for example is very different to that of the mine owner; the farm worker to that of the farm owner and so on, such that like culture everyday life 'must be situated, placed in a context – historically, economically, politically' (Keesing 1987: 162).

Among the most significant aspects of the lifeworld of interest to anthropologists are those relating to the where, how and under what conditions people live out their lives. For example the spaces and places in which people live, the social relationships and beliefs by which they live and the political, economic and environmental conditions within and against which they live, including the systems adopted for maintaining order and social cohesion. These conditioning constituents inform, transform, maintain or disrupt human social activity and thereby frame the ways in which individuals engage with and in the world around them. This engagement in the world has been studied from a variety of different yet frequently interweaving perspectives. Perspectives that have become established themes within the pantheon of anthropological theory such as work, play, faith, customs, kinship and cosmology. However, these themes are not exhaustive as the scope of anthropological enquiry necessarily reaches far and wide in its uncovering of what it means to be human. So, alongside the established themes the richness and depth of the human experience is also revealed in theorising linked to aspects such as 'Power, Change . . . Oppression . . . Passion, Authority, Beauty, Violence, Love, Prestige' (Geertz 1973: 21); through aesthetics, the senses, language and technology, and as a consequence of acknowledging contested experiences of the world (Asad 1973; Herzfeld 2001).

The effect of tourism on culture is what first brought tourism to the attention of anthropologists (Nunez 1963; Boissevain 1977; Crick 1994). An early focus on tourism as an agent of cultural change predominantly in relation to the effect of Western cultures on the lives of non-Western peoples has evolved into what is now a substantial body of knowledge about tourism from a variety of perspectives (see, Graburn 1976; Selwyn 1996; Nadel-Klein 2003; Tucker 2003; Nyíri 2006; Kolas 2008; Andrews 2011; Picard 2011; Huberman 2012). Anthropologically, tourism is one of the ways in which people access physically and through imaginative reverie the social and cultural particularities of other people, places and times. It is also a means by which the tourist can access and experience identity as demonstrated by some fascinating studies of what being a tourist means (Harrison 2003; Andrews 2009; 2011).

It is no surprise, therefore, that anthropologists are interested in tourism and tourists, in destinations and resident communities. However, the 'other' in tourism is not necessarily far away since diversity and difference, the exotic and the extraordinary can be found next door to where people live, in the next street or the next town, such that anthropologists are as fascinated by the near as they are by the elsewhere (Augé 2008). Or as Clifford maintains '"[c]ultural" difference is no longer a stable, exotic otherness'; the exotic, the different and the unexpected are nearby; they can be encountered in the adjoining neighbourhood (1988: 14). Notions of the exotic are of course relational as Dennis O'Rourke's 1987 film *Cannibal Tours* clearly demonstrates the Western tourists appear exotic, strange and at times incomprehensible to the people of Papua New Guinea.

Difference that is near is characterised by the same sort of signifying practices associated with the elsewhere; it is reflected in where and how people choose to live, in the food they buy and how they choose to eat it, in the clothes they wear and the ways in which they use and adorn their bodies.

It is reflected in the choices people make about whether and how to engage in tourism about what travel and travelling *mean* within the totality of the lives people lead. In Western culture if we take aside travel associated with daily need such as shopping for food and clothes, going to work, collecting children from school, then non obligatory travel has long been associated with personal growth, relaxation and an expansion of self-awareness – whether this is in terms of spiritual development, or for reasons of intellectual, political or aesthetic advancement as with the eighteenth-century Grand Tour of an educated, wealthy European elite.

Of course non-Western cultures also travel for pleasure and it is important to remember that tourism is not a modern invention as people travelled in ancient and medieval times, and from within the Near and the Far East (Casson 1994; Guichard-Anguis and Moon 2008), but there are differences in the philosophical understanding of the role and purpose of travel between Western and non-Western peoples. Such differences reflect alternative approaches to the nature of existence and to the relationship between the self, the state, the ancestors and the natural world (Nyíri 2006; Morphy 1995). Tourism and travelling not only mean different things to different people, they are also understood differently depending upon the context and the perspective within which they take place. Early motivations for travel rooted in trade, migration and religious pilgrimage have evolved in different ways such that today a Christian worldview has for the most part interpreted tourism and travelling in relation to the playful pursuit of pleasure. Whereas an Islamic worldview interprets travel as a search for spiritual knowledge through pilgrimage and therefore distances itself from the type of behaviour associated with the indulgence and hedonism of international mass tourism (Aziz 2001; Din 1989) Although these generalisations belie the fact that international tourism does not have to be incompatible with Islam (Okhovat 2010; Sanad et al. 2010; Henderson 2010), both are illustrative of different understandings about how the world is constructed and how individuals should behave, what anthropologists refer to as cosmology.

Cosmology and tourism

Cosmology is a significant concept in anthropology because as Mary Douglas (1996) points out, it serves to justify and explain behaviour, which in turn reveals something about the basis upon which a society operates. As Wagner states:

> In every "culture", every community or communicating human enterprise, the range of conventional contexts is centered around a generalized image of man and human relationships, and it articulates that image. These contexts define and create meaning for human existence and human sociality by providing a *collective* relational base, one that can be actualized explicitly or implicitly through an infinite variety of

> possible expressions. They include such things as language, social "ideology", what is called cosmology.
>
> (1981: 40, original emphasis)

To talk about a cosmology is then to talk about the basic belief system or worldview of a particular group or society, how people live, how they think about, imagine and understand their place in the world, how power is exercised, the relationship between the social order, between production and consumption and so forth. Cosmology is not only a scientific term for the universe or cosmos beyond the boundary of the earth's dominion, it is also a religious and hence cultural term that speaks of the knowledge, ideas and beliefs a people have about how they came to be in the world, how the world is and should be organised and about the existence or otherwise of 'life' beyond the veil of death. Despite the clear synergies with religion and stories of creation that seek to explain human existence, I prefer to think in terms of faith as the means by which ideas about the sacred, spirituality and the supernatural are located within culture. Faith is less culturally specific than religion, although both are inherently cosmological.

A cosmological system is, therefore, concerned with the maintenance of order through the setting of boundaries as to what is acceptable and what is unacceptable in any given situation. The basic principles and values of a particular worldview define the rules that govern behaviour in terms of social relationships, gender divisions, economics and so forth. In addition, a society's understanding of and relationship with nature, animals, the physical and material environment as well as attitudes towards death and the notion of time all coalesce to form an overall cosmological system. Cosmology is then a way of situating the self in the whole; a way of being, thinking and doing that makes life meaningful for individuals on their journey between birth and death, including how the time before birth may be understood (Lytton 1989; Weiner 2001; Hornborg 2006).

A cosmology is made manifest in the practices and social arrangements enacted by a society as Comaroff and Comaroff (1992: 6) argue in relation to Western ways of being 'many of the concepts on which we rely to describe modern life – statistical models, rational choice and game theory . . . case studies and biographical narratives . . . are our own rationalizing cosmology posing as science, our culture posing as historical causality'. It is clear from this that questions about cosmology cannot be confined to indigenous tribal societies; they are just as pertinent for the contemporary world and for societies driven by technological innovation (Abramson and Holbraad 2014). The continuing relevance of cosmology should not be taken to imply that cosmologies are inherently stable. As Douglas reminds us, a cosmology is not fixed in stone; it is more a set of categories that are as it were 'in use':

> It is not a hard carapace which the tortoise has to carry for ever, but something very flexible and easily disjointed. Spare parts can be fitted

> and adjustments made without much trouble. Occasionally a major overhaul is necessary to bring obsolete sets of views into focus with new times and new company . . . most of the time adjustments are made so smoothly that one is hardly aware of the shifts of angle until they have developed an obvious disharmony between past and present.
>
> (1996: 158)

Although cosmologies can and do change, the means by which they change may not always be as straightforward or as smooth as Douglas suggests. For example Malkki (1995) provides an unsettling ethnography of the opposing narratives laying claim to the historical background that led to the 1972 massacre of Hutus by the Tutsi in Burundi. Arguing that the differing versions of history are not just a struggle over what happened but also a struggle over opposing cosmologies.

Despite this example, the concept of cosmology is useful for exploring the meaning-making potential of tourism because tourism provides the meeting grounds for particular worldviews. Through tourism different beliefs and values come into contact with each other within the context of what I have referred to elsewhere as 'tourist society' (Palmer 2009). In this society social relationships are made, remade, celebrated, tested and broken in relation to the values influencing what is considered to be acceptable ways of behaving. So is it possible, therefore, to talk of there being a cosmology of tourism? I think it is and my view here is inspired by Miller's (1998a) anthropological essay on the significance of shopping for understanding the values that influence and sustain social relationships. Miller's specific intention is to establish the cosmological foundations of routine shopping through an analysis of shopping practices on one street in North London. By drawing upon the analogy between shopping and the rituals associated with ancient sacrifice, Miller reveals the fundamental values inherent in a cosmology of shopping, values such as devotional love, the aesthetics of thrift and self-sacrifice. Although Miller's ethnography is highly circumscribed in relation to the confines of his study, it does illustrate how social order and social relationships can be maintained, reinforced and/or subtly transformed by a particular cosmology.

Transformation through travel whether in terms of the self or in relation to others is well documented in the literature (Cone 1995; Noy 2004; Devereux and Carnegie 2006; Smith and Kelly 2006; Østergaard and Christensen 2010; Picard and Robinson 2012), and the link between cosmology and the transformative potential of tourism is certainly worth investigating. As is the wider cosmological framework within which tourists interact with each other, with resident communities, with the destination and with the organisational components of travelling. However, cosmology as a concept has yet to be fully explored within tourism, although its applicability for understanding tourism, tourists and local people is to my mind obvious. For example, the denigration of tourists as reflective of a cosmology that associates the West and outsiders generally with corruption, depravity, hedonism and decay has been noted by Crick in relation to Sri Lanka such that '[i]nternational tourists, in this cosmology, are sometimes clearly seen as just another source of social ill, as are Tamils and anything else alien' (1994: 58). Likewise, in their introduction to the journal *Tourism and Cultural Change* Robinson and Phipps (2003) tantalisingly refer to tourism as the cosmological pursuit of pleasure, stimulation, relaxation and stories.

Cosmology is referred to but not explored at length in relation to tourists' exposure to and experience of indigenous cosmologies for example Medina (2003), Ryan and Crotts (1997), Wright et al. (2009). There is, however a desire to engage more specifically with the cosmological significance of tourism. Picard and Di Giovine (2014) argue that contemporary tourism is shaped by a modernist cosmology that shapes understandings of the Other and Otherness. Campo and Turbay (2015) offer a fascinating account of how the cosmology of the Kogi people of Colombia provides them with a rhetorical strategy of resistance, a strategy of silence when confronted by outsiders, which in this instance are the tourists.

A cosmological theme underpins Bird's (2011) research into tourism and remembrance within the context of the D-Day landing of Allied forces onto the beaches of Normandy in World War II. According to Bird the D-Day experience, the beaches, the guided tours, the cemeteries, museums, re-enactments, significant locations, landmarks and memorial events can be conceptualised as a cosmology of remembrance. Such a cosmology not only positions the beaches and associated landmarks as being worthy of remembrance, it also sets the framework for why the D-Day landings should be remembered at all. In this cosmology place, time and the senses are significant actors in the tourism industry's interpretation of what constitutes a meaningful experience for tourists (Bird 2011). Meaning in this context relates to an affirmation of the values and beliefs worth dying for and of the ultimate triumph of good over evil.

Cosmology as a system of values and beliefs is just as meaningful in relation to mundane taken-for-granted practices such as shopping and tourism as it is in relation to the divine. In highlighting the cosmological significance of shopping Miller presents a forceful counterpoint to the prevailing tendency to 'glibly' dismiss 'the world's favourite object of scorn' (1998a: 155). Tourism like shopping is frequently viewed as frivolous both as an activity and as a focus of academic study. But to say that tourism is mundane is not the same as saying it does not matter; it is rather an acknowledgement of the embeddedness of tourism in terms of what people do. As Scannell (2014: 208) illustrates in relation to watching TV '[t]elevision today is routinely experienced everywhere as part of the ordinary life-world of members of modern societies, and watching it is just one of those things that most of us do in the course of an ordinary day'.

Although, a debate can be had over the extent to which tourism (or watching television) is an activity open to all people, or one that is a recognisable feature in all cultures, as clearly it is not. However, despite the existence of inequalities across and within societies, to travel, to go on holiday, to visit places of interest is endemic. This is so beyond the usual borders of Western practice and thinking as illustrated by the body of research on the meaning and significance of tourism in Asia, Latin America, China, Africa and the Middle East (Tan et al. 2001; Nyíri 2006; Notar 2007; Winter et al. 2008; Guichard-Anguis and Moon 2009; Ryan and Huimin 2009).

Thinking as philosophy

In accepting that tourism does matter, my purpose here is to explore what thinking through tourism might contribute to an understanding of the cosmological significance of tourism. In so doing I am responding to the aim of Scott and Selwyn's (2010: 1) edited collection *Thinking Through Tourism* seeking 'to reflect on the contributions anthropology, tourism and tourism studies make to each other'. My approach to thinking is philosophical in that I intend to look beneath the surface of our individual and collective engagement with tourism to better understand why it matters beyond references to escapism, relaxation and so on. Henare et al. (2007) provide a useful illustration of what thinking anthropologically means in the introduction to their book *Thinking Through Things*. Here they argue that thinking is about method rather than theory, it is about bringing something to the surface as opposed to an analysis of things or objects *per se*. Miller's analysis of shopping as sacrifice rather than as an economic activity is a case in point, 'an analogy with sacrifice should open up the possibility that shopping is a practice that might have ritual structure, that might be involved in the creation of value and relationships and that might manifest elements of cosmology' (1998a: 113). Miller's approach resonates with the social scientific study of tourism, particularly in relation to concepts such as magic, pilgrimage, ritual and myth (Graburn 1983; Selwyn 1996; Picard 2011).

Although conceptual analogies are certainly useful, they need to be situated within a wider framework capable of elucidating what engaging in tourism might reveal about the human experience, a framework that draws inspiration from the theoretical intertwining of anthropology, philosophy and tourism studies. In this respect I wish to acknowledge the influence of the anthropologists Tim Ingold and Michael Jackson, both of whom have inspired me to explore what being human might look and feel like by subjecting the practical experiences of human existence to philosophical scrutiny. In this instance practical experience that comes through engagement with the activity of tourism. Their philosophical endeavours are firmly rooted in the familiar everyday lives of people, what Jackson refers to as 'practical skills and know-how' (2009: 244) rather than in the rarified world of conceptual distance. As Ingold argues philosophers rarely:

> enlist the help of ordinary people in their enterprise, or test their insights against the wisdom of common sense. Anthropology is a kind of philosophy too, but it is not so exclusive. There are, of course, as many

> definitions of anthropology as there are anthropologists but my own is as follows: *Anthropology is philosophy with the people in.*
>
> (1992: 696, original emphasis)

Whilst Ingold's critique of philosophers can be challenged by, for example the work of the political philosopher Michael Sandel, including his radio series for the BBC entitled *The Public Philosopher*, such a definition puts people, the everyday, the mundane and ordinary experiences of life firmly at the forefront of any attempt to understand the dynamics of the human condition. What Lakoff and Johnson (1999) refer to as 'philosophy in the flesh'. Philosophy is valued and is valuable for my purposes in so far as it helps to illuminate, rather than obscure, what it means to live as a human being. Or more precisely some of the ways in which being human is experienced because, as noted earlier there is not one universal human experience but rather a multitude of experiences, many of which are neither comfortable nor safe nor come anywhere near to an experience of what a 'good life' might mean.

This is an important point because I am not concerned with or even interested in subjecting philosophy and philosophical arguments to critical enquiry. I do not intend to engage with and in debates about the metaphysics of reality or truth; which is not to say that such things cannot or should not be undertaken but rather to state that this is not the type of philosophising in which I wish to engage. To do so would be to separate tourism from its moorings and set it adrift in a sea of mystery divorced from the very thing that gives it meaning and purpose, life as it is *lived* as it is experienced by human beings.

Concepts and complexity should not as Jackson argues (1995: 5) 'cut up experience' because this condenses the fullness of the lifeworld into just those aspects that can be named. And as numerous ethnographies have shown, words alone cannot describe or ever fully explain the lived experience of other people. This is because knowledge is not communicated solely through linguistics but also through showing, doing and imagining, through myths, symbols and images, through art, nature and the senses (see Wierzbicka 2008; Boivin et al 2007; Geurts 2002; Bloch 1991; Levi-Strauss 1986). Concepts and the search for wisdom should illuminate a path through a forest rather than push us further on into the forest. According to Dewey, an assessment of the value of narrative abstraction in philosophy should be based upon the following test:

> Does it end in conclusions which, when they are referred back to ordinary life-experiences and their predicaments, render them more significant, more luminous to us, and make our dealings with them more fruitful? Or does it terminate in rendering the things of ordinary experience more opaque than they were before, and in depriving them of having in "reality" even the significance they had previously seemed to

> have? Does it yield the enrichment and increase of power of ordinary things . . . Or does it become a mystery that these ordinary things should be what they are; and are philosophic concepts left to dwell in separation in some technical realm of their own?
>
> (1958: 7)

Any search for meaning through tourism cannot be divorced from the activity and pursuit of tourism from the moving *and* the standing still, from the doing, thinking, reflecting, feeling and sensing that permeate engagement with tourism. My anthropological unravelling of the cosmological significance of tourism thus takes shape from within what Ingold (1993, 1995, 2011b) has referred to as a dwelling perspective, a perspective that owes its inception to the German philosopher Martin Heidegger's (2001) concept of dwelling-in-the-world. Heidegger's philosophy has proved fruitful for social scientists from a wide range of subject areas and disciplines such as geography, anthropology, archaeology, architecture, sociology, environmental sciences, media and communication, business and management, nursing and health. Despite the fact that many of Heidegger's ideas 'have filtered down into the culture at large' (White 2005), the significance of a dwelling perspective for tourism studies has yet to be fully explored or developed.

In saying this I do not mean that Heidegger's work has not been influential, as clearly it has. One of the reasons why his ideas continue to resonate is because he puts the practical everydayness of life centre stage, as part and parcel of what *being-in* the world means. Our mode of existence, our being-in or being-there in the world is referred to by Heidegger (1962) as *Dasein*, a derivative of the German words *da* meaning here and *sein* meaning to be. According to Heidegger we are not alone in the world; we are engaged in and with the world around us as part of a wider community. In this sense he is arguing that people are not bystanders or spectators in life but engaged actors whose very existence is understood through encounters with things and with others (Steiner 1989; Polt 1999). Given that tourism is a well-established human activity as opposed to something that is separate to or outside of the everyday, then it is understandable that Heidegger has influenced scholars of tourism. My point is rather that this influence is confined and concentrated, albeit in the form of some thoughtful and intelligent explorations of Heidegger's relevance for tourism.

In this respect I would highlight the work of Steiner and Reisinger, who have published several stimulating analyses of the significance of Heidegger in relation to existential authenticity, the search for an 'authentic' self (Reisinger and Steiner 2006; Steiner and Reisinger 2006a, 2006b). However, Cohen (2012) has criticised their use of obscure and highly abstract Heideggerian terms whose relevance for the theoretical and empirical study of tourism is unclear. Shepherd makes a more specific critique of discussions linking existential authenticity in tourism with Heidegger, arguing that these are based on a misreading of Heidegger. However, he goes on to state that his concerns are not about the relevancy of existential authenticity, but with the relevancy of Heidegger to the field of tourism studies.

These critiques notwithstanding, Heidegger's philosophy has provided a conceptual framework based around existential authenticity and the concept of *Dasein,* most notably in relation to the metaphorical essence of *Being* in tourism, or in terms of objects or wellness (Lau 2010; Larsen 2008; Kim and Jamal 2007; Wang 1999; Harkin 1995). Likewise, Pernecky (2010) opens up an interesting avenue in his exploration of the relationship between the being of tourism and peace, and there has been a call to recognise the significance of Heidegger for phenomenological research with a particular focus on hermeneutics (Pernecky and Jamal 2010; Ablett and Dyer 2009). Indeed, Pernecky and Jamal provide an astute analysis of the value of hermeneutic phenomenology for tourism by drawing upon the differing phenomenological positions of Heidegger and his mentor Husserl.

A concept of dwelling and travelling derived from Clifford (1997) as opposed to Heidegger is discussed by Ingold, whose own influence within tourism studies is emerging, most notably in the work of Vannini (2012). Lury (1997) employs 'dwelling-in-travelling and travelling-in-dwelling' to illustrate the implications for tourism of the capacity of objects such as souvenirs, T-shirts, postcards and photographs to both travel *and* to stay still. In terms of Heidegger's concept of dwelling, Urry (2000, 2007), Obrador-Pons (2003) and Jamal and Stronza (2009) are notable in exploring the dwelling concept beyond the level of brief references to it, as is the case with some of the studies mentioned above. However, Urry's focus on dwelling is part of his wider sociological analysis of mobility and Obrador-Pons has so far confined his use of dwelling to a discussion of embodiment and tourist agency. Finally, Edensor's (2002) dwellingscapes draws from Ingold to illustrate how understandings of identity are constructed in and through engagement with the spaces and places that are part of daily life.

Interestingly, Steiner and Reisinger (2006a) criticise Obrador-Pons for what they see as his inadequate engagement with philosophical concepts because he changes Heidegger's concept of existential dwelling to dwelling as metaphor. Such a view highlights the minefield that awaits anyone attempting to bring philosophical abstractions into lived experience. There will always be questions asked as to whether this should or even can be done and how effective or otherwise is the end result. As Al-Mohammad rather pointedly puts it, the metaphysical is not an ontic category, it is not a body or a thing to be investigated, it is ontological:

> We cannot use our experiences, nor the experiences of others, to support or negate Heidegger's (or any metaphysician's) claim as there can be no phenomenal basis for critiquing claims about the nature of reality, the nature of human beings and the nature of their constitution.
>
> (2011: 126)

The difficulty I have with such a view, however obvious it might seem on the surface, is that the value and usefulness of philosophy lies in its ability to open up a dialogue around fundamental questions of human existence, '[a]s Heidegger likes to put it, the task of a philosopher is to alert us to what is worthy of questioning' (Polt 1999: 7) and in so doing enrich understanding of what being human means *in relation to* life as it is lived, experienced and imagined. Metaphor can be very useful here, as Jackson argues metaphors make people whole by revealing the unities that bring self and world, mind and body together, 'metaphors coalesce social, personal, and natural aspects of Being, as well as unifying ideas and practices' (1989: 149).

I would have thought that the experiences of self and other are crucial here and indeed have been shown to be so through several significant ethnographies inspired by and interpreted within a philosophical framework. For example, Jackson's (1995) ethnographic exploration of the meaning of home both existentially and metaphorically, Ingold's (1995) *Building, Dwelling, Living: How Animals and People Make Themselves at Home in the World* and Weiner's (2001) Heideggerian anthropology of the Foi language of Papua New Guinea. In addition, Willerslev's (2007: 22) interpretation of the Yukaghirs of northeastern Siberia, employs Heidegger's theory of being-in-the-world to re-evaluate what he refers to as 'the animism problem' in anthropology. Basso (1996) draws on Husserl and Heidegger as inspiration for his goal of creating an 'ethnography of lived topographies' in relation to the ways in which Apache peoples use names and stories to create places in the landscape. Gray's (1999) ethnography of sheep farm practices employs Heidegger's dwelling concept and his use of *Umwelt*. So, if using a concept like dwelling as a metaphor helps to further the philosophical imperative then so be it, as Lakoff and Johnson argue in their book *Metaphors We live By*:

> The concepts that govern our thought are not just matters of the intellect. They also govern our everyday functioning, down to the most mundane details . . . how we get around in the world, and how we relate to other people . . . the way we think, what we experience, and what we do every day is very much a matter of metaphor.
>
> (1980: 103)

Furthermore taking concepts derived from one field and applying them to another is not necessarily a problem as long as their origins and their reuse is explained and justified. Turner (1978) used selected concepts from Freud's *The Interpretation of Dreams* to help him in his analysis of Ndembu ritual symbols such as the Blood Tree and the Milk Tree. Freudian concepts such as sublimation and projection were used analogously and metaphorically by Turner as a way of gaining some initial purchase on his data. However, Turner makes it clear that he was inspired by Freud's way of thinking rather than by his hypotheses, arguing that although psychology cannot be used to explain social facts:

> one can learn a great deal from the way a master thinker and craftsman works with data . . . It was his *style* of thinking and working which gave me encouragement rather than his actual inventory of concepts and hypotheses. None of these could be applied mechanically or literally to the data I had collected.
>
> (1978: 582, original emphasis)

Thinking and Heidegger

In bringing tourism within the realm of anthropology and philosophy I am aligning myself with Jackson's view that philosophy 'is a mode of being-in-the-world, and as such is inextricably a part of what we do, what we feel, and what we reckon with in the course of our everyday lives' (2009: 246). Although Heidegger's philosophy provides the inspiration for my thinking, as much as I like the intellectual challenge of my encounters with his work the at times dense impenetrability of his writing leaves me a little cold. I find that I cannot warm to his soul completely. Supporters of Heidegger such as Dreyfus (1991), White (2005), and Malpas (2008) all acknowledge the difficulties in reading, let alone interpreting, his thinking with White using adjectives such as 'murky', 'cryptic' and 'misleading' to describe Heidegger's style of writing. It is no surprise, therefore, when critics highlight this problem of language, which has variously been described as full of 'baffling complexity' (Philipse 1998: 3), as comprising 'mind-boggling abstractions' (Morris 1997: 323) and as the translation of 'meaningless German into meaningless English' (Edwards 1989: 470).

Within anthropology Miller finds Heidegger's writing 'incomprehensible and obscure, and much of its contemporary use pretentious' (2007: 24). Even Ingold limits his engagement with Heidegger and considers it a waste of time to read all of his work, 'I never read the whole corpus of Heidegger's work. . . . People who read too much of it get infected with a kind of virus and can't write coherently any more. So I've kept Heidegger at a distance' (2003: 11). However, White concludes that criticisms of philosophical language are rather boring and beside the point if there is something interesting to be said and 'Heidegger does have something insightful to say, and his dense writing results from the complexity and depth of the issues with which he is dealing' (2005: li).

While this may be so, philosophy about the meaning of life, about what it means to be human, needs to capture and communicate the liveliness and *livedness* of life, the vitality and warmth as well as the weary coldness that far too many people experience as life. So, although Heidegger's philosophy may be seeking to question the meaning of life in terms of its ontological construction, it is not life as it is lived. In many ways Heidegger's thinking resembles the artistic skill required to produce a still life painting. Such exquisite and minutely constructed executions of food, flowers and game may communicate realism through exactitude and thereby stimulate the imagination, but they can never recreate the experience of eating the fruit, smelling the flowers; plucking, cooking and eating the game depicted by the artist. The realism of the *Peach Twig* by the German painter Flegel (1566–1638) may dazzle the eye and move the mind with the velvety fuzzyness of peach skin, but it can never be soft to the touch and sweet to the taste; the juice from its peaches will never be caught by a hand as they escape from the mouth and run through the fingers.

I value Heidegger for the originality of his insights and completely agree with others who have highlighted the relevance of his work for tourism studies. However, I seek to draw from him rather than decipher him, to use him to question and explore rather than to translate what tourism *is*. The anthropologist Paul Rabinow states the case quite succinctly when explaining how he intends to use philosophical abstractions to interrogate contemporary life as it is lived in the here and now 'I am trying to appropriate conceptual tools that had been forged for certain problems, and to refashion them in the hope that they will provide analytic purchase for different problems' (2008: 7). In bringing tourism within the realm of anthropology and philosophy, I am aligning myself with the views of Turner, Jackson, Ingold and Rabinow. I am using philosophy as inspiration rather than as a means of abstract contemplation.

Hence, I will not debate the philosophical technicalities of what Heidegger 'means' or make judgements as to the merits of his philosophy; others are far more qualified than I to do so (see Bourdieu 1991; Dreyfus 1991; Philipse 1998; Malpas 2008). Neither will I use tourism to produce a 'reading' of Heidegger. Instead I use Heidegger as the starting point from which to fashion an anthropological interrogation of tourism as an expression of what it means to dwell in the world. Dwelling is understood here as a way of being human and tourism is one of the ways in which the experience of being human is made and remade. Heidegger may have started my journey but he does not define the journey. As Harrison argues 'although there can be no doubt that in its contemporary form the discourse on dwelling is founded by and in Heidegger's writing, it both *does not* and *should not* be allowed to end there' (2007: 626, original emphasis). I do not use Heidegger as a set of rules with which to straightjacket my mind; I use him to feel my way in examining what dwelling through tourism might mean as well as feel like when, to borrow a phrase from Jackson, it is anchored in rather than abstracted from the lifeworld.

Dwelling-in-the-world

While anthropology is my guiding ethos, the theoretical approach is drawn from Heidegger's (2001) philosophical essay from the 1950s *Building Dwelling Thinking*. This work is one of several essays delivered as lecturers in the late 1940s to early 1950s and seeks to explore the thinking that emerges from an analysis of building and dwelling. I first became aware of the actual significance of Heidegger for tourism studies through reading the work of Tim Ingold (1993, 1995, 2011b), who largely confines his use of Heidegger to the ideas of *Dasein* and dwelling. It was Ingold who introduced me to Heidegger's essay through his appropriation of dwelling and building into what he called *a dwelling perspective*. Before discussing my application of Heidegger and Ingold to tourism, it is first necessary to establish the foundations from which my thinking has developed.

Although the below discussion primarily focuses on *Building Dwelling Thinking,* Heidegger's work is interlinked in that he frequently follows up on, refines and also reinterprets ideas introduced in earlier writing (see Malpas 2008; Clarke 2002; Polt 1999; Dreyfus 1991). Indeed, Heidegger's overarching preoccupation with questioning the meaning of Being, as detailed in his major work *Being and Time*, is one to which he comes back time and again. How we are to question and understand Being is something that permeates much of his later writing, including *Building Dwelling Thinking, The Question Concerning Technology, The Thing* and *Poetically Man Dwells*. It is important therefore to offer a brief contextual discussion of Heidegger's questioning of Being in *Being and Time* so that the link with dwelling can be understood.

For Heidegger (1962), Being is hugely significant, it is the most universal but at the same time the least understood concept because what it means is all too often mistakenly interpreted as self-evidently obvious. In focusing attention on the meaning of Being, Heidegger is not referring to a category nor is he asking about the subjective consciousness of human individuals. He is instead posing an ontological question about the meaning of that which transcends the entity human being, as Malpas illustrates 'what is at issue in the question of being is, in the simplest of terms, how anything can be the thing that it is' (2008: 9). For Heidegger, in order to question something there must be an understanding of what the question is asking about, which in turn presupposes that there is something to be discovered by the question. Heidegger introduces the concept of *Dasein* to illustrate what is meant here:

> The best way to understand what Heidegger means by *Dasein* is to think of our term "human being", which can refer to a way of being that is characteristic of all people or to a specific person – a human being. . . . Heidegger is interested in the human *way of being*, which he calls "being-there" or *Dasein*.
>
> (Dreyfus 1991: 14, original emphasis)

As briefly mentioned earlier, for Heidegger *Dasein's* way of being, its fundamental structure is what he refers to as *being-in-the-world*. However, 'world' is not meant to be a specific place but is rather indicative of a holistic relationship with familiar everydayness, a 'sense of being absorbed in the world' (1962: 80) that Heidegger defines in terms of residing, inhabiting or dwelling. Thus *Dasein's* way of being-in-the-world can be understood as involvement on the basis of dwelling (Dreyfus 1991). To be involved is to be engaged with people, with things and practices from which a meaningful life is made and through which an individual is able to locate her/himself in the world, to feel at home as it were. Dwelling thus comes about through encountering and living with things that matter to people such as 'this page in this book, that office building, a pencil, a rabbit, a street' (Halliburton 1981: 4). However, dwelling comes about through engaging with not just things but also activities such as tourism and the range of experiences associated with it: going on holiday, visiting museums and attractions, day trips to places of interest, skiing, walking, painting and so on and so forth.

In *Building Dwelling Thinking* Heidegger traces the German word *bauen*, meaning to build, back to its etymological roots to the word *buan*, meaning to dwell. He thus liberates the verb 'to build' from a purely architectural association with structural forms and reclaims it as a way of being-in and thinking about the world. Thus, for Heidegger, to dwell is to experience what it means to be human '[t]he way in which you are and I am, the manner in which we humans *are* on the earth, is *buan*, dwelling. To be a human being means to be on the earth as a mortal. It means to dwell' (2001: 145, original emphasis).

For Heidegger contemporary usage separates the words building and dwelling into two quite different but related things where dwelling occurs as a result of building. However, such usage merely conceals the original meaning of dwelling as an expression of human existence and of building as the means by which humans articulate their existence as dwellers in the world. 'We do not dwell because we have built, but we build and have built because we dwell, that is, because we are *dwellers*' (2001: 146, original emphasis). Hence, dwelling is not tied to structures such as the buildings or houses in which people live or work, such places merely 'serve man's dwelling' (2001: 144); dwelling is instead a way of being-in-the-world that goes beyond mere occupation of a building or a space.

Dwelling is not just about *being-in,* it is also about *being in relation to* other people, places and contexts. The most significant of which is being in relation to the earth in terms of inhabiting the earth '[b]uilding as dwelling, that is, as being on the earth, however, remains for man's everyday experience that which is from the outset "habitual" – we inhabit it' (Heidegger 2001:145). There is thus an intimate connection between human existence and space-place such that to be human is to occupy both the earth as a spatial reality and more specifically place as the familiar locations in which people actual live. In Heidegger's thinking the nature of dwelling is made manifest through everyday engagement with places and with things and by the ways in which built things such as bridges situate dwellers within a landscape and thereby bring people into contact with each other, with things and with activities that sustain life:

> Bridges lead in many ways. The city bridge leads from the precincts of the castle to the cathedral square; the river bridge near the country town brings wagons and horse teams to the surrounding villages. The old stone bridge's humble brook crossing gives to the harvest wagon its passage from the fields into the village and carries the lumber cart from the field path to the road. The highway bridge is tied into the network of long-distance traffic, paced as calculated for maximum yield. Always and ever differently the bridge escorts the lingering and hastening ways of men to and fro, so that they may get to other banks and in the end, as mortals, to the other side.
>
> (Heidegger 2001: 150)

The bridge not only supports life, it also transforms the land into a location. It 'builds' a location out of the riverbank and the stream, it 'brings stream and bank and land into each other's neighborhood. The bridge *gathers* the earth as landscape around the stream' (2001: 150, original emphasis). However, the bridge illustrates a way of dwelling that connects individuals to more than the land such that to dwell is to experience more than the earth; it 'encompasses that which is other than the human' (Malpas 2008: 232). The other than human is what Heidegger refers to as 'the four we call *the fourfold*' – mortals, sky, earth and divinities – and to dwell is to unite with to be part of the 'simple oneness' of the fourfold (2001: 148, original emphasis). The fourfold concept appears in several essays and Heidegger illustrates its significance through various examples such as the bridge and a Jug. In crossing the bridge individuals are connected to the earth upon which the bridge rests and to the sky through the rain, which falls and swells the stream that flows under the bridge.

The divinities is an interesting concept not least because of the seemingly obvious connection to religion, to god/s and the sacred; however to read divinities in this way would, according to Malpas, be a mistake since 'Heidegger's gods should not be construed as "supernatural" in any of the usual ways' (2008: 274). Instead he suggests divinities should be interpreted more in terms of attunement in the sense of feeling at one with the world as individuals go about their daily lives immersed in the world around them. To talk of divinities is thus to talk of a mood of engagement that unites the elements together.

Dreyfus and Spinosa (1997) make a similar point when discussing the meaning of divinities in the context of a family meal. Such events or gatherings are a fundamental part of being a family and can engender a feeling of togetherness and 'graceful ease,' which may manifest itself as reverential sentiment in gratitude and thankfulness of the event. Heidegger's essay *The Nature of Language* seems to support such interpretations '[t]o undergo an experience with something – be it a thing, a person, or a god – means that this something befalls us, strikes us, comes over us, overwhelms and transforms us' (1982: 57). Thus, the fourfold illustrates Heidegger's argument that human existence depends upon a symbiotic relationship between key elements of the universe and in dwelling individuals engage in a relationship with a world that is above, beyond and alongside, holistic. The link with anthropology is clear here, given the discipline's overarching mission to seek a holistic understanding of human experience by locating experiences within their wider context; socio-cultural, political, technological, environmental and so on.

Heidegger's world is a community that is embedded in the 'soil and roots of a place', most memorably illustrated by his description of a farmhouse that has stood for over two hundred years in the Black Forest fixed through generations of use tending the land and the livestock (Shepherd 2015). The house is gathered together out of and in response to its surroundings, which for Heidegger encompass the ground (the earth), the elements (the sky), the toil of human labour (mortals) and the feeling of being attuned or connected to a place (the heavens and the divinities). Thus, 'the power to let heaven and earth, divinities and mortals enter in *simple oneness* into things, ordered the house' (Heidegger 2001: 157, original emphasis). This oneness caused the farmhouse to be built on a sheltered south-facing side of the mountain close to water and with a roof that protects the inhabitants from storms, rain and snow. This coming together 'designed for the different generations under one roof the character of their journey through time' (2001: 158). Building a life, building who we are as humans through dwelling in and as part of a community illustrates Heidegger's argument that being has to be understood in relation to a place, as being somewhere.

As humans dwell so they build through use for future generations and Heidegger's farmhouse was built or 'ordered' as he puts it by the coming together of humans and the environment. Use here refers to the uses to which the land is put, for example the growing of crops to provide food, grazing for animals, wood to build a home or shelter, water from the stream to drink or irrigate the crops. For Heidegger, then, to build is to cultivate the land and to care for and protect that which the land provides so as to sustain life in the present and in the future. To build is also to construct an inheritance to be passed on to the next generation. An inheritance of knowledge, skills, practices and values, as Ingold illustrates, '[h]uman children, like the young of many other species, grow up in environments furnished by the work of previous generations, and as they do so they come literally to carry the forms of their dwelling in their bodies – in specific skills, sensibilities and dispositions' (1995: 77).

So humans dwell through practical involvement with their surroundings through their appropriation and use of tools, machinery, objects, nature, animals as well as other humans, which are 'gathered' together to form what Heidegger refers to as the *Umwelt* (1962 84). Frequently translated as 'environing world' or 'surrounding world' *Umwelt* 'is a conception of world as a certain ordered realm within which one always stands in a certain orientation and with a certain directedness' (Malpas 2008: 55). World as environment, as *Umwelt*, in this sense is the significant whole in which people dwell (Polt 1999) and to be 'absorbed' in the world as noted earlier is to be absorbed in the familiar everydayness of work, family, home, neighbourhood, nature and so on.

This orientation or relationship to the familiar things of everydayness is what Heidegger refers to as 'Being-present-at-hand' (1962: 79). Here 'Things' occurring within the world combine to make life meaningful for individuals as part of their everyday experience, things such as trees, hills, rivers, rocks or birds (Halliburton 1981). Hence, to say that humans are *dwellers* and to describe the way in which they inhabit the earth as dwelling-in-the-world is to situate individuals within a totality of particularities or 'entities' as Heidegger refers to them rather than a specific location as such. World as *Umwelt* thus refers to 'the fundamental understanding within which individual things, people, history, texts, buildings, projects cohere together within a shared horizon of significances, purposes and connotations' (Clark 2002: 16).

For example, the world of the chef is an 'ordered realm' that carries within it a set of tangible and intangible rules for acknowledging belonging and conferring identity in terms of 'being a chef' (Palmer et al 2010). This realm is distinguished by certain specific configurations of kitchen space, within which specialised equipment – pots, pans, knives, spoons, mixers, moulds, fridges, freezers, ovens, and so forth – are organised in such a way as to turn food into dishes and dishes into a meal, a meal into a relationship. The layout of kitchen space establishes workflows and patterns based on the traditions of culinary practice. Movement within kitchen space mediates relationships with significant others, facilitating relations between other chefs, kitchen porters, restaurant staff and customers. This is the kitchen *unwelt*, the environing world gathered together to form the world of the chef. Dwelling as a way of being a chef is revealed as the chefs make and remake their world from that which is meaningful to them. Interestingly, the world of the chef and being a chef is no longer hidden behind closed doors, it has been opened up to other 'worlds' that enable customers to see into the kitchen. For example, the chef's table, restaurant windows into the kitchen and the conveyor belt delivery of Japanese sushi allow customers to see the chefs at work. In such circumstances being a chef is a being conditioned by surveillance.

Tourism also has a capacity to gather together a meaningful *Unwelt*, an environing world composed of places, activities, people and things. According to some scholars, this *Umwelt* is the result of the worldmaking influence of tourism (Hollinshead 2007; Hollinshead et al 2009). It is an ordered world, ordered by the structural, technological and linguistic activities of tour operators, marketing companies, transport networks, accommodation and food and entertainment providers (Franklin 2004, 2007). However, an ordered tourism world is very mechanical and process driven. It is devoid of the nuances, ebbs and flow of life; it is life as process, not flesh and blood. Order is about control and containment yet life is not completely controllable, that is just the myth of technological invention. Ordering is also about rationality, about organisation and bureaucracy and in this respect tourism as ordering is a good example of what Comaroff and Comaroff referred to earlier as the rationalising cosmology of Eastern thinking. As Winter (2009) notes, the framework of ordering privileges European and North American understandings of tourism and overlooks experiences in other parts of the world such as Africa, Latin America, Asia and the Middle East. What is needed, he argues, is a more pluralist approach, an approach that I argue can be found in the holistic endeavour that defines anthropology.

So in order to understand what it means to be human, it is necessary to study the activities, practices, spaces, places and things in and through which 'mortals' dwell on the earth. Dwelling speaks of engagement with the world, a world inhabited by humans as well as nonhumans, a world that is supported by and supports nature and the land. How we dwell is influenced by and in turn influences culture and politics, science and technology, biology and environment. Dwelling is about the collective 'we', about life and living, human, animal, plant and insect.

Dwelling through tourism

Given the above overview, it is clear that dwelling as a way of being-in-the-world is a particularly useful way of thinking through tourism because it enables tourism to be located within the totality of life and of living. Within this totality, gazing, mobility, identity, performance and so on are all aspects of being and dwelling through tourism because they are part of the experience of life and of living. In aligning myself with a dwelling perspective I argue that tourism can be conceptualised as a veil, the uncovering of which is capable of illuminating the intimacies of life along with the values, attitudes and beliefs by which people dwell and as they dwell they make and remake who they are. Given that a basic concern of anthropology is to understand how people who occupy the same space and time in terms of the history and geology of the earth can make very different lives, then it is surprising that anthropologists have yet to fully explore what dwelling through tourism might reveal about the experience of the human condition, the experience of being human.

Tourism enables a particular type of dwelling to occur that shapes the ways in which individuals think, feel and understand what it is to be human. The dwelling of away is very different to the dwelling of home it has a different rhythm and flow, as the routines, responsibilities and duties of daily life are interrupted, albeit temporarily. This altered form of dwelling brings with it numerous opportunities to engage in different types of activity and behaviour and for encountering other ways of living, thinking and being. In this way individuals continually make and remake the world around them and their place within it. People dwell as tourists and as members of what Tucker refers to as the '*toured* community' (2003:1, original emphasis). Hence, being and dwelling presuppose encounters between and interactions with people and cultures, with the environment and also 'things'. Through these encounters individuals come to explore who 'I am' and how 'I belong'. Being and dwelling are therefore closely intertwined with the concept of identity. However, in saying this I am using identity in its broadest, one might say in a cosmological sense to refer to what identifies us as human beings. Such a perspective opens up the possibility of a deeper consideration of the concept of identity as mediated by dwelling in the world through tourism.

Interestingly, since advocating a dwelling perspective, Ingold (2007, 2015) has pulled back from his preoccupation with it to focus on the significance of lines and knots in weaving together the threads of human existence. In moving on he has come to feel that he placed rather too much emphasis on dwelling as a way of describing how humans and nonhumans travel through life:

> Looking back, I rather regret having used the phrase. The trouble with 'dwelling' is that it sounds altogether too cosy and comfortable, conjuring up a haven of rest where all tensions are resolved, and where the solitary inhabitant can be at peace with the world – and with him or herself. This is not what I intended; for while we may acknowledge that dwelling is a way of being at home in the world, home is not necessarily a comfortable or pleasant place to be, nor are we alone there.
>
> (Ingold 2005: 503)

A similar point has been made by Cosgrove: '[t]he problem with the concept of 'dwelling' is that it can lead too easily to narrowing notions of localism, parochialism and intolerance of change and otherness' (1997: 28). In their analysis of a Somerset fruit orchard Cloke and Jones (2001:664) acknowledge that their use of the dwelling concept can be criticised as having the same romantic overtones as Heidegger's Black Forest farmhouse and Ingold's adaptation of the concept. Leading them to suggest that dwelling would look very different in harsher climates and in industrialised orchards and it would feel very different for workers in apartheid and post-apartheid South Africa. Mukhopadhyay (2006) provides an evocative example of an unromantic dwelling experience in relation to the slums of Calcutta, which he argues demonstrate that dwelling is not always as comfortable as Heidegger suggests, being more about survival than a nostalgic yearning to care for and preserve. In the slums, dwelling 'is better viewed as a relentless and quotidian *struggle* rather than an idyllic, lyrical, bucolic equilibrium' (Mukhopadhyay 2006: 225, original emphasis). In the slums there is no primal oneness with the fourfold of earth, sky, divinities and mortals not least because the sky, together with the sun and the light, rarely reach down to street level; 'these are luxuries reserved for those who live in the upper echelons of proper brick-built houses' (ibid.). Such views chime with criticisms of Heidegger's work and his focus on dwelling as being coloured by his rebellion against a changing world expressed as a romantic condemnation of modernity (Cloke and Jones 2001; Mukhopadhyay 2006; Willerslev 2007).

Thus, for Ingold (2008, 2011a), dwelling has given way to inhabiting and to wayfaring as the primary means by which human beings inhabit the earth. However, I argue that wayfaring also suffers from the same connotations as Ingold ascribes to dwelling. It too can conjure up images of gentle meanderings through a safe and scenic landscape, and habitation can be just as comfortable or uncomfortable as Mukhopadhyay's discussion of dwelling illustrates; it is a matter of perspective and experience. Furthermore, although there are clearly nomadic tribes and cultures whose whole way of life is spent following the herd or moving from place to place to find food or in time with the seasons such a form of wayfaring is in effect dwelling through moving. Similarly, although habitation may technically describe what humans do in terms of inhabiting the earth, for me it does not have the same philosophical and anthropological possibilities as dwelling. It is not as capable of elucidating the complex nuances of being-in-the-world. Habitation does not invoke the ebb and flow of life. It is too obvious, too blunt and too matter-of-fact for my taste. It is not as capable of bringing forth the value of tourism as a lens through which to explore the world in which life is lived, to explore life, death and the 'bits' in between.

I am arguing that dwelling should be set free from its association with stasis and the idea of living for long periods of time in one place, what anthropologists refer to as sedentism, and reconceptualised as a holistic expression of human existence. An expression that as indicated earlier involves moving and standing still as well as doing, thinking, feeling and sensing. Not to do so runs the risk of movement and mobility as somehow being seen as the 'other' in relation to dwelling, as if living in one place cannot lead to mobility whether in terms of physical movement or movement in relation to such as status, occupational aspiration or even movement as intellectual growth. As Ingold argues, '[t]his means that in dwelling in the world, we do not act upon it, or do things to it; rather we move along with it. Our actions do not transform the world, they are part and parcel of the world's transforming itself' (1993: 164). Dwelling in the world is not about stasis but about transformational possibilities.

In many ways debates that posit dwelling in opposition to wayfaring, stasis in opposition to movement, mirror discussions within the tourism literature that suggest tourism as a process of becoming is altogether more exciting than tourism as a process of being (Franklin 2004; Scarles 2009). Again my use of being should not be seen as suggesting a finished and less exciting state because to my mind being cannot be divorced from becoming. Being human or being a tourist involves a constant interplay and interchange of states, identities, experiences and feelings. As one Canadian tourist explains, foreign travel provides 'the opportunity to, even accidentally, bump into parts of yourself that you didn't know that you have . . . it's like having a limb go to sleep and then discovering it anew' (cited in Harrison 2003: 86). Similarly, I become a tourist for two weeks of the year before returning home to take up my job of being an academic. Being is always being and becoming, these two cannot be separated, or discussed as either or because they are inseparable; they are two sides of the same coin, as Andrews (2009) rather neatly puts it: tourism and being a tourist is a disrupted 'moment of being' full of potentiality.

Ultimately, being-in-the-world is not about ontological being but about being *human*-in-the-world, in effect putting the life back into being. I may be drawing on philosophy, I may describe my approach as philosophical, but it is an approach firmly rooted in the sort of activities and experiences associated with being a tourist. It is an anthropologically derived philosophy of what it means to be human by engaging with and through tourism.

Context and structure of the book

It is worth pausing briefly at this point to explain my use of context in relation to anthropology and in relation to tourism as the focus for exploring notions of being and dwelling. While context is certainly important, indeed anthropological knowledge is underpinned by ethnographic studies of cultures *in context*, we need to be mindful of the fact that context is not the sole container of knowledge, it is not 'a secure epistemic nest in which our knowledge-eggs are to be safely hatched' (Taussig 1990: 216). Neither is context a one-way perspective since contextualised ethnographies are themselves products of the context within which the anthropological gaze has come into focus; context in this sense is the window through which anthropologists look into the world of those they study. We can acknowledge the window's existence, challenge it and even change perspective, but we cannot deny the influencing hand of the original frame. Furthermore, because all contexts are fluid, they change and move over time, there is no one fixed context, social or otherwise, but a variety of contexts reflective of a particular historical moment, particular ways of seeing and thinking.

In referring to the context of tourism I am highlighting the associations and related components of a moment in time. A moment where tourism is seen as an important part of how we come to understand and experience what a 'good life' should look and feel like. This is important because it highlights the point made by Wagner that contexts are created out of experience '[a] context is a part of experience-and also something that our experience constructs' (1981: 37). As neither experience nor context is a singular expression of human culture, then to speak of context is to acknowledge the moveable nature of knowledge and hence the multiple and shifting patterns of meaning that emerge as a result. This book is therefore a moment in time rather than a fixed point in time and the arguments made are constructed out of a contextualised reading of selected examples of the type of behaviours and activities associated with being a tourist and with doing tourism.

The book is thematically structured to provide an analysis of the foundational elements of dwelling rather than every possible way in which being and dwelling through tourism can be examined. Although each chapter focuses on a different theme, this does not mean there is a neat dividing line between each chapter. They are all interrelated and intertwined. For example, Chapter 2's theme of sensuous dwelling focuses on the role of the body and embodiment in tourism but clearly the body of the tourist visits Hever Castle as discussed in Chapter 3. The body of the tourist also uses airports and takes day trips to museums, the focus of Chapters 4 and 5, so each chapter helps to construct my overall argument and as such each one follows the same structure. A discussion of the overarching theoretical framework for each theme is followed by an illustrative focus on a specific aspect/s of tourism.

This introductory chapter has set out the focus, purpose and the theoretical framework for the book and with Chapter 2 I move on to focus on what I refer to as sensuous dwelling, the intimacy of being that results from the dwelling relationship between mind, body and the senses. Sensuous dwelling is an exploration of embodied practices such as moving, thinking, feeling and doing; practices that create and are played out in and through a variety of social contexts, including the social context of tourism. Sensuous dwelling focuses attention on the relationships that structure and articulate how being human is brought forth through the body of the tourist. My arguments are discussed in relation to the activities of walking and sightseeing, both of which are among the most recognisable of activities, representing as they do ways of moving, looking and being a tourist.

Chapter 3 moves on from embodied dwelling to material dwelling, how being and dwelling is intertwined with materiality. Material dwelling concerns the ways in which objects, structures and the settings in which they are to be found are put to use; how they are employed to construct a 'world', and in so doing create and reinforce the fundamental values that define what matters in that world. Through a focus on heritage tourism, specifically *Hever Castle* in England, I explore how the objects, buildings and landscapes of heritage are *gathered* together and used to create a world that is essentially English and Protestant, and where individual liberty is a defining characteristic. Dwelling through materiality is a dwelling in relation to heritage time. Heritage time as socially constructed time illustrates the human need to create ways of locating the self within a wider temporality of people and events. In effect to establish, maintain and perpetuate the lineage of human existence.

In Chapter 4 I take a step back from 'things' per se to explore how the thinking and making function of architecture is a way of organising, knowing and describing the world. Buildings, structures and landscapes are creations of a process of imagining that I refer to as architectural dwelling, a way of being human-in-the-world based on the interweaving strands that connect architecture with human behaviour, thinking and feeling. Architecture plays a significant role in attracting and structuring the tourist experience. It both draws people towards a destination and provides the structures that support tourism such as hotels and airports. I argue that airports are designed to create a unique sense of place, one that articulates a relationship between people, place and cosmos. In this sense airports are sacred buildings because, like churches, temples and mosques, they are physical manifestations of the border between life and death.

Chapter 5 moves on from singular aspects of being and dwelling through tourism and adopts a more holistic approach referred to as earthly dwelling. Earthly dwelling focuses on the significance of the human-earth relationship for understanding not just what makes us human but also *how* we are made human in relation to the earth as world. Earthly dwelling highlights the relational totality of being human-in-the-world and by way of illustration I focus on some of the primary meaning-making referents through which this relationship is understood, namely, time, place, history and memory. This tourism fourfold is experienced in and through the places, people, buildings, souvenirs, landscapes and activities that are part of what tourists do. By focusing on the museum, the chapter argues that the collection and display of culture, nature and ways of thinking and being reflect particular configurations of time, place, history and memory. Configurations that speak of the diverse ways in which human subjects come to make and remake who they are in the world. In this sense museums are highly visible expressions of particular understandings, and more precisely particular moments, of earthly dwelling.

Although Chapter 6 synthesises the key themes discussed in the previous chapters, I argue that the chapter should be read as a pause in the argument rather than as a point of closure. This is because the body, things, the built environment and the four interrelated elements of earthly dwelling are not the only examples of being and dwelling through tourism. This chapter also sets out ideas for future research and argues that such research should look far and wide to acknowledge other cultures and other ways of being and dwelling through tourism.

2 Sensuous dwelling

Introduction

I start my journey through the lifeworld of tourism by focusing on the intimacy of being that results from the dwelling relationship between the senses and the body, a relationship encapsulated in the concept of embodiment. Although Heidegger has been criticised for either ignoring or failing to appreciate the place of the body and embodiment in relation to his articulation of being-in-the-world (Malpas 2008), they are inseparable from any discussion of how dwelling influences the experience of being human. This is so because we encounter and experience the world through the body and this body shapes and is shaped by the enveloping environment, in effect the body and world unfold together. In this sense lived experience is inextricably tied to both having and being a body: '[o]ur everyday life is dominated by the details of our corporeal existence . . . a constant labour of eating, washing, grooming, dressing and sleeping' (Turner 1996: 37).

While the body maybe the means by which humans physically encounter and engage with the world, it is the senses that define the nature of human dwelling, it is through the senses that the body makes meaning out of experience. Lived experience is thus predicated on a continual and complex harmony of exchange between body, world and the senses. In effect the body both meets the world and makes the world as it sees, moves, feels, hears, touches and thinks through the myriad of encounters and interactions that are part and parcel of daily life. It is this interplay between the corporeal and the sensory that brings body, mind and world together as a composition of being and dwelling. However, in focusing on the materiality of the body, it is important not to ignore the human subject, the actual person because it is the values, beliefs, ways of seeing, thinking and doing of each individual that give life to the world. Body, mind and senses animate the world of mountains, rocks and lakes, and they create, build, alter and sadly destroy the tangible and intangible places, structures, things and ideas that contribute to the world of human experience.

The joining of body, mind and senses is a holistic approach because the senses do not operate in isolation, they require a body to feel and a mind to interpret that which the world makes available. Serres (2008) argues that the senses, what he refers to as '*le sensible*', are an interconnected totality that cannot be separated from or discussed in isolation to each other or from the body and mind within which they are knotted together or from the world to which they are connected. The sense of smell requires lungs to inhale and a nose through which to draw in the aromas of life and living. Hearing uses ears to catch and contain the vibrations and resonances created by humans, nature and the animal world, although for the hearing impaired these vibrations are conducted via bone, or the surface of the skin. Touch requires fingers or toes to reach out and make contact through what is the largest element of the human sensorium, the skin. Sight requires eyes to bring order to refractions of light. Taste requires a mouth to take in what the palette then decodes, and all sense impressions are interpreted through what Lakoff and Johnson (1999) refer to as an embodied mind, the coming together of reason, thinking and perception.

Over the years the concept of an embodied mind has proved to be a topic of fascination for researchers ranging from neuroscientists to social scientists (see Jackson 1983; Scheper-Hughes and Lock 1987; Martin 1992; Lambek 1998; Shilling 2003; Damasio 2010). This is because it raises fundamental questions of ontology and of the differences between humans and nonhumans, which, as Lloyd (2011) argues, is not as straightforward as it might seem. Following an analysis of Western, Greek and Chinese approaches to the question of human distinctiveness, he concludes that there is no simple way to identify what might be distinctly human and attempts to do so are continually thwarted by an amazing proliferation of examples that undermine assertions of human uniqueness. Although claims of human distinctiveness might be difficult to evidence, the union of mind, body and the senses, together with language, are fundamental to human consciousness. This is because to be human is to consciously know that this body is my body and to possess the capacity to reflect upon the self as an individual within a wider world of other people, things, ideas and experiences; in effect to recognise my body as *my*self. Serres provides a good example of self-body awareness as he describes the terrifying experience of escaping a burning ship by squeezing his body through a porthole into the freezing ocean beyond:

> I push my head through, then one arm, not yet as far as my shoulder, only my hand and wrist. The angle of my elbow is a problem in the small space between my neck and the rim of brass around the pothole. I cannot get out, I have to get out. Everything is burning and my head is frozen.
>
> I remain there, motionless, vibrating, pinioned, gesticulating within the confines of the fixed neckpiece, long enough for me to think, no, for my body to learn once and for all to say 'I' in the truest sense of the word. . . . If I slide a leg through, I am still inside, while my leg, thigh

> and knee are outside. . . . My pelvis goes through, my genitals, buttocks and navel are almost certainly outside but I remain inside. I know what it is to be a man without legs; I know for a moment what phantom limbs feel like. At a precise moment, the very moment when the totality of the divided body shouts *ego* in a toppling movement, I slide out and can drag through the remainder of my body.
>
> (2008: 18, 20, original emphasis)

Interestingly, Heidegger argues that what we 'hear' is not sound but what that sound tells us about the world in which we live, '[w]hat we "first" hear is never noises or complexes of sounds, but the creaking wagon, the motorcycle. We hear the column on the march, the north wind, the woodpecker tapping, the fire crackling. It requires a very artificial and complicated frame of mind to 'hear' a 'pure noise" (1962: 207). A similar argument can be made in relation to the perception of odours such that what we smell is not merely a foul or fragrant odour but the composition of a particular world, the very structure and order of a society. In his analysis of the history of smell in French society Corbin (1986) highlights the relationship between smell and public order. During the summer of 1880, there was a public revolt over the stench in Paris, '[a]bhorrence of smells produces its own form of social power. Foul smelling rubbish appears to threaten the social order, whereas the reassuring victory of the hygienic and the fragrant promises to buttress its stability' (1986: 5).

Embodied sense impressions also influence understandings of identity and the ability to distinguish who we are from who you are, including how people differentiate between status, class or caste. Over the centuries Russian identity has been conceived and experienced as a sensory relationship through such as the smell and taste of cigarettes, the invisibility of deafness, the severity of the climate, the fermented sourness of cabbage, the stench of dead and wounded wartime bodies and the visceral experience of life under Stalin (Romaniello and Starks 2016). Such aspects not only influenced how Russians conceived of and experienced their sense of individual and collective identity, they also reflected the social changes within Russia brought about by the forces of modernity. These changes disrupted the previously accepted rules and hierarchies that defined the relationship between the state, the urban elites and the rural peasantry (Martin 2016).

Identity and social order as defined through the senses reveal how embodied experience shapes and is shaped by the relationship between self and world. The self-world relationship resonates through the body, causing it to react to what it sees, hears, tastes, smells and feels. In many ways the body 'hears' the world through the senses and what it hears influences lived experience. Interestingly, Serres has referred to the body as a tympanic membrane where the body-skin vibrates to the sound of the world, '[w]e hear through our skin and feet. We hear through our skull, abdomen and thorax.

We hear through our muscles, nerves and tendons. Our body-box, strung tight, is covered head to toe with a tympanum' (2008: 141). The same argument can be made in relation to the other senses because they too are part of the body-skin membrane that covers and incorporates bone, organ, tissue and muscle. What we see, touch or taste causes a reaction in the body. Even the anticipation or the memory of a positive or negative sensory experience causes the body to react in a certain way. I remember having to eat Brussels sprouts as a child, a hated green vegetable that to my palette tasted bitter. My body would go rigid as I stared at my plate knowing I had to eat the vegetable and the only way I could 'get it down' was to screw up my eyes, hold my breath and swallow it whole. Quickly followed by a drink of water or a large mouthful of mashed potato. Even today my body reacts with a slight shudder at the sight and even the thought of this vegetable, a vegetable that tasted sweet to other members of my family. The Brussels sprout is certainly a deeply embodied experience.

The significance of the senses generally and as part of the body's perceptual engagement with the world is a significant strand of scholarly interest (Classen 1993; Rodaway 1994; Geurts 2002; Howes 2005; Howes and Classen 2014). Indeed, Seremetakis argues that '[t]he senses represent inner states not shown on the surface. They are also located in a social-material field outside of the body' (1996a: 5). While the senses may be internal in a biological sense, reactions to our sensory encounters with the world are shown on the surface of the body: for example joy, pain, disgust and delight are revealed in the face and through contortions of the body such that the body speaks its presence as a form of language, as Classen notes:

> The exploration of how we grope to express sensory experience through language, and to convey non-sensory experiences through sensory metaphors, is revealing, not only of how we process and organize sensory data, but also of the sensory underpinnings of our culture.
>
> (1993: 59)

The body is a language where linguistic expressions are embodied through metaphor such that we 'see' through our eyes and through the imaginative power of the mind as illustrated by the phrase 'the mind's eye'. Even talking about out of body experiences presupposes that there is a body to be out of. Body metaphors such as 'heart ache', 'pain in the neck' and body practices such as lighting a fire, chopping wood, hunting for food and walking are forms of embodied language that not only communicate the relationship between culture and experience, they also enable individuals to make and remake the connection between body, person and world in effect '[t]o recognise the embodiedness of our Being-in-the-world' (Jackson 1983: 340). Even when the body is immobilised or restricted by injury or illness, it can find ways to communicate to others through minute movements of body parts and to the self through the imagination (Edwards 1998; Dudzinski 2001;

Sandström 2007). The imagination is a bodily experience that enables an individual to construct and to plan ways of engaging with the world. I can imagine how I might react in a particular situation or plan what I need to do to get from *a* to *b*. This is especially important if my body is restricted in some way such that a person may need to know if there will be stairs to climb or doors wide enough to take a wheelchair.

The importance of the imagination is highlighted by the experience of stroke patients diagnosed with what is referred to as locked-in syndrome, alert and intellectually competent yet immobile and unable to speak (Bauby 1998; Marsh and Hudson 2014). Likewise, Irving (2005) discusses how individuals with HIV/AIDS have to continually re-evaluate the relationship between body, self and world as they struggle to live with the cycles of illness and recovery associated with the illness. These cycles bring with them moments of self-conscious reflection about the body that is and the body that was that disrupt understandings of being a body-in-the-world. The account of Yudaya, a mother of four children from Uganda illustrates this well:

> *the first thing Yudaya does when she wakes up is test out and 're-inhabit' her body by walking around the house and if she feels 'fine' she goes to pick the sweet potatoes, still checking her body step-by-step . . . On other days a radical discontinuity soon emerges between body and world . . . the sweet potatoes go untended with all the accompanying consequences for her family. Most mornings Yudaya wakes up not knowing whether she can dig or not, and it takes her a while to feel part of the day, part of the world.*
>
> (2005: 322, original italics)

In such circumstances imagination and memory cause both pleasure and pain, constant reminders of the body before and the body after. The enforced sense of bodily awareness experienced by Marsh, Bauby and Yudaya is predicated upon the senses, which become the means by which to interpret body and world. So, even in extreme circumstances the senses bring life to the body. Without sensory impressions the body is closed in rather than open to the world, in darkness as opposed to the light. So while the senses can be described as the gateway to the world, the body and the mind are the means by which the world is turned into embodied experience. The union of body, mind and senses is what I refer to as sensuous dwelling.

Sensuous dwelling

Sensuous dwelling concerns the intimacy of being that results from the relationship between mind, body and the senses, it is a way of being in and engaging with the world as an embodied self that lives and breathes, thinks and speaks, moves and acts. It is a bodily experience that engages reason as well as emotion; that is physical as well as psychological; tangible as well as imaginary. As such it is both intimate and personal since we cannot know what it is to move, feel, smell, touch, taste, remember and imagine as others do. In her ethnography of the relationship between the senses and cultural identity in Ghana, Geurts (2002: 236) writes that because she is not an Anlo-Ewe person she was never able to smell the precise odour that marked someone as having an 'improper upbringing, thereby creating a stigma for the lineage'; this odour could only be detected by the Anlo-Ewe people. Like all the senses odour is culturally constituted but culture alone cannot always explain the experience of *my* body. Wendell describes how her own disabling illness forced her to rethink her relationship with her body '[o]f course, my illness occurred in a social and cultural context . . . but a major aspect of my experience was precisely that of being forced to acknowledge and learn to live with *bodily*, not cultural, limitation' (1996: 169, original emphasis).

Sensuous dwelling is also about the inner body of blood, bones, joints, tendons, muscles and organs, those aspects of inner 'flesh' that enable the body to live and to move. As such sensuous dwelling highlights the materiality of the flesh as a complex harmony of body, mind and senses. It is the means by which a body becomes fully human, how it learns to feel and to know that it is human through the coming together of the corporeal and the sensory, the cognitive and the linguistic, the emotional and the imaginary. Sensuous dwelling is a phenomenological expression of being human; it is, to borrow a phrase from Lakoff and Johnson (1999), 'philosophy in the flesh'.

Anthropologically, the centrality of body, mind and senses to an understanding of being-human-in-the-world is about culture in its broadest sense where culture is embedded in but not wholly constitutive of lived experience. In this sense the concept of sensuous dwelling responds to Jackson's (1983) desire to reconstitute culture as embodied experience rather than seeing culture as an isolated self-contained world of qualities, attributes and language or as the products of human societies. For Jackson, 'human experience is grounded in bodily movement within a social and material environment' (1983: 330), and individuals actively body forth the world through patterns of body use as they interact with this environment. By arguing that people actively body forth the world, Jackson is highlighting the active nature of the relationship between body and world, and as argued earlier the body makes and is made by the world such that 'bodies are not passively shaped by or made to fit the world's purposes' (1989: 135). In effect life is made meaningful by what our bodies *do*, such that the world is made by the practices of bodies, it is made by the ways in which people move, think and perceive the world as embodied lived experience. Embodiment is, therefore, an ongoing process; ongoing through a lifetime, such that 'our embodied being enables us to remake ourselves by remaking the world around us' (Shilling 2003: 182).

Explorations of culture are therefore explorations of how bodies shape and are shaped by lived experience of and *in* the world, and in this respect it is interesting to explore what the environment or social context of tourism may reveal about the embodiment of lived experience. As Kissell illustrates:

> Phenomenologists urge us to explore the experience of being a living body; to think about what it means to have an upright posture; for a body to be *my body*; to determine what are the physical boundaries of our living bodies; how the living body learns about the world; how it expresses itself in the world as an embodied self; what it means for a body to be *here* and *now*; how an embodied being is necessarily a being embedded in a social context, and so forth.
>
> (2001: 2, original emphasis)

The interweaving of culture, body and being lies at the heart of phenomenological approaches to understanding the lifeworld as embodied experience (Merleau-Ponty 2002; Csordas 1990, 1999; Jackson 1983). An embodied understanding of culture means that the body is not something to be studied in relation to culture as if it were an object, it is the very subject of culture – 'studies under the rubric of embodiment are not about the body per se. Instead, they are about culture and experience insofar as these can be understood from the standpoint of bodily being-in-the-world' (Csordas 1999: 143). This is important because understanding lived experience should not be limited to representations of the body in terms of how the body is employed to distinguish, classify and categorise but should encompass individual and collective experiences of being a 'lived body' (Merleau-Ponty 2002); the experience of embodying the world through sensuous dwelling. As Turner argues, the body is more than a rich source of social, cultural, and religious metaphor '[i]t is constitutive of our being-in-the-world' (2008: 16). The concept of sensuous dwelling focuses attention on the importance of coming to know, understand and value other cultures in terms of how they body forth their world. This is because culture affects body and mind and as such Howes (2005) argues that a focus on sensing cultures as opposed to reading cultures is perhaps a more fruitful way of exploring other realities and ways of organising the world.

As argued above people dwell first and foremost through the senses, and in Western cosmology these are invariably defined as sight, touch, taste, hearing and smell. These five senses are the primary means by which people perceive the world around them; they provide the perceptual stimuli connecting the individual to his or her surroundings. People learn about themselves and about their world through their senses and what they learn is turned into accumulated knowledge that influences how and why individuals, groups and societies behave the way they do. Individuals learn to make judgements, reasoned or otherwise, to discriminate and to distinguish on the basis of acquired sensory knowledge. As Seremetakis notes '[t]he senses in modernity are the switching place where the structure of experience and the structure of knowledge converge and cross' (1996b: vii). Thus, we know that fire, which can burn, can also provide us with warmth to survive. We develop skills to help us differentiate food that can harm us from that which is good to eat and to help us decide when to be wary and when to stride forth, when to speak and when to listen.

All such judgements are formed through the touchstone of sensory impressions such that sense and sensitivity combine with intuition and all of which are informed by culturally acquired knowledge (Guerts 2002; Willerslev 2007). The senses are intertwined with emotion and with feeling as they expose us to the pleasure and pain of the here and now, triggering memories that link individuals to people, places and moments in time. Visits to museums or places of conflict pull on the imagination, on memory and emotion to transport the body of those individuals with personal experience of the events depicted back to when they occurred. Hence, displaced Palestinians returning to the houses and villages now occupied by Jewish settlers find it difficult to cope with the memories and emotions of their own or their descendant's lost lives (Kadman and Kabha 2016).

This coalescence of imagination, memory and emotion are the building blocks, the structures of feeling that reveal how dwelling through the senses defines and influences the experience of being human. This is illustrated by Powles's (2005) work among Angolan refugees living in a settlement scheme in Zambia. Here social memories of catching, smelling and eating fish are primarily embodied rather than narrated. These embodied memories became 'incorporated into people's very being' through the frequent repetition of particular fishing practices, practices that help to maintain a sense of home, history and cultural identity (2005: 335).

In a similar vein, Stephenson (2004) has shown how Jamaican members of the UK Caribbean diaspora make embodied connections with Jamaica through engagement with the British countryside. In particular, the smell of fresh air and pollen and the sound of birds and farm animals enable ethnic minorities to reminisce about and connect with the ancestral homeland. For tourists, the imagination can enable the body to 'feel' a connection with a longed for homeland as Basu illustrates through his research into the relationship between roots tourism and the Scottish diaspora. Following a trip to Scotland, Brenda, a Canadian of Scottish descent, brought back a stone from the river bed in Glencoe. 'First and foremost, I hold my red stone and close my eyes. I can go back in my heart and the feelings come to the forefront once again' (cited in Basu 2007: 103). Interestingly, Basu argues that memory triggers, whether physical objects or virtual screensaver images should be understood as attempts to re-embody a disembodied identity; disembodied by time, distance and geography. This is significant because it illustrates that the intimacy of being that underpins sensuous dwelling is as much imaginary as it is physical.

Imagined intimacy is not always benign, it can be highly political as Ben-Ze'ev illustrates through his discussion of the role of food in connecting Palestinian refugees to a way of life that has been lost as a result of the war with Israel. 'Refugees carry with them an 'internal Palestinian map' of tastes and smells . . . signifiers of their contexts – the house, the village and the region' (Ben-Ze'ev 2004: 148). For the Palestinians, the tastes and smells associated with plants and food are embodied anchors of memory linking them to the villages they once called home, villages since demolished or occupied by settlers.

To link sensuous dwelling to the five senses touch, taste, hearing sight and smell is to limit the experience of being human to those senses that predominate in Western modes of thinking. Yet studies of alternative cosmologies clearly show that the nature and range of human senses is fluid, relational and contingent upon context and practice (Stoller 1984, 1989; Kensinger 1995; Willerslev 2007). Thus, proprioception – the unconscious awareness of the body in relation to its surroundings – balance, feeling and emotion can also serve as perceptual sensors connecting the embodied self to the world. In looking beyond Western traditions of thought, alternative cosmologies of the body highlight the significance and interconnectedness of the physical body with an inner body of soul and spirit.

Numerous ethnographies illustrate the coming together of soul and spirit in both humans and nonhumans, for example the animal world, such that the existence of ecstatic out of body experiences or of spirits remind people that understandings of the body transcend the material (Lambek 1998; Tsintjilonis 2006). In the world of the Siberian Yukaghirs humans, animals and inanimate objects all have an *ayibii* or souls and are considered to be persons albeit persons who think differently 'because each species has its own corporeal nature that provides it with a particular bodily presence and orientation in relation to the world' (Willerslev 2007: 81). Moreover, bodies can turn in on themselves through trance and be possessed by other 'beings' or spirits, for example the Cashinahua of Peru believe that every individual comprises a body and at least five spirits, or *yushin*, which although invisible cast an aura reflective of a person's state of health and wellbeing (Kensinger 1995). Such studies are interesting because they demonstrate the limitations of Western modes of thinking that frequently link discussions of human embodiment to the experience of a tangible conception of world.

This point notwithstanding, the body, the mind and the senses are intertwined and interdependent such that a balance is required to maintain equilibrium and health. This balance is maintained through what Cannon (1963) refers to as 'the wisdom of the body', the ability of the body to regulate itself through an intimacy of knowing that stimulates the pores on the skin to open or close in order to cool down or heat up the body, and prompts the movement of hands and feet to maintain balance. It is through the minutiae of such sensory regulation that we perceive the world, they create sense impressions or what Merleau-Ponty (2002) refers to as sense-experience, knowledge about the world that enables judgements to be made about how to react, how to behave. In this way the senses link individuals to the world, they are the connective tissue joining person and world together by enabling that which is encountered to be translated into the knowledge that informs reason and judgement and which underpins action, experience and ultimately survival. As Willerslev argues, for hunting peoples survival depends upon the senses working together to ensure the provision of enough food. There is no sense hierarchy but rather a coming together of the different registers of sensation 'into that synergic system that is the phenomenal body itself' (2007: 81). What this illustrates is 'system' as sensuous dwelling and sensuous dwelling enables the body to move through the world; it is the means by which humans (and nonhumans) navigate their way from birth to death.

Sensuous dwelling is, therefore, an exploration of practices of embodiment such as moving, thinking, feeling and doing that create and are played out in and through the social contexts referred to in the quote by Kissell. My argument here is that tourism is itself a particular social context embodied by tourists as they engage in the practices that define the tourist habitus. As Pallasmaa (2012: 76) argues, '[w]e transfer all the cities and towns that we have visited, all the places that we have recognised, into the incarnate memory of our body'. In unpicking the sensory threads outlined above this chapter positions body, mind and the senses at the forefront of how people dwell through tourism.

The sensory habitus

Sensory knowledge is inseparable from embodied knowledge, what Mauss (1979) first referred to as a *habitus*, the repertoire of culturally patterned uses and techniques of the body specific to a society. Ways of digging, running, swimming, dancing and hunting reflect the embodiment of cultural knowledge such that squatting mankind can be distinguished from sitting mankind (Mauss 1979). The Anlo-Ewe talk of *seselelame*, feeling or hearing skin sensations linked to intuition and premonition (Geurts 2002) and the Cashinahua of Peru speak of heart knowledge, ear knowledge, eye knowledge, hand knowledge, skin knowledge and so on (Kensinger 1995).

Influenced by Mauss, Bourdieu's (1977) concept of *habitus* focuses on the structures and processes that create and internalise body behaviours and in so doing illustrates how embodied knowledge is formed through practices constitutive of social life. That is through engagement with everyday practices that coalesce to produce an embodied history of behaviours and dispositions that are passed on and down to form a common sense view of what is acceptable and what is not within any given group. According to Bourdieu (1977), the codes of a particular habitus prescribe how aspects such as class structures and matters of taste and judgement should be understood. Such codes are learnt from childhood, perfected through reinforcement to form a collective history that presents itself as a pre-existing world of accepted ways of thinking and being. As Bourdieu illustrates, bodies are culturally marshalled, ordered and regulated:

> the values given body, *made* body by the hidden persuasion of an implicit pedagogy which can instil a whole cosmology, through injunctions as insignificant as 'sit up straight' or 'don't hold your knife in your left hand' and inscribe the most fundamental principles . . . of a culture in seemingly innocuous details of bearing or physical and verbal manners, so putting them beyond the reach of consciousness.
>
> (1990: 69, original emphasis)

The repetition of such seemingly reasonable bodily restrictions is an example of how societies remember how to behave and how group members perpetuate their particular ways of being, what Connerton (1989) refers to as history sedimented in the body. Even though accepted codes are continually being challenged, as can be seen in the experiences of transgender and transsexual individuals, they still have a powerful, normative conditioning influence (Schrock and Boyd 2006). The ability of behaviour codes to prescribe and control behaviour is demonstrated in the social production of a gendered body, a process that begins in childhood and continues through the experiences of adulthood. From a young age girls and boys are socialised to think about and use their bodies in ways that conform to the particular societal belief system into which they are born. This belief system structures and organises the role and status of the male and female body and in this way bodies acquire 'value' in relation to the given social formation or field (Crossley 2001). Young (1980) argues that a patriarchal culture teaches girls and women to move in different ways to boys, ways that inhibit, confine and objectify the female body. In such cultures a girl acquires the habits of a feminine approach to body comportment and movement, described by Young as throwing like a girl, walking like a girl, sitting still like a girl and taking care of her body like a girl. Such forms of behaviour are an illustration of the embodiment of gender in relation to a particular habitus, a particular 'system of inseparably cognitive and evaluative structures which organizes the vision of the world in accordance with the objective structures of a determinate state of the social world' (Bourdieu 1977: 174).

Bourdieu is important here because tourism and being a tourist is associated with and defined in relation to specific activities, practices and behaviours, which coalesce to form the tourist habitus. The tourist habitus is an embodied history of how to behave as a tourist reinforced by the reactions of other tourists that this is the correct way of being a tourist. Sunbathing, for example, is emblematic of being a tourist, it is one of the things tourists are expected to do and its origins lie in the desire to return home with a tanned body as a sign of having been away and of possessing the financial means to travel. Interestingly, Andrews argues that tourism represents a disrupted habitus as the flow of everyday life is momentarily halted such that tourism is experienced as a 'moment of being' providing opportunities 'for increased reflexivity and heightened awareness of individual and collective identity' (2009: 17). The codes of the tourist habitus are created, confirmed and reproduced from childhood through the medium of the family holiday. Despite the fact that going on holiday is culturally constituted, the beliefs, values and practices associated with being on holiday are passed down from one generation to the next. Hence, decisions about the type of clothes to wear, what activities to engage in, how to move, behave, and even how to *feel* about being on holiday, are all influenced by the tourist habitus. In this way the tourist habitus produces what Bourdieu refers to as a *socially informed body*, which in this instance is the body of the tourist, yet this body is a sensing body firmly rooted in the world of feeling and experience:

> the *socially informed body*, with its tastes and distastes, its compulsions and repulsions, with, in a word, all its *senses*, that is to say, not only the traditional five senses . . . but also the sense of necessity and the sense of duty, the sense of direction and the sense of reality, the sense of balance and the sense of beauty, common sense and the sense of the sacred, tactical sense and the sense of responsibility, business sense and the sense of propriety, the sense of humour and the sense of absurdity, moral; sense and the sense of practicality, and so on.
>
> (1977: 124, original emphasis)

The socially informed body experiences the world through a range of senses, both the sense impressions underpinning perception, as discussed by Merleau-Ponty and the wider societal sensibilities of practice that structure the relationship between body and world, as discussed by Bourdieu. The coming together of perception and practice, as sensuous dwelling is illustrated by Lande's (2007) ethnography of military culture. Here cadets are taught how to command and how to fight not just with the body but through the body as they learn to give orders and learn how to move and to fight through a process of bodily transformation referred to as 'breathing like a soldier'. For example, orders are understood as being orders by learning specific breathing techniques, as one cadet is instructed 'don't speak from your throat. No-one will hear what you say as a command. Breathe from your stomach' (quoted in Lande 2007: 95). Likewise, effective marksmanship is about breathing 'rightly' because '[i]rregular breathing and breathing that moves the body up and down too much will lead to misplaced shots' (2007: 102).

In a similar vein Adey (2010a) demonstrates how the training of British air cadets in the early part of the twentieth century served to produce an aerial body with the set of bodily instincts and patriotic attitudes necessary for defending the nation. As with the army cadets an aerial body and character was built by body discipline, such as a cold bath and exercises that strengthened both muscle and brain, 'the ultimate goal of the embodied performance of drilling was not spectacle, but so that the cadets could develop certain qualities of an aerial character' (2010a: 44). In controlling bodily functions in this way there is a conscious awareness of both the physical and the sensuous body interacting with the mind to bring about the desired effect, the inculcation of military culture. The embodiment of martial qualities produces a form of sensuous dwelling based upon the practices and techniques of military culture; a culture that ensures individuals body forth a particular way of being human-in-the-world, the sensuous being of soldier or pilot.

To say that human dwelling is a sensuous experience is therefore to speak of a sensory habitus in and through which people body forth their world. In Greek culture a sensory habitus is created through a process of sensory enculturation such that commensality is not solely defined by practices of consumption but '*as the exchange of sensory memories and emotions, and of substances and objects incarnating remembrance and feeling*' (Seremetakis 1996c: 37, original emphasis). The disappearance of one specific 'object', a variety of peach known as the 'breast of Aphrodite', illustrates the importance of a sensory habitus for connecting the past with the present:

> I grew up with the peach. It had a thin skin touched with fuzz, and a soft matte off-white color alternating with rosy hues . . . It was well rounded and smooth like a small clay vase, fitting perfectly into your palm. Its interior was firm yet moist, offering a soft resistance to the teeth. A bit sweet and a bit sour, it exuded a distinct fragrance.
>
> (Seremetakis 1996a: 1)

Seremetakis is possessed and consumed by the cultural memory of the peach and although this particular variety of peach no longer exists, it continues to live on through her memories, observations and stories of the feel and taste of the peach and of the role it played in her life. In remembering the peach, Seremetakis is recognising those aspects of the past constitutive of the history of a Greek sensory habitus and in the stories she tells about the peach she is bringing the peach back to life. 'The younger generation . . . heard these stories as if listening to a captivating fairytale. For me the peach had been both eaten and remembered, but for the younger generation it was now digested through memory and language' (1996a: 2).

In travelling from the city to the country Seremetakis describes how the body is not only transported by the train, it is also transported by the senses. Every station is identified by the smell and taste of particular foods. On arrival the smell of the city has been replaced by the smell of the ocean and the lemon tree, by the braying sound of the donkey and the high-pitched song of the cicadas, by the feel of wind on skin and of earth under feet. To pass through these 'sensory gates' (1996c: 29) is to pass from one way of being to another in much the same way as the individual moves from a world of obligation and duty to a world defined by a more leisured existence that of being a tourist. In becoming a tourist the individual passes through numerous sensory gates, both actual (hot to cold) and psychological (fear of flying) such that within tourism a sensory habitus exists in the taste, sound, smell and feel of the holiday experience. How the individual understands, relates and responds to certain smells, sounds, images and tastes shapes cultural practices.

For example, clothes suited to a daily life lived in a cold climate are changed to those more suited to the hot climate of a holiday destination; bodies unused to heat can be overwhelmed by high temperatures or unsettled by crowds of people whose language and behaviour are very different to that of home. Odours of both the visitor and the visited bring difference and similarity into sharp relief as illustrated by the phrase 'the smell of the continent' frequently employed by early British travellers to distinguish home from abroad (Mullen and Munson 2009). Heat is linked to sunshine and sunbathing, cold to snow and skiing, bodily imbalance to the turbulence of air travel. Aural connections to the past are made possible through the stories of tour guides both human and electronic. The body propels the tourist from place to place by walking up, down, on, through and around attractions, parks and gardens. Bodies 'fly' through the air in planes, they lie on beaches, turning and twisting to ensure an even tan, they bend and stretch, rise and fall as the swell of the sea moves swimmer or surfer on and through the water. Such activities represent an intimate poetic engagement of a sensuous body. An experience of being human-in-the-world through a body that is deeply embedded in and with the world in the sense described by Merleau-Ponty '[o]ur own body is in the world as the heart is in the organism' (2002: 235).

Sensuous tourism

Despite Merleau-Ponty's assertion, the body of the tourist has not always been at the heart of tourism research. Indeed, the absence of the body in sociological studies of tourism and tourists was initially highlighted by Veijola and Jokinen (1994) in an article written in the form of a holiday diary based upon imaginary conversations with noted sociologists of tourism. The diary, presented as 'methodological play', not only highlighted the absence of the tourist body in many seminal analyses of tourism, it also questioned the absence of the researcher's body when analysing the results of tourism research:

> So far the tourist has lacked a body because the analyses have tended to concentrate on the *gaze* and/or structures of *waged labour* societies. Furthermore, judged by the *discursive postures* given to the *writing subject* of most of the analyses, the analyst himself, has, likewise, lacked a body.
>
> (Veijola and Jokinen 1994: 149, original emphasis)

Since 1994 the body of the tourist has been uncovered through numerous insightful explorations of the relationship between the body and the places, practices and experiences associated with tourism (see Crouch 2000; Crouch and Desforges 2003; Obrador-Pons 2003; Andrews 2005; Chronis 2006; Matteucci 2014; O'Regan 2016). There is also an emerging focus on embodiment in relation to tourists with physical and/or visual impairment (Small and Darcy 2011; Small et al 2012; Richards et al 2010).

Although some studies focus on one or two senses in particular, such as vision, touch or hearing, it is clearly impossible to dislocate one sense from all the others. In any given experience a particular sense may dominate but overall the body of the tourist engages in a multisensory relationship with the world. Even the influential organising concept of the tourist gaze has been reconceptualised as an embodied and multisensory performance because '[t]he embodied travelling eye cannot be separated from the body that moves and touches the ground with 'performed' tourist gazes involving other sensescapes' (Larsen and Urry 2011: 1112). Similarly, Lagerkvist (2007) illustrates how activities such as eating and drinking draw Western visitors into a multisensory relationship with the city of Shanghai. This relationship collapses time and space by encouraging an experience of dwelling through nostalgia based on a never lived but covertly desired past drawn from selected memories of hedonism, affluence and Western self-perceptions of colonial superiority:

> the nostalgia for cosmopolitan Shanghai . . . offers visitors a colonial escape, a temporal displacement through multisensory means, which, in fact, holds a promise for them to stay at center stage – even though the future of the planet will most certainly be Asian.
>
> (Lagerkvist 2007: 168)

Although the body of the tourist and that of the researcher are now more visible in tourism research, the unity of body, mind and senses as a way of being and dwelling is frequently subordinate to the specific sense or embodied experience under discussion. This is not to say that embodiment is not linked to or mentioned alongside a concept of dwelling in some of the studies referred to earlier, but rather to argue that the philosophical possibilities of dwelling (sensuous or otherwise) are largely subordinate to the sense or senses under discussion. Likewise, whilst it is clearly important to explore and understand the interrelationship between tourism, embodiment and understandings of identity (whether self, individual or collective), what identity tells us about dwelling as a way of being human-in-the-world is less clear. Since *being* and identity are not the same thing, socially, culturally or philosophically.

Sensing the world through tourism invokes a particular understanding of dwelling based on the body's *immersion* in the world that goes beyond experience of the world. Immersion is a more nuanced and arguably a more productive way of exploring what we mean by *experience*, which to my mind tends to evoke an *of* rather than an *in* understanding of the encounter between self and world; an uninvolved and passive rather than an active encounter. Hence, my tendency to talk about experience *of and in* the world as a way of diluting the sense of detachment from the world that experience *of* can sometimes imply (see Turner and Bruner 1986 for a discussion of the relationship between anthropology, experience and culture).

Sensuous immersion of the tourist body occurs within spaces defined by moments of departure from many but not necessarily all of the practices, responsibilities, relationships and duties that structure daily life, such as work, relationships with family and with the wider community. In the spaces of interruption that tourism provides the body of the tourist has a different rhythm; it moves in different ways reflective of what has been referred to as 'flirting with space' (Crouch 2010). The concept of flirting is interesting because flirting is sensual as well as corporeal with transitory almost fleeting connotations suggestive of how tourists might experience and embody the moments of interruption that tourism provides. Hence, the tourist body wears different or even no clothing as the freedom associated with being away is embodied through the sounds and smells of being on holiday and through the unbuckling and undressing of the tourist body (Obrador-Pons 2007; Andrews 2005, 2011); the tourist body experiences different and often heightened sensations and emotions in response to place, people and activity, as Skinner's (2007) ethnography of dance tourists to the English resort of Southport illustrates. One particular tourist called Helen expressed and displayed various emotions associated with the tourist stages of the trip such as fantasising over the weekend ahead and mood swings in response to the daily obligations of the dance floor then 'finally, upon return, post-tourism, the bodymind collapsed in a heap of muscular/mental memories of carrying cases learning dancing and being danced' (2007: 347).

Dance tourism demonstrates that the body of the tourist is also a social body, it engages with other bodies, things and activities, with other places and ways of living. So although embodiment may be personal in terms of *my* body, it is affected by the presence or absence of other bodies and by involvement with human sociality. It is also affected by experience of and engagement with nature and with the natural world of animals, insects, reptiles and so forth (Merchant 2011; Ben-David 2013; Schwartz 2013). A focus on sensuous dwelling is a focus on the relationships that shape and articulate how being human is brought forth through the body of the tourist.

Sensuous tourists

So how do tourists body forth the world as they engage with tourism? What are the habitual patterns of body use that Jackson (1983: 335) argues are 'socially implemented and publicly played out' through tourism? This section explores some of the ways in which the body of the tourist bodies forth the world as sensuous dwelling by exploring selected body practices of the tourist habitus: walking and sightseeing.

Of course there are numerous tourist practices and activities that can be drawn upon to illustrate the role of tourism in cultivating a sensuous relationship between body and world. For example, O'Regan's (2016: 333) work on backpacking culture demonstrates that, '[e]ven before the journey, the backpacker body is made fit-for-purpose, with vaccinations, travel insurance and first-aid kits incorporated, performed and rendered through the body as embodied expressions of backpacker consciousness'. However, walking and sightseeing are foundational tourist activities, being among the most recognisable of activities representing as they do ways of moving, looking and being a tourist. Furthermore, although walking and seeing are ordinary, routine activities of daily life, they are not understood as being particularly significant in the same way as they are when associated with tourism. Through tourism, walking and seeing acquire heightened significance because they are advertised as the means by which to uncover and discover the people, places, things and ideas not normally encountered as part of daily life. In effect tourism transforms them by making them visible, visible in the sense of being noticed and as such seeing becomes sightseeing and a walker is turned into an explorer.

In focusing on these two it is not my intention, nor is it possible, to discuss each one in terms of a specific sense, as the union of body, mind and senses is implicit in both activities. Furthermore, I do not intend to separate them from each other but rather to integrate them since walking is inextricably linked to sightseeing. Phrases such as 'look where you are going', 'mind the step' arise from the interplay of the physical and the visual, an interplay that shifts vision from the near to the far, from foreground to horizon. This is not to ignore the fact that sightseeing also occurs sitting down, through the window of a tour bus, a car or a train but rather to argue that walking engages the body with and in the world more completely than sitting because of its nature, it is a physical practice not a physical position. Walking brings with it awareness of the body – a body that sees through the feet, the hands, the arms and head as well as the eyes. Walking utilises the body's muscles, sinews and tendons; lifting a leg, striding forth, the pain of stretched, taut muscles, minute bodily movements in negotiating a rocky or narrow path. Tripping, stumbling, falling as body meets world. Of course the body is still active when sitting down but it is so in a different, more contemplative way than when engaged in walking.

Sightseeing moves the head back and forth to get a better view, sometimes it requires instant decisions about whether to move or to stay put and what is seen may delight or cause physical distress. Hence, my argument that these activities illustrate the harmony of body, mind and senses that is sensuous dwelling, the means by which a body feels and comes to know that it is human. In focusing down the discussion I am not arguing that every tourist body engages with these activities in the same way, as different cultures and belief systems influence how bodies become a tourist. Chinese tourists do not move in the same way as American tourists. Even non-tourists walk differently. A police officer walking the beat in an urban environment has a very different gait to a gamekeeper traversing the Scottish Highlands, thereby demonstrating that walking is conditioned by clothing, purpose and terrain. Similarly, visually impaired individuals navigate through touch and not just through the hands but also through the touch of their feet on the ground (Macpherson 2009; Small et al 2012). So, what matters is that walking and sightseeing are both identifiable with tourists and tourism despite culture not because of culture. They are activities that can cross as well as define cultures.

Walking seeing thinking

> Walking, ideally, is a state in which the mind, the body, and the whole world are aligned, as though they were characters finally in conversation together, three notes suddenly making a chord . . . Walking can also be imagined as a visual activity, every walk a tour leisurely enough both to see and to think over the sights, to assimilate the new into the known.
>
> (Solnit 2002: 5, 6)

Tourism and walking are characters in conversation with the world and this conversation takes place through the medium of a sensing body. Walking connects mind, body and the senses with the world through active engagement in the world. This engagement may occur through formalised walking tours of Israel or Belfast (Selwyn 1995; Skinner 2016), improvised walks through the ruins of industrial decay (Edensor 2008), or purposeful walking over a bridge (Irving 2013). All these examples demonstrate that walking and seeing are inextricably linked. Indeed, de Certeau notably argued in his essay *Walking in the City* that to walk is also to read the landscape since walking encourages a particular way of surveying the world as illustrated by the rhetorical question '*voyeurs or walkers*' (1988: 92, original emphasis). However, walking as seeing is not just a way of reading or narrating a landscape because a reading metaphor ignores the body's role in creating what is read using all the senses not just that of sight. As Edensor argues in his discussion of the serendipitous and fragmented experience of walking through ruins, '[i]n its quest for an orderly account, narrative cannot effectively capture the momentary impressions confronted, the peculiar evanescent atmospheres, the rhythms, immanent sensations and physical effects of walking' (2008: 137).

However, as indicated earlier the narratives of visually impaired tourists can capture and convey the sensations and physical effects of walking as seeing on the body leading to a viscerally different experience of the world to that of sighted individuals. This is illustrated by Keith, one of the walkers interviewed by Macpherson as part of her research into the experiences of blind and partially sighted members of a walking group:

> texture is very important . . . and obviously you can feel through your feet the texture of what you are walking through . . . and because you can't visualize where you are about to put your foot that's important . . . it is like your knees act as shock absorbers, so your body sort of takes on the role almost of an extra hand, you can feel through the shoe . . . instead of anticipating with the eyes and generating images with the brain . . . you have to analyse the texture and feel with your body.
>
> (Quoted in Macpherson 2009: 180)

Visually impaired tourists 'see' through the heightened awareness of their other senses and as their body makes actual physical contact with their environment. Hence, a visually impaired tourist describes her encounter with the Blarney Stone at Blarney Castle as being, '[f]or me, I need to touch it; if I can, I'll walk on it, sit on it, whatever. But I need to touch it' (quoted in Small et al 2012: 944). Through sitting and standing, the body touches the world as a way of navigating and making sense of that which it encounters and in so doing experience becomes embodied memory. The walking and seeing that occurs at a tourist attraction both creates memories of a day out and stimulates memories of what an individual tourist may once have experienced, or have read about or even been taught at school. Heritage attractions invite tourists to step back in time, to follow or walk in the footsteps of people from the past as if through walking the individual can physically embody and experience not just the past but the past as another person's life. Hence, Visit England's (2017) website invites tourists to '[f]ollow in the footsteps of prisoners at the Westgate Museum', to '[w]alk through 800 years of history in Southampton's Old Town', to '[t]ake a step back in time in Southsea' and to '[f]ollow in the footsteps of William the Conqueror'. These are examples of walking as time travel or more specifically walking is the means by which the body can travel back in time, a form of walking that resonates with what Ingold (2010) refers to as mind-walking, walking through the imagination.

The body acquires the technique of walking and seeing as a tourist through reading brochures of destinations and activities that are represented as worthwhile holiday experiences. Nielsen (2003) for example illustrates how tourist brochures of the Koli Mountain region of eastern Finland present nature as something to be seen and engaged with through sensuous activity rather than contemplated for its aesthetic qualities. Engagement is presented as an 'invitation to be embodied' (2007: 95) as visitors are encouraged to walk, hike, ride, ski, fish, row and camp in a landscape transformed over the years by the activity of lumberjacks, skiers and nature lovers. Here walking, hiking and camping are not just ways of seeing and experiencing the world; they are also ways of being human-in-the-world by reconstructing historic patterns of use both with and through a sensing body. Moreover, Nielsen argues that this sensing body moves and is moved by the landscape by connecting with the pulse or rhythm of the natural environment, by feeling the wind, rain, sun and snow of the natural world. Edensor (2010: 75) makes a similar point in relation to the rhythmic dimension of walking. Drawing on the works of three walking artists, Edensor argues that as the lively moving body of the walker weaves itself in with the sounds, smells, animals and rocks encountered on the walk, the walking body not only sees the landscape through the eyes it also senses the landscape as a rhythmic pulsing space.

The concept of pulse is interesting in relation to the previously cited quote from Merleau-Ponty that '[o]ur own body is in the world as the heart is in the organism' (2002: 235) because it enables walking to be understood as a form of rhythmic embodiment of the landscape as something akin to the pulse of the heart as it pushes the blood around the body. Walking and seeing through tourism quickens the pulse of the lived body by engaging all the senses and this is particularly so with political walking tours to places of past and ongoing conflict. The Falls Road in the city of Belfast plays a significant role in the struggle between the Unionists and the Republicans that became known as The Troubles – 'a seething, and still simmering, ethno-nationalist conflict on the streets of Northern Ireland' (Skinner 2016: 24). Walkers guided through the Nationalist Falls Road by Republican ex-prisoner Liam experience a visceral and conflicted understanding of their tour guide's relationship with the road. As Liam recounts his experience of being arrested as a teenager and sent to goal, the bodies of the tourist 'start to grow cold and tremble' (2016: 30). In walking, seeing and listening 'we all had an 'Oh my God' moment with him. Here was someone before us 'who had taken the bullet' and who had given the bullet. Here was a martyr. Here was an ally. Here was an enemy' (Skinner 2016: 26).

Although this is a good example of the link between walking and seeing, it is also an example of walking as a way of thinking and expressing the human condition. The bodies of the Falls Road tourists feel Liam's experiences as a political prisoner through imaginative thinking that connects the present to the past in another example of walking as time travel.

Skinner further argues that Liam's walking is the personification of his Republican ideology embedded in and through his bodily movements around the landscapes of political conflict. A similar argument has been made by Gros (2014) in relation to Mahatma Ghandi, whose constant walking was a political statement and a non-violent protest against Great Britain's colonial occupation of India that personified the strength and the humility of the man. This is interesting because the walking of Ghandi, the walking of Liam and that of the Falls Road tourists are ways of connecting people, place and time and this explains why phrases such as 'walk in the footsteps of' are so appealing. A good illustration of the ability of walking and seeing to connect people place and time and hence to attract tourists is provided by the following walking tour of Delhi:

> Much loved, oft-quoted, sorely missed, inspirational Gandhi was possibly India's most influential (not to mention inspiring) figure. This Delhi tour honours the great man, his work, his words, and enduring legacy.

Highlights

- Discover Gandhi's Delhi, and walk in his footsteps through the city
- Visit places in Delhi associated with Gandhi
- Hear stories of Gandhi's courageous life
- Discover Gandhi's philosophies of non-violent protest
- Pore over documents and artefacts at the National Gandhi Museum
- Experience the city through the father of Indian independence

(Urban Adventures 2017)

The tours of Ghandi's Delhi and that of Liam's Belfast illustrate the link between walking and knowing, walking and knowledge because both are predicated on the exchange of knowledge as ideology; Liam's Republican ideology and Ghandi's ideology of non-violent protest embedded in their bodily movements. Walking and seeing combine to create a sense of place and time that engenders a physical link with the past as the tourists' bodies react to their experiences on the tour. Liam's actual body and Ghandi's imagined body choreograph this link with and experience of place and time by bringing together the materiality of past events with the stories about what took place. This ideological choreography resembles the coming together of what Seamon (1979: 54) has referred to as '*body ballets* and *time-space routines*', a set of habitual and integrated gestures and bodily movements that fuse together to create '*place ballet*'. Seamon's concept of place ballet refers to the regular routines of life that bring people together as, for example, when parents who meet other parents as strangers at the school gate every day may over time become acquaintances and then friends. Nonetheless the walking tours of Delhi and the Falls Road also involve the regular and habitual bodily movements of Ghandi and Liam. Through these movements Ghandi and Liam body forth the world of colonial India and The Troubles of Northern Ireland for the tourists. In this way ideology is transferred from the past to the future through the sensuous dwelling of tourists, 'supporting a time-space continuity grounded in patterns of the past' (Seamon 1979: 57).

The walking and seeing body ballets of tourism illustrate what Ingold (2004) refers to as 'circumambulatory knowing' – a way of understanding the world based upon a responsive relationship between body and world. This relationship is not only mediated by stories and materiality but also by walking tools such as shoes, boots, skies, skates and so forth (Ingold

2004: 331). These tools influence the body's relationship with the world because they structure how the world is experienced and how it is *felt* as the soles of the feet meet the ground beneath. Rigid shoes and boots separate the individual from the ground by creating an insulating barrier between body and world, a barrier not experienced by those individuals and groups who walk or run barefoot. Feeling and sensing the ground through the sole of a shoe produces a different sensory relationship with and knowledge of the world because the consequences of stepping on something sharp or tripping over an obstacle are not understood in the same way as they are for the barefoot walker. Of course shoe walkers also have to look where they are going, but what and how they know through walking is predicated upon a different experience of sensuous dwelling.

The idea of knowing through walking is further illustrated by Irving's (2013) ethnography of walking, thinking and being in relation to the bridges of New York. Irving asked a number of individuals to wear a microphone into which each recorded their thoughts as they walked across a particular bridge. In thinking while walking Irving's walkers demonstrate how emotion, mood and memory combine with movement to constitute lived experience. The bridges wove themselves into and through the thought process of each individual, creating a dialogue in the form of a conversation with the self. The ongoing streams of inner dialogue and imaginative reverie captured in the recordings reveal how walking, thinking and seeing stimulate knowledge of the relationship between self and world. This knowledge is expressed in the form of opinions and reflections about the state of the economy, work, relationships and childhood memories. As the following excerpt from Yuri's recording on the Brooklyn Bridge illustrates:

> I've lived this life for the past thirty-seven years and the outcome has always been trial by trial by trial. But at the same time I get a calming sense walking on the Brooklyn Bridge. It's perhaps where I got the idea of being propelled up into heaven by an invisible line. But hopefully today's job will work out fine. I have to go in tomorrow for orientation. I have a chance to move up and it's in sales and hopefully everything will be peachy and I can set my problems aside and I can learn how to become a New Yorker.
>
> (Quoted in Irving 2013: 298)

Irving's bridge walkers illustrate walking as therapy, walking as confessional, walking as seeing and thinking, '[w]hile walking, you hold yourself to account: you correct yourself, challenge yourself, assess yourself' (Gros 2014: 196). Through walking an individual *sees* her/himself as well as the immediate environment and in so doing thinks about the self in relation to that environment, that particular 'world'. Walking, seeing and thinking also occurs as visitors walk around tourist attractions. In my conversations with and observations of visitors and staff at three English heritage sites, people frequently linked their life to the person, event/time and the materiality of the particular place visited. These connections between people and place drew on memories of times past or on aspects of the present and were often expressed through anger, laughter, smiles and shrugs. The following examples illustrate what I mean here. Both are excerpts from recorded conversations, the first with a group of visitors to Chartwell, the home of Sir Winston Churchill and the second with a member of staff at Battle Abbey, the site of a significant medieval battle between the French and the English:

Chartwell

MAN: I tell you one thing I once remember reading about Winston Churchill. It must of been when I was about ten and not getting very good school reports.

WOMAN: Were you comforted by his? [Laughs]

MAN: I was comforted, because I read somewhere a copy of his school report which said he was lazy, not very bright and wasn't a good leader of men and was easily led, that was it, was easily led and . . . I got this appalling report saying but I was a good leader and I remember showing it me mother and saying, well it was better than Churchill's [both laugh] that must of been in the early fifties.

Battle Abbey

Oh yes, I think all of us custodians we, you know, it becomes part of your blood if you're away from it and you're at a different site you think no, my monuments Battle Abbey or whatever, but yeah it does become part of you . . . the historical feel . . . it's lovely getting out in the grounds and walking around seeing that lovely roof vaulting and all the rest of it, yeah, it does give you a lot.

These embodied emotions are the biological connective tissue between the past and the present and like all such tissue they stretch, loosen, tighten or breakdown as the act of walking and seeing causes visitors and employees to think about and respond to their encounter with people, time and place. As Solnit notes '[t[he rhythm of walking generates a kind of rhythm of thinking, and the passage through a landscape echoes or stimulates the passage through a series of thoughts' (2002: 5–6).

The rhythm of walking is a form of writing on the landscape where the body is the pen and the senses the ink to write the thoughts that come to mind as someone walks. Walking-seeing-thinking is, then, a rhythmic composition and what is being composed is the activity of tourism and being a tourist. Walking around the Acropolis in Greece is a dialogic embodied performance between people and place that serves to construct the Acropolis as a tourist site; 'both tourists and locals took similar routes in their embodied exploration of the place and engaged in similar 'performances' of activities many of which reflected the construction and consumption of the Acropolis as a 'touristic' place' (Rakić and Chambers 2012: 1628). Activities such as walking and sightseeing are constitutive of what tourists are expected to do, and in their embodiment of the Acropolis both tourists and locals are confirming and reproducing walking and sightseeing as accepted practices of the tourist habitus.

However, Bourdieu notes that the concept of learnt habitus should not imply passive acceptance as individuals and groups can act to subvert the codes of a particular habitus. In order to be subversive an individual must have something to subvert, there must be a rejection of a particular set of accepted dispositions. Being against something is an acknowledgement that there are accepted ways of doing something, accepted ways of being a tourist and of doing tourism. So, although bodies can be manipulated by technology and advertising, bodies also disrupt and create their own rules by choosing to subvert or challenge what may be understood as accepted ways of walking and sightseeing. Elastic City is an American company that offers local residents and tourists artist-led walking tours of New York based around the creation of a participatory, sensory relationship between body and world. Through poetry, performance, sound and movement participants on the walks actively shape how they experience and come to know the city through encounters with the park, museums and monuments. In doing so they discover alternative ways of knowing, seeing and experiencing the city, as the following website testimonial illustrates:

> Navigating through a park with one's eyes closed, using only the sense of sound, creates an adventure through a sea of squealing children and squeaking swings. Movement starts to feel vertiginous and unpredictable, directional orientation becomes an outright adventure. I can't wait to try it again.
>
> (Elastic City 2017)

Such alternative forms of walking challenge the usual depiction of the tourist as *flâneur*. Based upon Walter Benjamin's (1973) adaptation of the concept the tourist is represented as passively strolling through the urban environment, watching and observing what goes on (see Wearing et al 2010). The tourist as *flâneur*, whether male or female, has always seemed to me to present a particularly disembodied theorisation of the actual experience of walking generally and specifically in relation to sightseeing. The experience of sensory-impaired tourists is instructive here; Elizabeth Dann has written that despite a total loss of vision and with limited hearing, she is nonetheless able to participate in tourism by employing her other senses, namely, touch, taste and smell. Since losing her sight in 2008 she has documented and categorised her sensory experiences according to the sense judged to be dominant at any given time. So although she touches the Christmas trees in Cologne cathedral she categorises the experience as being predominantly one of smell because 'I consider their seasonal aroma more evocative than the reassurance of touching them, important though the latter undoubtedly may be in another set of circumstances' (Dann and Dann 2011: 10).

This example illustrates the active nature of embodiment since Elizabeth is selecting which one of her sense experiences most connects her to the world around her. She does not ignore the fact that her experiences are multisensory, but rather she is an active participant in her own sensory dwelling. The experiences of the blind and visually impaired suggest that sightseeing is too narrowly defined and is perhaps better understood as sense-seeing. As Howes noted earlier in relation to the means by which anthropologists explore other realities, walking and sightseeing are ways of sensing rather than reading people and place. These activities are indicative of embodied ways of knowing the world and also of learning how to be a tourist in the world.

In learning how to be a tourist through walking and sightseeing the individual is also learning about ways to body forth the world through the imagination; Ingold's notion of mind-walking. This is important because doing tourism is not solely defined in relation to specific activities and behaviours; it is also an imaginative doing as the places and things of tourism are frequently imagined before they are experienced and this produces a form of knowledge about doing tourism and about being a tourist that is not concerned with 'sense so much as sensuousness, an embodied and somewhat automatic "knowledge" that functions like peripheral vision, not studied contemplation, a knowledge that is imageric and sensate rather than ideational' (Taussig 1992: 141). Mind-walking through tourist brochures and websites is a sensuous preparation for the experience to come, a preparation that provides the foundations needed to turn the body of daily life into the body of a tourist. In this sense brochures, websites and travel programmes serve to create the tourist habitus by conditioning the body to think, move and feel like a tourist.

Knowing how to be a tourist thus comes about through walking as a form of embodied seeing. As the body of the tourist walks, it sees and responds to the rise and fall of the landscape by walking up or down a hill, over stones or uneven ground and in so doing it both creates and communicates this relationship between self and world – '[t]he rigid walk of the urban pedestrian reveals the dense, impacting weight of city walls; the lambent grace of the stroller in the meadows shows the lightness of a natural space' (Grange 2000: 72). The body is responding not just to the materiality of walls and the ground beneath the feet but also to environmental conditions such as sunshine, rain, fog, sleet and snow. Tourism creates experiences that body forth an enchanted body by manipulating the environment through the use of technology. *The Enchanted Forest* is an annual light and sound spectacle set in Faskally Wood in Pitlochry, Scotland: '[w]ith dazzling visuals and innovative design set against an original music score . . . explore the stunning autumn woodland setting . . . Using the forest as a natural backdrop, you will experience a lighting show that is, quite simply, out of this world' (*The Enchanted Forest* 2017). Spectacle produces a heightened form of embodied engagement with the world such that walking through an enchanted forest produces a different form of sightseeing because what is being seen is not the forest but the sensory spectacle of light and sound. *The Enchanted Forest* attraction is sensuous dwelling in technicolour.

Conclusion

What I have argued here is that human dwelling is essentially experienced through the senses through the coming together of body, mind and senses as sensuous dwelling. It is a way of engaging in a conversation with the world about how particular sensory orientations influence ways of being human-in-the-world. However, sensuous conversations with the world are, as previously argued, formed by and through culture, by particular ways of knowing and understanding the world and in this regard what I have presented here is a predominantly Western approach to sensuous dwelling. This is important because the sensory habitus of tourism is not the same for all tourists and in experiencing the world through tourism people not only encounter familiarity, they also encounter difference in terms of different smells, sounds, textures and so forth. Familiarity and difference are sensory compass points for working out who I am, who we are and how we should live in and with the world.

The world I am referring to is a world gathered together through the coming together of body, mind and senses, and what is gathered are flesh and feeling, bone and body. In effect sensuous dwelling makes the body available to be someone in the world, what Heidegger refers to as ready-to-hand. Although Heidegger explains ready-to-hand in terms of things as tools or equipment, body, mind and senses are the basic equipment of lived experience, and as equipment they are used to create, recreate and enliven the circumstances of human dwelling.

Tourism is one of the ways in which human dwelling is expressed, and the form this dwelling takes is based around the bodily practices and activities that over time have come to define the tourist habitus, define what it is to do tourism and to be a tourist; activities such as walking, sightseeing, and also diving, skiing, sunbathing and so on. The tourist habitus is fundamentally a sensuous habitus because tourism is the sensory engagement with different ways of living, thinking and knowing. Tourists encounter people, places and things through the senses, through the sights, smells, sounds and tastes that represent being away. However, I do not mean away in terms of geography or time, but away in a more visceral sense where tourism is a sensuous departure from that which is familiar towards an unfamiliar sensory orientation, towards other ways of dwelling and being human-in-the-world.

It is in the sensuous realm of leaving and returning that we come to feel and to know who we are. Hence, to say that our return journey is by train, car, boat or train is to miss the point of what homecoming really means, of what it is to come home. Coming home is not about transport, it is about reconnecting with a particular embodied understanding of the world. It is a sensuous homecoming to those familiar sensations individuals subjectively choose to refer to and rely upon as a means of locating the self in the world. Transport may facilitate homecoming, but it is not the only means by which we return home from our travels. We can travel home through the imagination, through memories of home and through anticipation of a return to home.

Sensuous dwelling is, then, a way of engaging in a conversation with the world and with the self and into this conversation we invite or visit other people, things and places. It is a conversation about ways of grasping the diversity of human experience, although it is important to acknowledge that encountering diversity is not the same as accepting and embracing diversity. In this respect, sensuous dwelling should not be seen as a static understanding of the relationship between body and world because as with any conversation the topic changes, individuals leave or join, they choose to agree or disagree; location and time influence when a conversation begins or ends, conversations are interrupted, broken up and even prohibited. The conversation between walking and sightseeing offers a more nuanced understanding of these activities as embodied expressions of being a tourist-in-the-world.

Walking and sightseeing also illustrates that being in and understanding the world is not merely about movement, despite what the movement-mobility paradigm might suggest in relation to the doing of tourism. We move because we have a body, we move because something in the world stimulates us to move. Movement is thus a response to being human-in-the-world, it is not a prerequisite for being human-in-the-world. Nevertheless, movement is part of the rhythmic pulse that propels the body of the tourist towards and around destinations, and in this sense, it is a contributor to the conversation about how dwelling through the body of a tourist influences the experience of being human.

3 Material dwelling

Introduction

From embodied aspects of dwelling I now move to the material to discuss how being and dwelling is intertwined with materiality. By materiality I mean the world of objects and 'things', the wider physical world of structures such as buildings, landscape and the natural environment. All such elements are brought into being, infused with meaning or affected in some way by human activity and thus by the social and cultural framings that transform how they are created, thought about, put to use and even destroyed (Miller 1998b; Thomas 1999). Dwelling through materiality encourages an engaged and involved experience of being human in relation to the 'stuff' of tourism – souvenirs, postcards and brochures; photographs, films and mementoes; travel tickets, T-shirts and mugs; rugs, carpets and pottery – that are bought, sold, collected, collated and displayed. All such 'things' mediate knowledge and understanding in terms of the self as an individual and as a social being.

Dwelling also occurs through encountering the material spaces and places of tourism, through visits to ruins, sites of industrial activity, palaces, pagodas, gardens and so forth. The objects and 'things' of tourism, therefore, cannot be separated from the wider material setting in which they are located and experienced. Museums, art galleries, castles, country houses and such like are not only repositories of objects, they are also material settings in their own right, which when taken together speak of relationships between people, between people and time, people and place, people and memory. This is important because my intention here is not to analyse a tourism object or set of objects *per se* or to focus on material culture as a general interpretive frame since there is a wide body of literature on such aspects already (Pearce 1994; Palmer 1998; Miller 1998b; Haldrup and Larsen 2006). My intention is rather to explore how dwelling through *materiality* as outlined above influences the experience of being human. Specifically, I am concerned with the *gathering* capacity of materiality and with how the objects, buildings and landscapes of tourism *gather* together a 'world' in and through which being human is experienced. The nature of the world so created is of interest here because it illustrates the connective links between building, dwelling and thinking.

Before moving on I need to say something about my use of the word 'thing' as this is pertinent to the ensuing discussion. By using 'thing' to refer to a variety of material objects my intention is to encapsulate both the physical and the phenomenological characteristics of their presence in the world. Heidegger's (2001) essay '*The Thing*' provides a useful contextual framing, given his focus on how humans encounter the world through practical, everyday forms of materiality. However, I do not intend to deconstruct Heidegger's ontological examination of 'the thing', or what he refers to as 'thingness' but rather to consider how his philosophical approach influences my thinking in relation to how human dwelling is revealed through the everyday material world of tourism.

As argued in Chapter 1, tourism is embedded in the everyday, it is what many people do, think about and experience either directly or indirectly through for example, tourism advertising, through recollections of trips made and through contemplation of those yet to come. The objects, things and 'stuff' of tourism are inseparable from the thinking, doing and experiencing of tourism. Heidegger's discussion of two specific 'things', a jug and a lectern are of particular relevance here.

For Heidegger (2001: 164) 'being-there' in terms of being-in-the-world should be understood as a process of 'nearness', a process of bringing person and world together through encounters with what is near to us and '[n]ear to us are what we usually call things'. However, Heidegger's interpretation of 'thing' goes beyond objects such as works of art, books or photographs to encompass the concrete phenomena encountered in everyday life (Polt 1999; Malpas 2008). Heidegger's 'things' range from a bench, footbridge and plow to tree, pond and hill. However, his primary illustration of 'the thing' is a jug. Things like a jug are important not only because they have a practical use but also because they are endowed with a 'holding nature' that gathers person and world together, '[t]he jug is not a vessel because it was made; rather, the jug had to be made because it is this holding vessel' (2001: 166). In other words, the jug was made because a 'thing' was needed to hold water and other liquids; however before the water can be held, it first has to be gathered by something, presaging the need for a 'holding vessel'. Hence, the jug holds or gathers together the world 'through the way in which the thing 'works' in its essential character as a thing' (Malpas 2008: 233).

In this sense thing creates world and as argued in Chapter 1, 'world' is indicative of a holistic relationship with familiar everydayness, a relationship with what is encountered in the immediate environment. What the jug gathers or brings together is a set of ordered relations that create the location for and the experience of drinking, socialising and such like. For example, the jug 'gathers' because a table or dresser is required on which to place the jug, a cup or glass is needed from which to drink and someone has to drink from the cup. What eventually emerges is a setting in which to drink and this setting has many different manifestations such as a kitchen, a home, a café, a bar, a restaurant and so forth. Each setting is reflective of the wider world from and to which the jug belongs, the world of the kitchen, restaurant, hotel or bar:

> in which the jug is kept, the shop from which it was bought, the character of its making, the mode of decoration that it bears, the cups and glasses into which it pours . . . the occasions of its use, the needs to which it responds, the people who make use of it or who are served by it . . . and so on.
>
> (Malpas 2008: 240)

In this respect the jug is suggestive of the role of materiality in relation to its use value, in terms of what it does or how it works to bring a meaningful world in to being. By meaningful I am referring to the practices, purposes, values and beliefs that underpin how people choose to live and what they choose to make of life. Such elements bring about or reveal particular configurations of the world depending upon the thing or things gathered. The world of the chef was discussed in Chapter 1, but things also cohere and gather together other worlds such as the world of the teacher or a scientific world; 'the way in which scientific practice and scientific things gather the world together is a different form of gathering from that which we see in the gathering of the jug, but it is a form of gathering nonetheless' (Malpas 2008: 240). As such, the settings and experiences brought together by things such as a jug are reflective of the cultural particularities of the world in and from which they came into being. The world so created enables those who experience it to *be* someone and to have an identity in the sense of being a host, a guest, a scientist or a tourist; as well as being English, Russian or Chinese.

The second example of 'things' as connectors of human and world is Heidegger's (2008) examination of a lectern. Here, Heidegger argues that in coming into contact with the lectern we do not encounter or see the lectern, we do not see a set of brown shapes or boxes constructed as an academic lecturing desk, rather what we 'see' is the experience of speaking and of being received, the experience of being asked questions and of having to provide answers. In other words we 'see' who we are in relation to how we experience and use 'things' in the world, and through what we do in the world. As Heidegger (2008: 57) argues 'I see the lectern in an orientation, an illumination, a background'.

In standing at a lectern – however it may be configured – I see myself as an academic, as someone who reveals, generates and challenges that which is referred to as knowledge. Whereas in encountering the lectern, the members of my audience see the reason why they are in the audience, they see the reason why they are there. Depending upon the occasion, this may be the experience of being a student, of being a fellow academic or an interested member of the public. Thus, a particular world – in this instance the world of education and of learning – is gathered out of the immediate environment, what Heidegger memorably referred to as 'worlding', a gathering together of things as a particular world or environmental milieu:

> In the experience of seeing the lectern something is given to *me* from out of an immediate environment [*Umwelt*]. This environmental milieu (lectern, book, blackboard, notebook, fountain pen, caretaker, student fraternity, tram-car, motor-car, etc.) does not consist just of things, objects, which are then conceived as meaning this and this; rather . . . Living in an environment, it signifies to me everywhere and always . . . the character of world.
>
> (2008: 58, original emphasis)

Both the jug and the lectern illustrate that although objects as 'things' have a practical role in terms of use, what is meant by use goes beyond function to mean use value in relation to the particular world gathered by the object. In this respect the relationship between person, object and world underpins how human dwelling occurs through materiality. Richardson's (1982) ethnography of the market and the Plaza in Cartago, Costa Rica illustrates what I mean here. By drawing from Heidegger, he demonstrates how encounters with the material setting of each place bring about different ways of being-in-the-world; different ways of being and living as a South American. Through an analysis of interactions and behaviour at each site, being-in-the market is expressed as *listo* – meaning smart, clever or opportunistic, whereas being-in-the plaza is expressed as *cultura* – meaning proper, ordered, behaved, '[t]hrough our actions, our *inter*actions, we bring about the world in which we then are' particular persons (Richardson 1982: 421, original emphasis).

To speak of material dwelling is therefore to speak of the ways in which things, whether objects or structures and the settings in which they are to be found are put to use, how they are employed to construct a world, a life and in so doing create and reinforce the fundamental values that define what matters in that world. Such an argument resonates with much of the literature focusing on aspects of the material world (Appadurai 1986; Miller 1998b; Palmer 2003). Dwelling in this sense comes about through immersion of the individual in the lifeworld on the basis of encounters with things and hence with culture. As Ingold (2011a) argues, dwelling concerns the ways in which people singly and together produce their own lives, and as they do so, produce who they *are*. Such a comment resonates with the work of Richardson above.

In terms of the material world of tourism, the objects of tourism enable an individual to *be* a tourist through encountering and experiencing objects as part of the social world. Through encounters with the objects of tourism we 'see' the experience of being a tourist and in so doing experience how the people we choose to visit structure their world. We experience what matters to them, their values and beliefs and this is so even when encountering a world that is familiar to *me*, when I am a person in and from that world. This is not to deny accepted caveats that the world created for tourists is frequently invented, politicised, exclusive and selective, but such criticisms can be directed at other aspects of life that have nothing to do with tourism. The materiality of tourism is drawn from an already imperfect world and some visitors will understand and acknowledge that, whilst others will not even notice or be concerned. Humans dwell as they engage with, make and transform the materiality of their everyday world wherever it is to be found. By way of illustration I now move on to discuss a specific example of being and dwelling in relation to the material world of tourism. My example is based upon rethinking my own ethnographic work at Hever Castle in England, part of a wider study of Englishness and heritage tourism (Palmer 1998, 2005).

By focusing on heritage I do not intend to reiterate arguments that are already well established in the literature, as there are numerous excellent sources examining the heritage phenomenon from a variety of perspectives, such as politics, history, identity, gender, visuality and performance (Wright 1985; Nadel-Klein 2003; Winter 2007; Waterton and Watson 2010; MacDonald 2013; Terry 2013). My intention is rather to explore what kind of dwelling world is created through the *gathering* capacity of heritage materiality. More specifically, what does this gathering build, how do tourists experience that which is built and what thinking occurs as a result.

Dwelling through heritage

Heritage is an interesting phenomenon expressive of what I referred to earlier as the relationship between people and time, people and place, people and memory. It is a complex conglomeration of history and culture that exists on a continuum ranging from romantic nostalgia to political and contested (Hoelscher 2011). History presented as heritage produces ways of being through dwelling based upon a particular translation and interpretation of the relationship between the past, the present and the future; resembling what Macdonald (2013) has referred to as 'past presencing'. However, the objects, ideas, meanings and associations labelled heritage are selective translations of particular times and the associated individuals, groups and events. Translation of the past is hugely political because it depends upon the person or people influencing what is to be selected and translated and the underlying purpose for doing so. As a result heritage and politics are conjoined twins, members of a dysfunctional family that never quite see eye to eye.

Within tourism, history provides the material that is presented as heritage. For Lowenthal (1998: 120) there are clear differences between history and heritage. Heritage utilises what he refers to as the spoils of history, whereas the history of historians is accessible and testable '[o]ther kinds of history – tribal, exclusive, patriotic, redemptive, or self-aggrandizing – are, by and large, heritage masquerading as history'. Heritage thus provides a perspective on the past as seen through the eyes of the present and as such heritage should be understood as an approach to the past, an approach that is heavily coloured by the ideas and values that preoccupy the present and which are seen to influence the future.

However imperfect the concept and components of heritage might be, their use within tourism enables people to encounter and experience the past of self, other and world. What is experienced are those aspects of the past highlighted as being significant, distinctive and meaningful at any given time. Heritage has cultural value and in this sense it has much in common with what Annette Weiner (1985) describes as inalienable wealth. Here certain possessions have significance because they authenticate a group's right to exist in relation to other groups and this turns them into treasured possessions to be handed down through the generations. The similarity with contemporary understandings of the purpose and function of heritage is clear and this is best illustrated by Hever Castle's continuing significance, which is and has been variously described as a treasured part of the nation's heritage and as containing rare Tudor treasures (Hever Castle and Gardens 1995, 2008, 2015). Hever Castle has cultural value because it possesses a significant heritage handed down from one generation to the next, a heritage that legitimises the right to exercise power over the political and religious foundations of nation-ness.

In terms of translating the past as cultural wealth, guidebook descriptions of people and place are the most 'ready to hand' sources of information for past and present tourists and this is so whether these are provided in print form or provided online to be accessed via iPhones and iPads. No matter the format, what they 'say' about a particular attraction has a significant influence on the relationship between people and place. As Adams (1984) memorably argued, travel brochures work to reinforce images and stereotypes of people and place because the tourist lacks the time and incentive to question what is presented. Of course more detailed historical accounts may also be read, but such sources are not the main translators of history for the vast majority of tourists visiting heritage attractions. What I am highlighting here is the need to understand Hever Castle from sources purposefully targeted at tourists because these provide an interpretive framework for translating experience into meaning.

Hever Castle, located in the English countryside in the county of Kent, is an interesting example of heritage translated as *being* English. Interestingly, Kent is widely promoted as the *Garden of England* by official and unofficial tourism promotion agencies and guides such as visitbritain.com, visitkent.co.uk, travelaboutbritain.com and *Lonely Planet*, based upon the abundance of fruit and hop flower orchards and gardens. The intertwining of nation with landscape generally and specifically in relation to the practice of gardening is deeply embedded in the English imagination, firmly associated with identity and with being English (Matless 1998; Tilley 2009). However, it is important to note that England is not Great Britain and Great Britain is not the United Kingdom and these identities are not interchangeable. They refer to particular configurations of the wider nation, which also includes Wales, Scotland, Northern Ireland and the Channel Islands. Nevertheless, there is a long tradition of use whereby English and British are seen as synonymous terms (Haseler 1996; Aslet 1997; Taylor 2001). Even the castle guidebook and website refer to both England and Britain, giving the impression that they are one and the same entity 'Hever formed the unlikely backdrop to a sequence of tumultuous events that changed the course of Britain's history, monarchy and religion' (Hever Castle and Gardens 2012: 3). Likewise, '[j]ousting tournaments take place over the summer holidays every year when the brave Knights of Royal England return to battle it out' (www.hevercastle.co.uk 2017).

The conflation of English with British is not a recent phenomenon, as Davies (1999) argues over the years travellers, historians, advertisers, domestic and foreign publics have used England as a shorthand for Great Britain and in the process upset the Welsh, the Scots and the Northern Irish. Thus, to talk of Englishness is to open up a world of contested understandings and interpretations of what being English actually means in relation to Great Britain and the wider United Kingdom. However, such a world is absent from the discourse of heritage tourism.

History and the world of Englishness

Whilst the origins of Hever Castle date back to the thirteenth century, in terms of English history the most significant owners were the Bullen or Boleyn family, who bought the castle in 1452. Hever is the family home of Anne Boleyn, the second wife of King Henry VIII, and it is this relationship that provided the catalyst for the King's decision to break with the Catholic Church in Rome. When Henry succeeded to the throne, England was a Catholic country subject to the laws of Rome and to the ultimate authority of the Pope. Henry's first wife, Catherine of Aragon, had failed to produce the required male heir and the King's relationship with Anne Boleyn was in part prompted by his desire to rectify this situation by marrying Anne (Ives 2005). As a Catholic Henry needed the approval of the Pope, so he petitioned for a divorce but the Pope refused. This refusal set in motion a series of events that precipitated the break with Rome; however, the timeframe of the Reformation and the wider religious and political issues that contributed to its progress are matters of debate amongst historians (Haigh 1987, 1993; Jones 2001).

The violent Reformation that resulted from the King's decision rewrote the relationship between church and state as it enshrined Protestantism as the nation's official faith referred to then and still today as the Church of England. The break with Rome is hugely significant because control over the internal religious and political affairs of England was re-invested with the monarch. Henry became the supreme head of the church in England, 'there can be no doubt at all that it was the combination of Nationalism and Protestantism which determined the peculiar character of the Reformation in England' (Sykes 1953: 9).

The English Reformation is a seminal event in the building of the English nation-state because the monarch, and thereby the country, were no longer subject to the dictates of Rome (Haseler 1996; Weir 2002). Henceforth, not only did the king rule absolutely, but England was also identified as an independent Protestant nation free from foreign intervention in the affairs of both church and state. The break with Rome not only brought religious and political freedom, it also helped to establish the principle of individual liberty as a core foundation of Englishness, thereby ensuring that liberty and Englishness were inextricably interlinked (Elton 1974). As Haseler argues, '[e]ver since Henry VIII the idea of a Protestant England set against a Catholic continent had been a subtle, though powerful, image in the forging of national identity' (1996: 23).

Hever Castle still physically intact and thus stands as a reminder of the basis upon which the battle with Rome was fought and of who was the eventual victor. It is a tangible reminder of the birth of the English nation's religious identity and its independence from external religious authority. 'It was Henry's love for Anne and her insistence that she became his wife rather than his mistress that led to the King renouncing Catholicism and creating the Church of England' (Hever Castle and Gardens 2012: 3). It is the memory of this birth that is brought to mind and brought to life through guidebook descriptions of the castle, its history and contents and by themed events such as Tudor tales and jousting, and talks by historians of the Tudor period. Henry's ability to marry, divorce or execute his wives means that the castle is also a reminder of the power of monarchy, although nowadays this is contained and circumscribed by the supremacy of the British Parliament and the House of Commons. Hever remained in the background of the nation's religious upheavals as the battle between a Protestant nation and a Catholic continent continued during Anne Boleyn's time as Queen of England, through the reign of Henry's eldest daughter Queen Mary and into the reign of Anne's daughter Elizabeth I.

Elizabeth I's reign firmly entrenched Protestantism and its associated freedoms as the nation's defining characteristic, most notably through Sir Francis Drake's naval defeat of the Armada of Catholic Spain in 1558. This fleet of Spanish ships had originally set sail with the intention of invading England to overthrow the Queen and restore Catholic rule. Events such as this reinforce the significance of Elizabeth's reign as being a period of time when England dominated politically and militarily (Somerset 1997; Starkey 2001). The naval battle referred to in history books as the defeat of the Spanish Armada contributes to a mythology of invincibility based upon the nation's naval history and immortalised in patriotic songs and anthems such as *Rule Britannia!*, which includes the lines *Britannia rule the waves. Britons, never, never, never will be slaves*. The importance of this for Hever Castle is illustrated by one guidebook, which states:

> the defeat of the Armada destroyed the power of Spain, the British colonies in America were established, and England rose to Supreme heights of greatness . . . So this little moated manor house is full of romance, and has helped to weave a chapter both sad and great in the annals of medieval England.
>
> (Hever Castle and Gardens 1966: 6)

The castle's history is significant not only for its links to Protestantism but also because it serves as a reminder of past glory, power and influence through its association with events that preceded the nation's rise to dominance on the world stage. References to nation here illustrate the interweaving relationship between the past and the present. The castle's Tudor history is English but its use and interpretation in the present is in relation to the history of Great Britain. This is illustrated by the previously referred to guidebook reference to the castle's role in changing the course of British history.

The holding vessel

Structurally, the oldest parts of Hever Castle comprise the Gatehouse, a walled bailey or outer wall and the surrounding moat. Despite the 'castle' epithet, Hever is not what might be understood as a real castle in the sense of a structure built as both a fortress and as a place in which to live. This is because the main part of the castle is quite small being a Tudor manor house built by the Bullen family and accessed through the moated Gatehouse. As such, Hever Castle is more a fortified manor house than a place from which invaders can be repelled,

> Hever was never really much more than a manor house, although it is embattled and moated and possesses some of the stern features of what we call a Castle. It has been described as a 'castle in miniature', or a 'castle-ette' of the feminine gender.
>
> (Hever Castle and Gardens 1972: 17)

References to castle thus refer to the protective wall, moat and castellated Gatehouse rather than to the small manor house that lies behind the wall. In effect the castle is a medieval facade, an illusion of strength that masks a soft inner core; it is a feminine rather than a masculine structure. As such Hever Castle presents a dual nationality through a juxtaposition of images that have both masculine/feminine, mother/father connotations. A castle is an overtly masculine structure both physically and symbolically signifying the power and authority derived through battle. It is a source of protection and resistance and a means by which to exercise control over people and land. Such complex associations adhere to castles over time and serve to reinforce the nation as ancient, powerful, strong and enduring based on masculine characteristics associated with domination and control. As Easthope (1992) has argued, in the last four hundred years of Western culture the masculine ego is generally imagined as a military fortification such as a castle. The phrase 'an Englishman's home is his castle', which evolved out of a declaration by Sir Edward Coke, the seventeenth-century English barrister and judge, still resonates, despite the obvious gender bias (Behr 2010; Stretch 2014).

However, this particular feminine castle-ette represents the nation's alter ego, the nation as a feminine construct. This feminine identity is reinforced by the landscape that surrounds the castle and in particular the Tudor herb garden through its association with home and hearth, with the kitchen and with cooking. Hever is then, a medieval facade because its supposedly strong outer masculine shell hides an inner feminine core, a home, a place of women and domestic life. This is the nation as a feminine entity, homely, domestic, a mother.

At the beginning of the twentieth century a Tudor-style 'village' was added to the medieval structure by William Waldorf Astor, the American businessman, politician and publisher who bought the estate in 1903. The village is made up of 'haphazard cottages' designed to resemble 'a real village of small individual dwellings' (Hever Castle and Gardens 1966: 22, 6) and as such it illustrates what Strathern (1992) refers to as Tudorism, Englishness as an architectural form. Each, apparently separate cottage was built by a different person so that the village would be made up of varying materials, shapes, angles and styles within the whole Tudor concept. Craftsmen created panelling, carved screens, stone fireplaces, plasterwork, marquetry, stained and painted glass. All the ceilings, including those in the main castle, were formed as far as possible from materials that would have been used in Tudor times with the workmen forbidden to use any form of straight edge, meaning that everything had to be done by eye (Hever Castle 1995). The overall effect is one of 'quaint roofs, gables and chimneys . . . so old and crooked' and possessing 'such individuality that they might have grown up one by one in various ages instead of in three years' (Hever Castle and Gardens 1972: 21). Inside, however all the rooms are joined by corridors and service areas providing bathrooms, bedrooms, servants' quarters and estate offices (Hever Castle and Gardens 1995). Overall, the Tudor village is a very impressive sight:

> Every chimney stack is different. Some of the roofs are tiled, some covered with stone slates. Every carved gable and barge-board is different. Almost every leaded window is of a different pattern. There are little internal courtyards, dormer windows, projecting first storeys – and

> perhaps more important than anything else, the whole 'village' has been kept down to a scale which allows Hever Castle, small as it is, to remain the dominant building.
>
> (1995: 11)

The Tudor village thus personifies an idealised English village community. An idea of village-ness can command a powerful emotional attachment to the existence of both a core of 'real' villagers and of 'real' village concerns and in so doing reflect and magnify notions of kinship, belonging and class, both in terms of the village itself and the wider society of which it is a part (Strathern 1982):

> Villages . . . are traditionally associated with a close-knit society centred on a hall, which serves as a kind of community centre, a market, parish church, pub and a 'green', which is a grass area for fairs, shows, cricket matches and other sporting events, or public gatherings . . . A village's focus is likely to be on continuity and familiarity, and it is often said that everyone will know everyone else's business.
>
> (Childs 2017: 64)

Visitors frequently mistake this imitation village as being part of the original structure; however, although its location is identified on the plan of the castle in the current guidebook, it is not a feature of the public tour and has been renamed the Astor Wing. The Astor Wing is used for corporate events and as a luxury bed and breakfast operation for temporary 'villagers'. As far as the day visitor is concerned the Tudor village can only be gazed upon. It is an enchanting and romantic spectacle, an idealised vision of the nation as a country of villages with a distinctive way of life. Its *use* therefore is as a site for contemplative reverie, a component of the overall holding vessel gathering together a meaningful world, a world of Englishness as seen through the prism of Tudorism 'visible in the landscape and indubitably English' (Strathern 1992: 32).

The world of an English gentleman

Nineteenth century travel books and guides discuss Hever Castle in relation to the society and class structure of the time by depicting it as a home for English gentlemen (Amsinck 1810; Blencowe 1858; Kershaw 1880). Amsinck notes that the castle is interesting not for the beauty of its location, or for the magnificent building, but for the view it gives of a particular lifestyle. Hever was also seen as a good example of how the character of the English had changed over the centuries, changes that mirrored the changing use of a castle from that of a fortress used to repel an attack, 'the sterner features of defence . . . are greatly modified; the proud keep has disappeared, and there are no dungeons to tell of cruelty and suffering. A century or two had exerted some influence upon the savage character of our countrymen' (Blencowe 1858: 118).

According to a former manager of the present-day Hever Castle, Astor was a great follower of Englishness and the castle represented the home of a typical English country gentleman, '[w]e understand from what the Astors themselves have written that he determined that to be a gentleman one had to live in England . . . at which point he sought a property of suitable standing' (personal interview, 1996). Astor's love of England and indeed of Europe dates back to his time as the American Ambassador to Italy in the mid nineteenth century. This period coincided with a growing disenchantment with his homeland and a public declaration that in his opinion 'America (was) no longer a fit place for a gentleman to live' (quoted in Hever Castle and Gardens 1995: 7). Over the years Astor was becoming more English than the English and in 1890 his Englishness ambitions took a significant step forward with his formal acceptance as a British citizen (Kavaler 2000).

In Hever Castle Astor saw a particularly English way of life and his transformation from uncivilised American to civilised English gentleman was complete when he was made Viscount Astor in 1917 (Kavaler 2000; Kaplan, J. 2007). In restoring Hever, Astor not only appropriated a significant piece of the nation's identity rooted in the Tudor past, he also turned himself into a custodian on behalf of the nation and more specifically a custodian of Englishness because of the castle's associations with Henry VIII and the English Reformation. As the historian David Starkey (1998) has argued 'above all Henry defines our sense of England and Englishness'. For a man determined to be an English gentleman, living at Hever Castle was like wearing a coat of Tudor Englishness.

In his desire to become English Astor needed a suitable English heritage so he followed in the footsteps of his adopted class by embarking on a Grand Tour filling Hever with antiques, furniture, paintings, tapestries and Italian sculptures. However, the Grand Tour was not merely a *rite of passage*, a ritual coming of age for the sons of the British aristocracy of the eighteenth and nineteenth centuries; it was also an opportunity for a Protestant nation to purchase and appropriate the artefacts, sculptures and paintings of a Catholic Europe. In this way, the Grand Tour represents a symbolic conquering of Catholicism by a Protestant people. In turning what would have been 'a picturesque unoccupied ruin' (Hever Castle and Gardens 1995: 6) into the home of an English gentleman, Astor created a mirror in which he could bask in the reflection of his own version of Englishness.

Moreover, in building the Tudor village Astor resurrects the castle's historic significance, its association with the Tudor period and the nation's struggle for religious supremacy over a Catholic Europe. In effect he was laying claim to a Protestant heritage as his ownership of Hever was a form of public declaration that this past is also my past. Astor's Englishness is essentially Protestant, reinforced by his association with the religious values of his adopted nation. Furthermore, the size and scope of the village turns Hever Castle into a more substantial property than when in its original state. This increased stature enhances its role as a beacon of English Protestantism. As holding vessels, Hever Castle and the Tudor village gather together the nation's core religious values, values inseparable from those of being an English gentleman.

Gathering the nation

Things as materiality gather together a world wherein visitors are provided with the opportunity to recognise and experience the kinship ties that bind the nation's past, present and future. The gathering of Englishness is based around the organisation of the castle and the sequence in which rooms, objects and events are to be encountered. The guidebook and website describe the tour and highlight the not to be missed objects of significance: renowned Tudor portraits such as those of Henry VIII, Mary and Anne Boleyn, Anne Boleyn's prayer book or Book of Hours, a twentieth-century replica of the silver clock Henry gave to Anne as a wedding present and a door lock that belonged to the King and which was carried with him when he travelled.

A tour of the castle is predominantly a tour of the manor house that lies behind the protective outer wall, although visitors do pass through the original thirteenth-century portcullis on their way in and the Gatehouse on their way out. For the most part, the tour follows the layout described in the guidebook and on the website and visitors can read about each room, its contents and history as they walk through the house. The tour is quite extensive and comprises the Entrance Hall, Inner Hall, Drawing Room, Dining Hall, Library, Morning Room, Anne Boleyn's Bedroom, the 'Book of Hours' Room, the Waldegrave Room, the Staircase Gallery, King Henry VIII's Bedchamber, the Long Gallery, the Astor Suite and Family Bedrooms, and the Gatehouse. Over the years some rooms have been renamed for example the early guidebooks included the Rochford Room and the Anne of Cleves Room whereas by 2012 these had been replaced by the Waldegrave Room and Book of Hours Room. Henry's marriage to his fourth wife Anne of Cleves only lasted around six months because the King felt he had been misled as to her appearance. Although Anne of Cleves was given the castle as part of her divorce settlement, she is not associated with any significant moment in the national story so a connection with the Waldegrave family who took ownership of the castle after her death enables the Tudor thread to stretch into the eighteenth century. Thereby reinforcing the endurance and significance of the Tudor period. The past as heritage time is, it seems expandable.

Clearly, any historic attraction will change over time and the changes inside the house are not confined to the names of certain rooms. Heritage like history evolves and this is so for the ways in which the Tudor connection and the royal romance are presented to visitors. Past exhibitions such as the costumed figures in the Long Gallery showing scenes from the life and times of Anne Boleyn, scenes such as courtly intrigue, feasting and merrymaking, accused and condemned have given way to updated representations of the castle's historic significance. The current guidebook includes pages telling the story of Henry VIII and Anne Boleyn's relationship, portraits and a brief biography of each of Henry's six wives together with a family tree of the Tudor dynasty. The website includes two key timelines, one telling the story of Hever Castle, its owners and key renovations up to 2009 and another setting out an Anne Boleyn timeline focusing on her life and relationship with the King. The format may change over time, but the flag of Tudorism still waves gently in the breeze as a reminder of the nation's historic roots.

At the end of the tour visitors pass through the Gatehouse on their way out of the house. The Gatehouse includes the Council Chamber where a collection of instruments of medieval torture, discipline and correction are displayed. These instruments include scolds' bridles, which 'were designed for outspoken women who defied authority . . . Bridles prevented them from speaking; some had a tongue plate . . . that prevented tongue movement, while others had a spiked iron bit' (Hever Castle and Gardens 2012: 58). A Scold's Bridle is a tangible demonstration of male power and whether a king or a peasant exercises that power, the message is the same. Even though this experience is of a past that no longer aligns with the values of the present, the playful nature of this experience is nonetheless significant because it is a reminder of how women have had to struggle for equal recognition.

On the tour the visitor encounters a variety of different eras or timelines that encompass medieval, Tudor, the seventeenth and twentieth centuries, all of which are presented within the confines of a twenty-first-century style of living; although the Tudor connection is more evident in certain parts of the house, for example in the Staircase Gallery, which contains a portrait of Anne's daughter Queen Elizabeth I, a bedroom identified as one in which the King might have slept and in Anne Boleyn's bedroom what is believed to be a Victorian replica bed carved with the words 'Part of Anne Boleyn's bed from Hever 1520' (Hever Castle and Gardens 2012: 28).

After the Long Gallery the visitors pass into the corridor leading to the Astor Suite, containing the memorabilia and possessions of four generations of Astors and three bedrooms once occupied by members of the Astor family. The tour ends with a visit to the Council Chamber where visitors exit the castle via the original spiral stone staircase, which re-emphasises the medieval aspects of the tour as a counter balance to the twentieth-century history of the Astors that has gone before. Outside the house the visitor's experience of times past continues with what is described as a unique collection of miniature model houses, which 'are set in a permanent display and journey through medieval times to the Victorian age' (Hever Castle and Gardens 2012: 82).

These miniature houses, people, contents and room settings are so fantastically precise that they resemble mirrored reflections of a world that appears to exist alongside that of the present day. The juxtaposition of a castle-house that can be entered, walked through and embodied with houses that can only be embodied through the gaze is interesting. In the castle-house visitors can actively engage with a materiality of Englishness that was or might have been actually used. Not necessarily in the same time period but as part of everyday life. Whereas the materiality of exactitude offers a more passive engagement with times past, something to be marvelled at from a distance, something abstracted from everyday life rather than part of life. The world gathered together by the materiality of exactitude is the world of the skilled craftsman and not the world of Englishness.

The gathering of nation also includes the materiality of the gardens, lakes, mazes, fountains, ponds and sculptures, which surround the castle with a seasonally renewed mantle of Tudor Englishness. In addition to the Tudor Herb garden and Anne Boleyn's Walk there is the Italian Garden. This garden is of particular significance because it was built by William Waldorf Astor to display his collection of Italian sculptures bought on his Grand Tour of the continent and during his time as the American Ambassador to Italy. Over one thousand men took two years to build the garden, which includes a pergola, grottos, marble pavements, Roman sarcophagi and Roman bath. The garden is a physical reminder of an Englishman's rite of passage and as such its design resembles an ideology of Englishness based on the appropriation and display of cultural superiority. The superiority of the English aristocracy and the superiority of wealth, both of which provide the ability to travel and the means to purchase the culturally significant products of other nations.

The Italian gardens also demonstrate the superiority of religion and in particular Protestantism, the garden and the collection of statues and sculpture illustrate 'that complicated interweaving of Greek, Asiatic, Etruscan and Roman strands which marked the transition from Paganism to Christianity' (Hever Castle an Gardens 1966: 28). Astor's ideological transformation of the gardens aligns with Sommer's (2010) discussion of landscape architecture in the eighteenth century, which she argues is characterised by a fundamental change in the relationship between nature and culture in response to the ideological basis of the Enlightenment. Through an analysis of the design and construction of the Russian park Pavlovsk near St Petersburg, given by Catherine the Great in 1777 to her son and his wife, Sommer argues that nature was choreographed to represent the glory days of imperial Russia:

> Choreographed nature refers to the elaborate and exquisite landscape gardens of the eighteenth century that were conceived as nature incarnate and the epitome of all the best of nature, but carefully contrived by a combination of ingenious gardeners and wealthy landowners. In fact these landscaped gardens were not at all natural but a knowing and

> splendid staging of the environment according to principles of aesthetic ideals. Nature, in this instance, was a highly skilled construction originated by eighteenth-century men of taste.
>
> (Sommer 2010: 228)

At over a thousand acres, Pavlovsk Park is much larger than the castle gardens at Hever; nevertheless the transformation of nature at the park has much in common with what Astor set out to achieve at Hever Castle. Influenced by Russian and European design principles, Pavlovsk was transformed into an imperial residence including a castle, villages for peasant workers and a landscaped park with decorative and ornamental elements, forests and rivers. The overall result reflects the well-known, familiar traditions of architectural design combining carefully selected influences from abroad that include pavilions inspired by ancient Greek and Roman cultures (Sommer 2010). There are obvious similarities here with Astor's renovation of Hever Castle, the design and construction of the Italian Garden and the Tudor village. According to Sommer, Pavlovsk Park unites the local and the universal, the world of nature and the world of culture through a 'masterly choreography' of 'cultural codes' drawn from Italian antiquity, the Russian national character and the cultural traditions of France and England. Astor's choreographed gathering of materiality at Hever Castle drew upon the cultural codes of his adopted class and nationality to reinforce his own status as an English gentleman. A status legitimised by association with and possession of a significant historic legacy. As Sommer (2010: 233) illustrates by reference to the Russian park 'Pavlovsk is a consciously created set-up, a grandiose interpretation of the world'. However, Astor's world is not the glory days of imperial Russia but the glorious foundations of religious and political Englishness.

Being human-in-the-nation

As with all tourist attractions, visitors come to Hever Castle for a variety of reasons encompassing a day out, a must see site, history as heritage, to entertain children, to visit the gardens, and the royal romance of the Anne and Henry association. In addition, for many visitors Hever Castle is part of an educationally sanctioned past and this is important because education not only legitimises the significance of that past, it also reinforces the values to be learnt from the past.

WOMAN: I don't know why it's significant, but it's certainly something that you're taught at school, there's a lot of emphasis on it. I can't speak for school in general, but mine did.

GIRL: Well everybody seems to study old Henry VIII at school so, and if you've got an idea of what he was like as in how he lived and everything then it helps.

WOMAN: . . . Well I'm interested in history anyway so,

MAN: Its history the kids can relate to, they've learnt about it at school, they can see it.

GIRL: Henry had lots of wives and had their heads cut off, we've just done that bit.

WOMAN: Yes, and learnt that funny rhyme about it haven't you, we did that when we were at school, funny isn't it, the same I mean.

The 'funny rhyme' referred to describes the fate of each one of Henry's wives.

Divorced	(Catherine of Aragon)
Beheaded	(Anne Boleyn)
Died	(Jane Seymour)
Divorced	(Anne of Cleves)
Beheaded	(Catherine Howard)
Survived	(Catherine Parr)

This rhyme is interesting for two reasons. Firstly because it highlights that a romance does not always have a happy ending. It can be dangerous, it can lead to death, and secondly, it illustrates the lessons and values handed down from history. Values reinforced and sanctioned by education which in terms of the Tudor period associated with the Castle relate to the masculine dominating the feminine, a masculine king dominating a feminine queen and the ultimate act of domination is the power to control life and death. In terms of identity this is the nation presented as a paternal construct, run and dominated by a male hierarchy.

The extent to which such an understanding of nation is recognised by individuals, even if unconsciously so, is highlighted by frequent references to Henry's predilection for beheading his wives. So, while the nation may be a combination of male and female characteristics, at Hever Castle it is those of the male that hold sway over those of the female. Henry VIII not only changed the nation's religious affiliation by breaking away from the Catholic Church, he also broke away from the matrimonial ties binding him to his various wives. In doing so he was asserting his *individual* rights as both a king and as a man; after all Henry's break with the Church of Rome was precipitated by his desire to be *personally* free from his first wife Catherine of Aragon. Thus, Hever Castle is significant or treasured history because it reinforces an important concept handed down from the Tudor era, that of freedom: individual, sexual and religious. Failure to recognise these fundamental 'principles' is punishable by death. The enduring resonance of male superiority is illustrated by the fate of George Bernard Shaw's *Joan of Arc* who was ultimately executed for encroaching upon male territory. She engaged in war, she marched with and commanded troops, she fought like a man and 'she wears men's clothes, which is indecent, unnatural, and abominable' (Shaw 1946: 131). She thus appropriated not only male clothes, but also male characteristics together with their implicit elements of power and control, as the wording of her 'confession' states 'I have blasphemed abominably by wearing an immodest dress . . . I have clipped my hair in the style of a man, and . . . have taken up the sword . . . inciting men to slay each other' (Shaw 1946: 136).

Despite the plethora of reasons for visiting the castle, when talking with, listening to or observing visitors the notion of heritage as a form of inheritance handed down through the generations is something that people experience and understand:

WOMAN 1: very interesting, all those wives and many rooms to see and pictures.
WOMAN 2: it's very interesting this history, isn't it? It gives you a sense of yourself, you know, like tracing your family tree. My Albert was always interested in history.
WOMAN 3: yes, it is, isn't it? My brother traced our family once, took a long time though.

WOMAN: yes, I think it sort of brings it home more, because they're names that you've heard of and then you sort of tend to see where they lived and . . . it perhaps gives you an interest to follow it through a little bit more.

MAN: oh I never really thought about it before, but yes, I suppose so, places like this remind you of who you are because they tell of where you have come from, you know, like a family tree almost.
WOMAN: yes I suppose we came here because it's of interest to us, although I can't say we consciously thought so at the time, but it's interesting as our heritage, England really.
MAN: yes England, the Scots and the Welsh etc., they have their own historical places and everything, but this, this is English.
RESEARCHER: what is it that's English?
WOMAN: oh you know, the knights and the building, the castle, the intrigue at court, the religious changes, yes they were, I suppose what changed us to how we are today.

However, not everyone will recognise a connection between self and nation as many people are capable of imagining an historic past without feeling it necessarily represents their identity. Overseas visitors may recognise the ancestral line reflected by Hever Castle; as one American commented, 'hey look, there's Elizabeth I. She's related to the present Queen isn't she?', but this recognition is in terms of *your* kinship ties not *my* kinship ties. Despite the fact that not every visitor will feel the same connective links, what is important is that everyone is presented with a version of the nation's past that they can choose to connect with or not depending upon what resonates with their sense of self. Walker Connor (1993) highlights the importance of such felt history by arguing that attachment to the nation is not triggered by appeals to reason but by appeals to emotion, experienced as an intuitive feeling that I belong and that we are a nation of related individuals:

MAN: oh fascinating, fascinating how they all lived and that.
WOMAN: yes, and to think it all happened here, it makes you think doesn't it?
RESEARCHER: what does it make you think about?
WOMAN: er, well, er,
MAN: well, for me this is about us, isn't it, our history, national history, the French have their Versailles etc., and the Germans their, their, well you know.
WOMAN: yes and we have this.

Felt history is experienced and understood in terms of the recognition of kinship ties, what Connor (1993) refers to as the sense of consanguinity that binds individuals together. The creation of felt kinship is a key component of heritage tourism as its fundamental raison d'être is the selection, preservation and display of nationally significant sites and objects designed to promote an idea of nation (Walsh 1992). The notion of felt history is significant here because heritage tourism provides imaginative encounters with nation-ness creating what Anderson (1991) memorably referred to as imagined communities where each individual imagines their fellow compatriots as having the same basic understanding of what the nation stands for. In this sense the spaces and places of heritage tourism resemble what Smith (1991) refers to as sacred centres, centres that reveal the uniqueness of the nation's moral geography.

Hever Castle promotes imaginative, felt kinship ties based on familiarity whereby the house behind the wall and its contents are recognisable to visitors. The layout of the furniture invites people to imagine themselves 'at home'. Visitors were heard describing the house as 'cosy', 'really live-able' and 'warm'; a place where you can 'squash all the cushions down' and imagine yourself 'being in there lying out on the sofa'. Such descriptions of homely familiarity extend to the type of mundane activities associated with being at home. Memories of relatives were recalled and forthcoming family events discussed for example the layout and furniture in the Drawing Room prompted two women to discuss a family get-together. They queried how many guests would fit into their house, who was likely to attend, who it was not appropriate to invite and generally gossiped about the behaviour and activities of family members. Some women commented upon the arrangement of particular rooms and the amount of housework needed to maintain the house, 'look at this lovely gallery here, a lot of dusting', and 'lovely table. I'd like one in my window to put flowers on'. Whereas for other visitors features such as wood panelling brought to mind occupations undertaken by family members, 'my uncle used to do all this woodwork stuff up in Tooting, he worked in all the big houses he did'.

Hever Castle is familiar to visitors because the proportions of the house, the range and type of furnishings resemble those to be found in many a family home such as sofas, tables, chairs, wall lights, beds, books, house plants and flowers. Felt kinship ties were not only expressed through references to the homeliness of specific furnishings, they were also evident in the ways in which visitors discussed the Tudors as if they were related to them in some way. In the *Inner Hall*, portraits of key historic figures such as Henry VII, Henry VIII, Edward VI, Anne Boleyn and her sister Mary were talked about as if they were familiar friends or relatives. Such family portraits have their contemporary equivalent in the family photograph album:

CHILD: Who are these people? How did he die?
MAN: [At Henry VII portrait) that's Henry's dad.

WOMAN: Henry's a massive man, recognised him. That's Anne Boleyn I'd recognise her anywhere.

MAN: There's another one of his wives, let's go and see another.
CHILD: Where's the knights in armour?

Such comments illustrate the type of family rituals that define the boundaries between those who belong and those who do not. As numerous ethnographies demonstrate, rituals can reinforce the social ties between individuals by revealing the mechanisms by which the structure of a group is strengthened and perpetuated as a result of the social values upon which the ritual is based (Geertz 1973; Okely 1983; Palmer 2003). Hence, visitors reacted to the portraits as if reviewing a set of family photographs. They recognised individuals as *my* relatives, *my* kith and kin by pointing out familiar portraits as if flicking through an album of long-deceased family members. Parents pointed out the pictures of Henry VIII, Anne and Mary Boleyn to their children and recounted the story of their lives. In turn the children questioned their parents about the people in the portraits. Furthermore, visitors often gossiped about their 'relatives', ascribed emotions to them and passed judgement on their behaviour; thereby demonstrating the structural boundaries demarcating us from them:

WOMAN: Mary Bullen [Anne sister], she was his mistress before Anne, but Anne stuck out for marriage, that was her fault.

WOMAN: [At spiral stairs leading to Anne's bedroom] it's amazing that someone of Henry VIII's size managed to get up these stairs.

WOMAN: [In the Staircase Gallery] Mary [sister of Queen Elizabeth 1], she kept on saying she was pregnant all the time, I think she really believed she was, and of course Philip [of Spain, Mary's husband] didn't want to be around her.

MAN: It says here he was over six foot tall and handsome, must have been when he was eighteen, he was a big fat lump after that.

WOMAN: It's the history, romance lasted twice as long as their marriage.
MAN: didn't he like her, then?
WOMAN: well he wanted someone to give him sons.

MAN: look Simon, did you know that Elizabeth the first was the daughter of Henry VIII and Anne Boleyn?
CHILD: it's boring in here.
MAN: not if you read it. You might learn something if you read.

This ritual identification of the ancestral line is supported by the existence of so-called family heirlooms. Just as many families bequeath significant objects and items to the next generation, so the contents of Hever represent heirlooms of the national family. The existence of heirlooms illustrates Weiner's argument that certain possessions are cosmologically significant because they authenticate a group's right to exist, '[t]he object acts as a vehicle for bringing past time into the present, so that the histories of ancestors, titles, or mythological events become an intimate part of a person's present identity' (Weiner 1985: 210). The significance or 'wealth' of particular objects and possessions are reinforced as they are inherited by and handed down within the same family or kinship group. Hever Castle has cultural value because it possesses a significant national heritage, a heritage of Englishness handed down through heritage tourism from one generation to the next. This heritage legitimises the existence of the English nation in relation to other nations and claims religious authority over Catholicism.

Weiner goes on to argue that even if an object is given away or borrowed, it retains its identity and attachment to the original owner. This is interesting because the contents of Hever are not necessarily the actual objects of Tudor England; some are replicas and some are pieces from a different time period altogether. This is interesting because it illustrates that cultural wealth, cultural value is transferable to objects and possessions that stand in for the real thing.

At Hever Castle, the heirlooms include several key objects referred to earlier such as a replica of Anne Boleyn's bed, her Book of Hours, the bedroom supposedly occupied by Henry VIII, and the most frequently reproduced portraits of Anne and Henry. People are introduced to these objects via the guidebook and the website. Some visitors actively look for these heirlooms as if searching for the belongings of a fondly remembered relative, while for other visitors a mere encounter is sufficient, nothing remarkable perhaps but must be pointed out nonetheless:

WOMAN 1: that's part of her bed, Jean.
WOMAN 2: fantastic it's survived so long really.

MAN: kept it all original.
CHILD: whose is this bed?
MAN: Anne Boleyn's I think, it was bought for Anne Boleyn.

MAN: do you think that is the bed he slept in, must have been a bit small for him.

WOMAN: mmh yes, it must have. You can sort of see him though and it feels really old, don't you think?

According to Weiner (1985), age adds value because it confers a claim on the past that legitimises identities in the present based upon the affective qualities of the object, qualities that establish the social and political identity of the group in relation to a past. Hence, people actively sought confirmation that the contents were old and of the Tudor period, to legitimise the objects' status as a component of national heritage. Anything restored or obviously modern is in many ways a disappointment, as when a seemingly valuable heirloom is found to be a fake, or a replica of the real thing sold off many years before. As such some visitors were unimpressed by the Astor Suite because this was seen as too modern, 'this is the Astor's then, he did this, made it I mean, modern. It doesn't seem old anymore'.

Being human-in-the-imagination

Although not open to the public, the Tudor village is part of the overall landscape due to its physical presence and in this sense it does form part of the tour. However, it is a tour that takes place within the confines of the imagination:

WOMAN 1: we were absolutely riveted by this, but it should be in inverted commas, shouldn't it? It's unbelievable that it was 1905 or whatever,

WOMAN 2: yes, looking from the castle it really does look authentic . . . they had servants or something there.

WOMAN 1: it's a kind of Disney world Tudor village, isn't it yes. But I suppose it is in keeping really, isn't it? I mean with England and all that.

WOMAN 2: mmh, yes, very much.

WOMAN 1: English makes me feel like a village person rather than a town person, for me English isn't towns like Doncaster it's this kind of setting I'm thinking about, small scale.

For these two women the setting of the Tudor village enhanced the Englishness of the castle. It conjured up images of home and nation at one and the same time because it represents a version of home to which they can relate, the nation as a small village community:

MAN: gosh, yes, I never noticed it before, we saw it on the way in, but thought it was part of the tour.

WOMAN: mmh wonderful, it reminds me of when we went to see Shakespear's house at Stratford that time.

MAN: yes, I see what you mean, sort of Cotswoldy, not like modern towns is it?

WOMAN: no, but it looks like that old drawing I found at home the other day of my great-grandmother's house, that was sort of higgeldy-piggeldy like that.

In referring to the Tudor village as 'Cotswoldy', a link is being made to the Cotswolds, a region of Great Britain frequently described as quintessentially English because it represents a seemingly unspoilt rural idyll (Brace 2003). Hence, the popularity of the Cotswold market town Chipping Campden can be attributed to the belief that it is 'a reservoir of an agricultural way of life and an honesty and depth of an unspoiled rural character . . . rapidly disappearing elsewhere' (Fees 1996: 128). In other words the towns and villages of the Cotswolds offer a dream of England that still ought to exist. So not only do villages like the Tudor village and Chipping Campden represent an image of Englishness generally, however idealised and selective this image may be, they also reflect a set of values and a way of life based on a rural rather than an urban outlook. Gazing upon the Tudor village provides an opportunity for visitors to connect with a particular sense of Englishness rooted in the ideals of continuity and community that village life is believed to represent.

Dwelling through heritage time

The materiality of Hever Castle and Gardens gathers together a meaningful world based upon values associated with the Tudor period. This gathering builds a version of nation-ness that is essentially English and Protestant, and where individual liberty is a defining characteristic. Visitors, particularly those for whom the site resonates, dwell in this world through the materiality of heritage – a materiality that enables an experience of felt kinship ties encouraged by a form of contemplative reverie that links self and nation. The world represented by the castle is recognisable because it is familiar to *me* and to *my* life. The manor house is just like *my* house, the portraits are of *my* relatives. Such familial connections are activated and expressed through the conversations that occur as visitors tour the castle-house and gardens, as they encounter the materiality of Hever. These conversations are reflective of the stories about past and present relatives and events that are told and re-told within many families, stories that are a key resource for understanding who *we* are both individually and collectively. As illustrated by the psychiatrist John Byng-Hall's discussion of the therapeutic importance of family stories, myths and legends:

> Family stories can give a feeling of continuity, of how the past led to the present, of rootedness and family tradition, and so help to make sense of a complicated and fraught family life in the present . . . it is not so much the story itself as the story-line which matters most, the family ethos which it transmits.
>
> (1990: 216, 220)

Dwelling as a way of being human is experienced and expressed through the stories or narratives we create, learn about, dispute and pass on as we encounter the world through materiality. However, objects as materiality are not just passive receptors for the stories we choose to live by; they also have stories of their own to tell and these stories circulate within culture, inform group members about their culture and influence the use and interpretation of other objects (Woodward 2001, 2009). The story of nationness at Hever Castle is created and narrated through the familiar trope of a romance. A romance or love-affair that leads to a divorce and re-marriage are circumstances people can relate to either through first-hand experience, or through knowing other people who have gone through such experiences. Of course not all visitors will recognise the story of Hever as being relevant, familiar or significant; it is after all merely one piece in the kaleidoscope of nation-ness. The point is that heritage tourism provides a range of pieces – industrial, maritime, rural and so forth – from which individuals can choose to build their story or version of the relationship between self and nation. In this sense dwelling can be understood as thinking, thinking through if, where and how *I* fit into the story presented to *me* and this thinking takes place in response to the materiality encountered in touring the site.

The tour of the castle-house encompasses a variety of historic periods: medieval, Tudor, the seventeenth and twenty-first centuries and these periods reinforce the ancient line of descent linking people from the past with those in the present. No matter which particular period is encountered at any one time, the visitor is continually reminded of or brought back to the Tudor era either by the name of a room, by the contents therein or by glimpsing the Tudor village through a window in the manor house. Such Tudor touchstones illustrate what was referred to earlier as temporal co-presence whereby certain historic associations may leak out and transfer from one period to the next (Macdonald 2013). The ritual repetitiveness of this Tudor leakage reinforces the associations and meanings embedded in the materiality of Hever Castle and the Tudor village.

Although the village represents the nation as a community, underneath the surface there is an inherent uncertainty, or danger because those individuals who do not conform to the prevailing codes governing political and/or sexual behaviour will suffer the full penalty of the state's (in this case the King's) condemnation. Hence, Anne Boleyn's failure to conform by providing a male heir resulted in her condemnation on the basis of sexual infidelity. Whether the accusations against her were true or not misses the point, the point being she failed to conform to the will of the state, to the King's will. An heir was required, the queen could not provide one, therefore she had to be sanctioned, side-lined and ultimately executed. Nowadays, the extent to which an understanding of the Tudor era is dominated by Henry's treatment of his wives on the basis of whether they conformed to his wishes or not, merely serves to reinforce the fact that the state holds the balance of power over the individual. Of course the contemporary British state no longer executes its citizens for not conforming, but ultimately the state *expects* the individual to conform. Revisiting a remembered school history entails a revisiting of the values and the societal characteristics associated with that history; values and characteristics that may still be relevant, even if they are thought about and acted upon differently.

William Waldorf Astor may not be significant historically or in terms of attracting visitors to the castle, but he is significant in terms of dwelling through heritage time because in renovating the castle and building the Tudor village he reaffirmed the religious roots of his and the nation's identity. He may have built the village to accommodate his family and friends, but he did not have to build a *Tudor* village. He could have chosen to construct a village with a medieval theme to reflect the origins of the castle and its structural architecture. Yet the result of his vision is to more firmly emphasise the importance of the Tudor period. In this respect Hever is typical of other heritage attractions where the character of the owner is intertwined with the culture and identity of the wider nation, attractions such as Chartwell, the home of Sir Winston Churchill (Palmer 2003).

So, although not part of the public tour, the Tudor village is important because it gathers together the nation's historic roots and in doing so it enables visitors to think of the nation in relation to the values associated with village life, namely community, tradition and continuity. By gazing upon the Tudor village, it is possible to imagine the whole nation living in similar traditional communities. Whilst it is accepted that the nation is not all villages and Tudor beams, the point is that the individual is able to experience the nation on the basis of a recognisable aspect of the national past. This may not represent the nation in the present, but it represents the nation as it once was and this is important because it highlights the continuity of ages that links the past with the present. As Connor (1993: 377 original emphasis) argues in relation to the construction of nation-ness 'it is not *what is* but *what people perceive as is*' that matters. In gazing upon the Tudor village the visitors are acknowledging the historical lineage that connects them to their ancestors.

Moreover, this lineage has a founding mother and father as represented by the feminine Tudor manor house and the masculine castle wall. Just as Anne and Henry physically produced an heir, Queen Elizabeth I, to carry on the (national) family line, so Hever's intermingling of images with both masculine-feminine, mother-father connotations symbolically reproduces the birth of the nation's religious identity. In visiting Hever Castle individuals are offered the potential to think about and locate their own ancestral links alongside those of the nation, and in so doing to remind themselves of the religious roots of the nation's identity, Protestantism.

As with Heidegger's jug and lectern, Hever Castle and the Tudor village can be conceptualised as a holding vessel gathering together and illuminating a world of Englishness. In wandering around and gazing upon the landscape of Hever Castle, visitors see and experience who they are, or who they are not, through recognition of the kinship ties of self or other. As Hall argues, it is through not outside difference that the boundaries of identity are to be experienced, '[e]very identity has at its 'margin', an excess, something more . . . every identity naming has its necessary, even if silenced and unspoken other, that which it 'lacks''. (1996: 5). The gathering of materiality as Englishness and the values and principles that cohere to it can be illustrated schematically (Figure 3.1).

Schematic representations of space feature in many anthropological works whereby the relational organisation of space, object and person is employed to illustrate a particular cultural cosmology (Levi-Strauss 1972; Bourdieu 1979; Keane 1995). The spatial orientation of the landscape of Hever Castle illustrates how the site is represented to and experienced by visitors. Initially approached as a fortress, Hever Castle represents the nation as strong, ancient and masculine. On passing through the castellated archway the

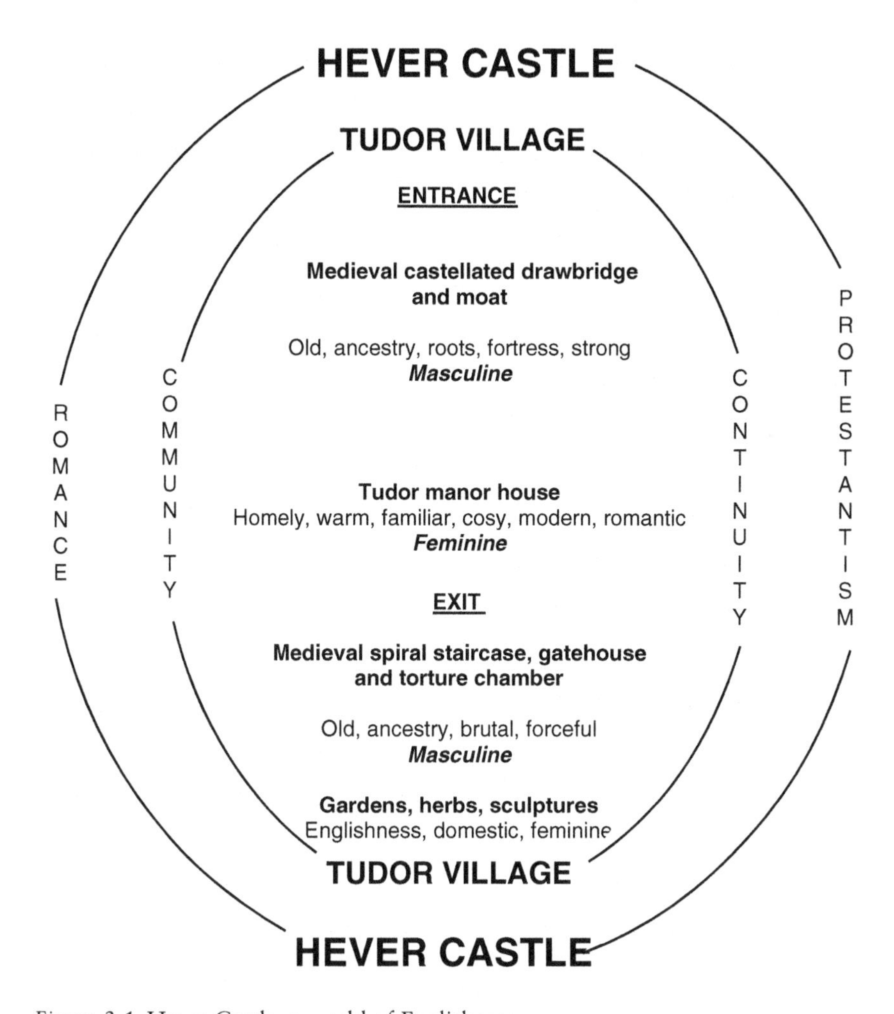

Figure 3.1 Hever Castle: a world of Englishness

masculine nation is juxtaposed alongside an image of the nation as homely, feminine and familiar. The dichotomy of masculine-feminine, mother-father is further enhanced by the gardens and the Tudor village, which in turn represent what the nation once stood for, namely community, tradition and a sense of continuity. Such images of nationhood are located within an historic timeframe that not only highlights the religious roots of the nation's identity but also symbolically reinforces the structures and moral codes seen as fundamental to the way society is, or should be organised.

Although William Waldorf Astor is absent from the above and is not important to the history of Englishness, he is actually highly significant. In building the Tudor village, in renovating the castle and the Tudor manor house and in creating the gardens, Astor is building in the sense meant by Heidegger (2001) to care for, cherish and protect, to cultivate, nurture and preserve. Astor choreographed, scripted and gathered together a world of Englishness through his painstaking and careful building and restoration of the material fabric of the castle and its surroundings. In so doing he preserved this world and laid the foundations for its continuation through heritage tourism because tourism provides the financial stability needed to maintain Hever Castle as a world of Englishness.

Conclusion

Astor's choreography of Hever and its subsequent evolution and commercial expansion brings together a variety of time periods and timelines. The different historic periods present at the castle illustrate the social uses of time, which Herzfeld (1991) defines as the time of formal relationships and of everyday experience and interaction. In contrast to social time is monumental time, the bureaucratic measure of history used by the state to make decisions as to what should be conserved, how and why. Monumental time is 'the time in which an entire cultural identity is framed' in relation to the material fabric of an historic past (Herzfeld 1991: 14). Although Herzfeld is referring to the legal processes by which the Greek state declared the Old Town of Rethemnos in Crete a national historic monument, his focus on time is relevant because heritage materiality reworks the past as the experience of time, more specifically as an experience of heritage time.

Heritage time is a combination of everyday social time and the time of historians. It is a temporal narrative of personal and collective identity. Heritage time is a socially constructed offering of essences and experiences, ideas and values, places and people, objects and performances. It is politically questionable, contested and debated. It is also highly significant and hugely enjoyable, as a visit to Hever Castle clearly demonstrates. Heritage time both makes the world and is of the world, because it creates a relationship between life in the present with life in the past and by extension life/lives to come. My use of life/lives is not restricted to human beings or to animals, because anthropologically supposedly inanimate structures and objects have lives. The natural world of the weather, of mountains, trees, oceans and rocks are all 'alive'. Heritage time makes use of the animate and the inanimate, the tangible and the intangible and in doing so it explains (inadvertently perhaps) what matters to human beings.

At Hever Castle heritage time reveals that belonging, community and identity matter, not necessarily in the same way for every visitor, as everyone is able to choose the extent to which something *matters*. Versailles matters to me for a whole range of interrelated and possibly contradictory reasons; it matters architecturally, aesthetically, and as a part of world culture but it does not matter in terms of my sense of belonging. I do not recognise aspects of myself in the heritage time of French identity. At Hever Castle dwelling through the gathering of materiality is a dwelling in relation to heritage time, and heritage time is a time where what matters from the past is brought into the present with all the inconsistencies and contradictions that entails. Material dwelling provides opportunities to engage with what matters and by extension to ignore, challenge and disagree with what this mattering might mean.

Ultimately, dwelling through the materiality of heritage time is about understanding that the present influences the future because it shows how past people and events have shaped the here and now. Of course heritage and what it shapes is selective, partial, open to manipulation and distortion so it provides a glimpse into the past rather than an interrogation of the past. Heritage time as socially constructed time illustrates the human need to create ways of locating the self within a wider temporality of people and events to those of the present. In effect to establish, maintain and perpetuate the lineage of human existence. In order to visualise a future, a continuity of me, you and the collective human us, there has to be a past through and against which to imagine the lives to come. Looking back provides reassurance because the present is the future of the past, the future of those people that have gone before, and the materiality of heritage time is one of the ways in which a future can be confirmed. Acknowledging that the past has an influence over the present demonstrates that what happens in the present, what we do now, will likewise have an influence on what is to come. This is not to say that everyone will see things in this way as some people will and some will not, but the possibility to do so is there nonetheless. Dwelling through the materiality of heritage time provides reassurance that there will be a future me as well as a collective we.

4 Architectural dwelling

Introduction

The previous chapter laid the foundations for understanding how dwelling through the materiality of heritage tourism gathers together a particular understanding and experience of time that offers a reassuring glimpse into the future. In this chapter I take a step back from 'things' per se to explore how the thinking and making function of architecture provides both a tangible and an intangible expression of the relationship between people and world. Specifically, I argue that buildings, structures and architectural landscapes are creations of a form of imagining that brings forth structure and order out of the material world; a form of imagining influenced by the principles, techniques and practices of architecture is what I refer to as architectural dwelling, a way of being human-in-the-world based on the interweaving strands that connect architecture with human behaviour, thinking and feeling. Given the plethora of architectural forms encountered through tourism, it is surprising that the cultural and philosophical dimensions of the relationship between architecture and tourism have not received more attention.

This is not to say that architecture is not recognised as an important part of what attracts tourists to particular places;, after all, contemporary structures and those of the past labelled as heritage provide a fascinating insight into different ways of thinking and living. Tourist architecture is diverse and eclectic, ranging from the classical architecture of the Acropolis in Athens to the postmodern brutalist style of the Pompidou Centre in Paris. There is landscape and sculptural architecture that includes parks and gardens, such as Pavlovsk Park discussed in the previous chapter, monuments and memorials. Indeed, the growth of leisure travel among the middle classes in Great Britain during the eighteenth and nineteenth centuries was fuelled in part by the desire to visit the great gardens and parks of the landed aristocracy. The gardens of the eighteenth-century English designer Capability Brown, most notably Blenheim Palace in Oxfordshire and Chatsworth in Derbyshire are enduring reminders of the social boundaries that define society. In effect, the parks and gardens of the aristocracy are examples of architecture employed to legitimise the prevailing social and economic structures governing society. The spectacular fountains, lakes, bridges, grassland and tree-lined avenues are visible reminders of who has the right to own, use and ultimately inherit the land.

In addition to buildings and parks tourists are also attracted by monuments and mausoleums designed to commemorate particular individuals or events. Monuments such as Lenin's Tomb in Moscow, the William Wallace memorial in Scotland and that to the Chinese American actor Bruce Lee in Hong Kong. Rodger (2015) refers to such structures as hero buildings because they not only serve to remind individuals of what took place, they are also tangible manifestations of the socio-cultural and ideological beliefs that brought them into being. Such an argument highlights the importance of architecture as language where buildings and structures are designed to 'speak' of specific beliefs and values and their audience includes those people who choose to visit them as part of a tourist itinerary. According to Neuman, the monolithic design of *Yad Vashem* – Israel's official memorial to the Holocaust – provides visitors with a redemption story that is narrated via a number of different pathways through the museum resulting in an experience that ' . . . maintains the presentation of the central ideological Zionist narrative, relating to the wartime events in terms of the Holocaust, heroism and resurrection' (2016: 95).

Despite the importance of architecture within tourism, little attention has been given to the ways in which architecture *works* to create and express particular dwelling worlds linked to tourism or to what the worlds so created reveal about the experience of being human. For example, cathedrals, mosques and temples, brick and stilt houses, work and leisure places are physical manifestations of a range of dwelling worlds encountered through tourism. In experiencing these worlds tourists are experiencing different ways of being human since '[t]he architecture of each culture is a model of that culture's world, not of the world's shape, but of its underlying form' (Lobell 1979: 60). Tourism brings people into contact with the underlying principles of other worlds as revealed through architecture, and in this sense architecture as a physical reflection of cosmology has an important role to play in building an expression of human dwelling for tourists.

My focus on architecture and tourism is contextualised within a wider discussion of the role of architecture in building literally, conceptually and philosophically a dwelling world reflective of what it is to be human. As the architect Juhani Pallasmaa argues, architecture is a way of touching the world and in so doing it expresses and communicates our experience of being human-in-the-world: '[a]rchitecture is deeply engaged in the metaphysical questions of the self and the world, interiority and exteriority, time and duration, life and death' (2005: 16). In order to engage with the conceptual possibilities such an understanding of architecture suggests, I intend to focus on an architectural structure that is inextricably linked to the rise of mass tourism and to the opening up of the world by enabling borders and boundaries to be crossed, namely the airport. By focusing on one type of structural form, it is possible to uncover meanings about the whole through the specific.

Hill (2012) provides a good illustration of what I mean here by arguing that a history of architecture is also a history of nature-culture relations generally and specifically in relation to the weather since environmental awareness is a central feature of the architectural imagination. Architects have to consider the weather when designing buildings to keep people dry, warm or cool. They also have to consider weathering in terms of the effect of the environment on the structure and component parts of a building. In turn, the weather and weathering connects architecture to understandings and experiences of time. Time that is seasonal and chronological in terms of the effect of the seasons on the fabric of a building and the people and events associated with a particular building over decades or centuries:

> Just as the intermingling of natural and human forces creates the contemporary climate and weather, a building results from the relations between nature and culture that arise during its conception, construction and use. . . *Weather Architecture* is a story of time.
>
> (2012: 310, original emphasis)

Thinking through architecture

As argued above, architectural dwelling is a way of organising, knowing and describing the world, a way of making out of the world what and how we are as humans in the world. Whether we are a mother, a father, a farmer, a hunter, a fisherman, a teacher, a banker, a builder or a tourist, architecture is a key component of our dwelling world because it actively shapes how we come to know self and world through the places, buildings and structures we encounter and engage with along the way. Indeed, numerous ethnographies demonstrate that people have always created a 'world' from their surroundings by drawing with and from nature and from material things to build places of shelter, places of worship, places of work and play, places for the dead and for the ancestors. Indeed, Ingold notes how archaeologists and anthropologists still search for evidence of the first human building because it 'marked the turning point at which humanity was set upon the road to culture and civilisation' (2011b: 182). In this sense architecture is the outward expression of people and place as community and whether the first building was made of mud, straw or wood, it enabled individuals to make a life out of the environment. As Tuan rather succinctly puts it, '[d]epending upon the resources at their command humans have turned nature into villages and fields, villages into towns, and towns into cities' (2005: 118). The how and why of such 'building' is a constitutive element of architectural dwelling since architecture is one of the ways in which humans transform their surroundings into a meaningful world. As such architecture, as an expression of human existence, both describes and reflects the cultural particularities of the systems of thought governing its creations.

Architecture is, then, the study of human beings and their relationship with the world. Through its ability to structure and organise ways of living, architecture mediates the relationship between people, place and nature (Lobell 1979; Harries 1993; Hill 2012) as illustrated by the ways in which the word architecture is used as both practice and as metaphor. Arguably, the most visible understanding of the word is as a set of practices and techniques underpinning the design and construction of tangible buildings, structures, monuments, public and private spaces. For example houses, mosques and temples, factories, offices and prisons, hotels, airports, cruise ships, parks and gardens. The word is also used in the sense of building or describing systems of structure and order associated with technology or biology. For example, a computer scientist may refer to neuromorphic architecture and a neuroscientist to neural architecture as in the architectural design of DNA (Mallgrave 2010; Arbid 2015; Eberhard 2015). In a similar vein, the theoretical physicist Carlo Rovelli (2015: vii) refers to the cosmos as 'the architecture of the universe which we inhabit'. As a final example, the ways in which websites are able to encourage people to remain on a site or to purchase the products and services advertised has been attributed to the persuasive architecture of website design (Morosan and Fesenmaier 2007).

The association of architecture with building and with notions of structure and order has resulted in its use as a conceptual device for interrogating aspects of human experience. In *The Architecture of the Visible* MacPhee (2002) explores the relationship between visual technology and human culture, and Costas and Grey (2016) demonstrate how an architecture of secrecy works to create and maintain the social world of organisations. Similarly, the word is employed to describe the ways in which individuals use technology to think about and construct imaginary worlds or imagined uses of the tangible spaces and places in which people live (Burdea and Coiffet 2003). It may, therefore, be more appropriate to refer to architecture in the plural, to *architectures*, as there are numerous ways of exploring dwelling as the experience of structure and order.

In this respect even nomadic peoples build in the sense of erecting the temporary structures of their mobile world. Although tents and caravans are mobile, the organisation of space and structure into a community of temporary dwellings is brought forth out of a culturally specific architectural imagining drawn from an acquired knowledge of practices, skills and traditions handed down through the generations (Ingold 2011a; Prussin 1995). Knowledge of where to set up camp, how to erect each dwelling tent, where and how to shelter the animals is architecture on the move. Whilst this is not architecture as it is understood in more static societies, such building-moving-building is nonetheless an example of architectural dwelling, a way of knowing and organising who *we* are through the way people build how and where to live.

My use of architecture encompasses both the conceptual and the tangible characteristics of the word, since dwelling, as being human-in-the world, is an interweaving dance between the abstract and the concrete, between thinking and doing. This approach sees architecture as a creative process that builds through the imagination, and the dwelling worlds so built reflect the values and beliefs underpinning the relationship between self and world. De Botton (2007: 72) describes this as the material articulation of wellbeing and happiness whereby 'works of design and architecture talk to us . . . They speak of visions of happiness . . . of our ideas of a good life'. We need to bear in mind, however, that because architecture can be employed to exercise power then what is built may not always provide such a rosy experience of life. For example, the architecture of death camps, of slavery, prisons and internment (see Macdonald 2006; Hagen 2010; Myers and Moshenska 2011).

Although architecture can be used as a weapon of war, it can be used as a force for good, and according to Wittgenstein (1980), good architecture encourages a tangible response, what he referred to as a gesture that influences how life is experienced. The ability of architecture to reveal, express and even nourish the self, defines the work of the architect Christopher Day (2002, 2004). For Day (2004), architectural design should be based on how bodies move, how they 'work' both physically and sensuously in carrying out the activities required of daily life because doing so brings not only health benefits but also improvements in productivity. Hence, buildings, such as schools, houses, churches, offices and hospitals together with public spaces such as parks and streets should be designed to 'create appropriate gestures: of welcome, privacy, activity, repose and so on' (2004: 162) and in doing so promote rather than blunt wellbeing. Such 'gestures' are achieved by bringing 'colour into conversation with the light' (2004: 73), by the use of forms, shapes and materials that 'fit' the surroundings and by the creation of spaces 'where silence can be a welcome guest' (2004: 213).

Day's approach to design is based on a view of architecture as a healing art illustrative of the interconnectedness of building, dwelling and the human condition. This approach is interesting because it suggests that architectural design is not solely about achieving the right balance between function, form and aesthetics. It is also, and perhaps more importantly, about creating a particular feeling or mood, which in turn influences how individuals think and how they behave. In this sense architecture is an influencing mechanism because of its ability to create responses to and feelings about particular places, as the architect-philosopher Christian Norberg-Schulz notes:

> different actions demand different places with a different character. A dwelling has to be "protective", an office "practical", a ball-room "festive" and a church "solemn". When we visit a foreign city, we are

> usually struck by its particular character, which becomes an important part of the experience.
>
> (1980: 14)

To talk about architecture is to take part in a conversation that goes beyond function and form to one that engages with architecture as both attitude and gesture. As an attitude about what buildings should say and how they should say it, and as a gesture that shapes and reflects the meaning, character or feel of a building's internal and external surroundings. In effect, an attitude and a gesture of dwelling that expresses what it is to be human. What gestures and attitudes are revealed through the engagement of tourists with architecture is something that will be explored later on.

To say that architecture shapes as well as reflects or symbolises a particular dwelling expression is important because it further highlights the ability of architecture to influence rather than merely respond to the experience of being human. A good illustration of what I mean here comes from Copertino's (2014) ethnography of architecture and materiality in relation to the restoration of Arab houses in Damascus Old Town, a UNESCO-designated World Heritage Site. Here, architectural techniques of building, rebuilding and restoration actively contribute not only to the construction of social groups and relationships but also to a foundational element of Arab identity, the possession of a distinctive cultural heritage; '[p]lans, scaffolding, logs, cobs and raw materials are not merely tools with which to build and restore houses: people and groups use them to construct themselves as social actors in their specific contexts' (2014: 344). Here architectural dwelling creates and expresses an experience of Arabness, albeit one that is subject to the controlling oversight of state regulation and UNESCO.

Building a dwelling world

Heidegger's essay *Building Dwelling Thinking* has had a significant influence on how I conceptualise the relationship between architectural dwelling and tourism. This essay, together with *The Origin of The Work of Art*, *The Thing*, and '. . . *Poetically Man Dwells*. . . ' has also played an important, although not uncontested, role in the development of a phenomenological understanding of architecture (Norberg-Schulz 1980; Harries 1997; Leach 2000; Pallasmaa 2005; Sharr 2007; Anderson 2011).

In *Building Dwelling Thinking* Heidegger (2001) argues that architecture has reduced building and dwelling to two distinct activities within a process of construction dominated by aesthetic ideals and engineering principles. In this view dwelling is the end goal of building, a functional process governed by systems of production and consumption. However, as argued in Chapter 1 such usage conceals the original meaning of dwelling as an expression of human existence and of building as the means by which humans articulate their existence as dwellers in the world. In a sense then, for Heidegger building and dwelling should be understood as attitudes towards and about the world (Lazarin 2008); they are what humans do in order to be human.

By focusing on the symbiotic relationship between building and dwelling, Heidegger highlights the importance of thinking to this relationship. However, for Heidegger thinking is not about problem solving but a means of questioning what and how we think, '[e]nough will have been gained if dwelling and building have become *worthy of questioning* and thus have remained *worthy of thought*' (2001: 158, original emphasis). This is important because my intention here is to question and think through the dwelling world created by the architectural gathering of materiality into the locations, structures and buildings that are woven into the experience of tourism. As an activity of the mind and as a set of practices, architecture helps to structure spaces, places and activities as a collective expression of the dwelling world of tourism.

The role of architecture as both practice and structure in creating and revealing the many ways in which human beings organise themselves is an established focus of sociological inquiry (Foucault 1977; Levi-Strauss 1983; Parker Pearson and Richards 1997; Carsten and Hugh-Jones 1995; Melhuish 2005). The ability of architecture to bring together and build from the scientific, social and cultural fabric of life helps to explain why thinking through architecture captures the imagination of social scientists. Within anthropology, architecture is a cosmological language speaking of, for and to people, place and ideas (Bourdieu 1979; Bloch 1995; Buchli 2013). Indeed, anthropology's role in highlighting the significance of architecture for understanding ways of thinking and being has come from its focus on culture rather than theories of structural design. For example analyses of the variety of dwellings to be found among the peoples of Southeast Asia, South America, Africa and Siberia demonstrate that culture, rather than the formalised codes of architect and planner, designs and builds places to live, work and pray (Carsten and Hugh-Jones 1995; Keane 1995; Prussin 1995; Waterson 1997; Willerslev 2007). However, Ingold (2013) argues that many such ethnographies are studies of not with architecture and as a result they do not say enough about the creative processes used in the construction process.

Nevertheless, Bourdieu's (1979) classic analysis of the Algerian Kabyle house illustrates that architecture as language speaks through the organisation of external and internal space and through the things, practices and activities that are contained within; practices that reveal and perpetuate the relational threads linking the structure and organisation of the house to wider truths embedded within Berber cosmology. This cosmology is of a highly regulated society organised on the basis of a series of binary opposites such as inside/outside, male/female, night/day, raw/cooked, fire/water, public/private, human/animal, dark/light, life/death and so forth. According to Bourdieu, '[t]hese relations of opposition are expressed through a whole set of convergent indices which both establish them and receive their meaning from them' (1979: 136). Indices refer to such as the materials from which the house is constructed, the division of labour in the house, the space set aside for human beings and that for animals, and the association of space with particular kinds of activity – all of which reflect and reinforce the social and cultural practices of self, group and community. In this sense the house is the world and the world is the house and the unspoken mediator is architecture, or more specifically the architectural ordering of people, place and environment, 'our house is our corner of the world . . . it is our first universe, a real cosmos in every sense of the word' (Bachelard 1994: 4).

Architectural cosmos

Architecture as universe speaks of both the practical and the metaphysical threads connecting people, place and cosmos. Many philosopher-architects have pointed out that architecture lies at the heart of the metaphysics of life because the structures it creates both reveal and question the relationship between life and death, heaven and earth (See the contributors to Goldblatt and Paden 2011). Sacred architecture is perhaps the most obvious illustration of the coming together of the physical and the spiritual largely because God was considered to be the real architect shaping the relationship between time, space and existence (Harries 1993). This view was based on the premise that sacred buildings are specifically designed as places for the ritual performance of acts of worship supporting adherence to a set of beliefs that speak of a common destiny. As such God, however conceived, could be the only architect because sacred buildings are the physical manifestation of fundamental laws governing human existence.

Hence, in common with other belief systems the architecture of a mosque, physically and symbolically embodies the Islamic worldview influenced by a sense of adoration for the creations of God (Erzen 2011). According to Erzen, most mosque architecture encapsulates four historically persistent symbols, all of which are designed to represent and recreate the perfect world given by God. These symbols are referred to as 'paradise regained', the 'heavenly theatre' wherein prayer is a ritual performance of adoration and prostration to God, the 'urban sculpture' as familiar landmark reminding individuals of their communal ties and finally the 'cosmic spiral' representing the basic, formal organising principle of a circle uniting heaven and God. In order to fully experience a mosque an individual needs to 'read' the culturally specific metaphors and symbols upon which Islamic architecture is based (Erzen 2011).

This example demonstrates that the practice of architecture is an artistic endeavour to produce buildings and landscapes that weave together the physical and the spiritual. Although places of worship, such as churches, temples or mosques may embody sacred beliefs and values, domestic dwellings can also embody sacred ideals and as such they too can be described as sacred architecture. This is so even in societies where culture, rather than a formal set of principles, techniques and practices labelled as architecture, builds places to live, eat and pray. For example, ceremonies associated with the construction of a Foi longhouse in Papua New Guinea include magic spells that serve to embed the body parts of several mythical hunters within the house and in so doing 'fixes the immortal cultural heroes corporeally into the very architecture of the house' (Weiner 2001: 61).

The intertwining of the vernacular and the sacred is also evident in the house of the Zafimaniry people of Madagascar, which supports and reflects kinship and reproductive beliefs sacred to the community (Bloch 1995). For the Zafimaniry the growth stages of a house reproduce the strength and compatibility of the union between a man and a woman. In the early stages of the relationship the house will be a simple construction of a three stone hearth within a wooden frame of three posts. At this stage it is flimsy and permeable as neighbours can see in through gaps in the woven bamboo walls. Over time, and as the fruitfulness of the union is strengthened by the production of children, the house is 'hardened', it acquires 'bones' as the woven bamboo is gradually replaced by huge wooden planks. Bloch refers to this process as 'house hardening', whereby the wood grows like human bones as each generation contributes to the decoration and maintenance of the house. As the house 'grows', it transcends human mortality because the last son of each generation gradually takes over the house to start and bring up his own family whilst looking after his parents until their death. In this way the link between the ancestors and their descendants is maintained through the generations:

> when this founding couple dies, their descendants gradually come to feel that they are present as the conjoined house itself rather than as two individual people. It is at this point that the house will be increasingly referred to as a 'holy house'.
>
> (Bloch 1995: 80)

The structural composition of the dwelling expressions discussed above reveals the intimate relationship between the body and the built form, whether in terms of the body as a living person, as mythic ancestor or as the body of a whole community. The anthropomorphic properties of houses, places of work or worship illustrate this intertwining of body, belief and structure. An intertwining that is seen as central to architectural thinking (Bloomer and Moore 1977; Dodds and Tavernor 2002), and it is this intertwining that links architecture to Heidegger's concept of the fourfold. The coming together of mortals, sky, earth and divinities, which, as discussed in Chapter 1, is a way of understanding human existence as a unifying relationship between people, environment and cosmos. Hence, to say that architectural dwelling is an expression of human existence is to acknowledge that what is built are not just the visible and tangible structures of the physical world, but also the invisible and intangible attachments to an underlying ethos. These invisible connections are made possible through the imagination and specifically the activity of dreaming.

Bachelard (1994) offers a profound illustration of the importance of dreaming for architecture through his analysis of a house as providing a home for both body and mind. Every nook and cranny is a resting place for daydreaming such that particular parts of the house are associated with certain dreams and these dreams are reflections of the way the world is. Thus, the attic is associated with daylight being at the top of the house and closest to the sky, and as such it is a place of rational dreaming. Whereas the cellar is underground, in the dark of the earth, a place of irrational fear and exaggerated dreams, '[u]p near the roof all our thoughts are clear . . . As for the cellar . . . it is first and foremost the *dark entity* of the house, the one that partakes of subterranean forces. When we dream there, we are in harmony with the irrationality of the depths' (Bachelard 1994: 18, original emphasis).

The ability to imagine and to dream is important because these two activities are fundamental to the creative force that underpins the *work* of architecture and the way in which tourism *works* to attract people to place. Imaginative dreaming creates shapes and structures in the mind before anything is built on the ground and tourists imagine experiences before they actually arrive. After all, that is the whole purpose of tourism marketing, as Dann argues:

> Via static and moving pictures, written texts and audio-visual offerings, the language of tourism attempts to persuade, lure, woo and seduce millions of human beings, and, in so doing, convert them from potential into actual clients. By addressing them in terms of their own culturally predicated needs and motivations, it hopes to push them out of the armchair and on to the plane – to turn them into tourists.
>
> (1996: 2)

In this sense the imagination designs and builds the tangible and intangible structures of dwelling as a way of being human-in-the-world, what Harries (2011) refers to as architectural fantasies. However, architectural dwelling is influenced by time because use both shapes and transforms character and purpose. Buildings fall into ruin, they 'die' and are reborn through a process of architectural imagining that reshapes them for a new purpose.

Indeed, Gieryn (2002) notes that buildings are deconstructed materially and semiologically all the time as they are (re)interpreted and (re)presented in response to changing circumstances. Churches are deconsecrated and reformed as houses or theatres, bars and pubs are turned into homes and even large utility structures such as water and electricity stations are decommissioned and reinvented in response to changing social and economic conditions. Architecture is part of the story of a building, a story about the relationship between people, time and context. It is a story that not only narrates the changing socio-economic, cultural and political influences surrounding a particular building or landscape, it also narrates the history of the people and events associated with it. Following its decommission in 1983, London's coal-fired Battersea power station, located on the south bank of the River Thames, was for many years the subject of heated debate, as various arguments jostled for supremacy over how the building and its surroundings should or could be reused. Eventually the site was sold based on redevelopment plans to provide luxury and affordable housing, shopping and leisure facilities (Kollewe 2017). The architectural story of the power station is a story about changing attitudes to the environment, about the politics of energy, globalised finance, community representation and engagement. Swirling around all these 'short stories' is a wider narrative about cultural value generally and in relation to a particular moment in time, a narrative about what a society or group considers to be worth saving in the first place.

The example of Battersea power station demonstrates that the world brought forth through architecture is neither fixed nor stable, being as it is subject to the social, political, economic and technological influences emanating from human activity. In this sense ruins, decommissioned and reworked buildings have an afterlife, an afterlife that often includes being part of the local and global panoply of tourist attractions. As is the case with Battersea power station, which, although undeveloped, is listed on the 2017 Visit London website as one of London's landmark architecture attractions. This listing demonstrates that architecture and tourism are inseparable, if not mutually dependent, because architecture can be 'sold' as experience to tourists and the income that visitors bring in is frequently used to maintain and conserve the material fabric of the buildings, structures and landscapes visited.

Architecture and tourism

Given the above discussion, what is of interest in relation to tourism is the idea of architecture as universe, as the physical manifestation of cosmology. The architecture of tourism brings people into contact with a particular conception of universe and in so doing enables them to linger within its borders and to touch, albeit briefly its underlying ethos. Initially, contact with this universe is made through the imagination, through dreaming about the holiday to come. Such dreams are triggered by the pictures of cities, hotels and places of interest that are pored over in anticipation of the experience, pictures of the places and locations that are brought into being by architecture. Architecture plays a significant role in attracting and structuring the tourist experience. It serves as both an object of fascination drawing people towards it and as a service providing the structures that support the activity of tourism, structures such as hotels and transport terminals. As architecture, like tourism, has a symbolic function, then its role as object and service within tourism extends to include what these structures and locations might communicate about the local, regional or global context within which they are designed, constructed and located. (Culler 1981; Picken 2010).

Whether as object, service or symbol, architecture influences the behaviour of tourists and thereby the experience of people and place because it guides and regulates, excites and repulses, encourages compliance and transgression. Tourists navigate around buildings and landscapes via maps, pathways and directional signs indicating where to go, what to do and what not to do. Transport architecture encourages contemplation of what is to come through viewing platforms in airports and overhead walkways connecting service stations either side of a motorway. The anonymity of the airport frees individuals from the constraints imposed by daily life, providing opportunities for escaping the 'me' associated with family, work and community. As a result, Gottdiener (2001) argues chance encounters at airports resonate with possibility fuelled in part by the lure of sex with a stranger exemplified by the phrase the 'Mile High Club'.

Such imagined possibilities may become actual experience encouraged as they are by the proximity of airport hotels. Indeed, the design and construction of hotels, what Pritchard and Morgan (2006: 770) refer to as 'architectural language', contribute to their place in the social imaginary as spaces where the norms of behaviour can be temporarily set aside. This is because hotels provide private spaces than can encourage acts of transgression, risk and sexual adventure, '[t]he sense of flux and mobility of human traffic in these anonymous yet public spaces . . . create conditions of freedom and opportunity for those open to such adventures' (2006: 762).

The architecture that so fascinates tourists and non-tourists alike comes in many forms. There are iconic contemporary buildings such as the Sydney Opera House and the Guggenheim Museum in Bilbao and the archaeological traces or ruins of a past sacralised as local, regional or world heritage such as the temples at Luxor, Machu Picchu, the Parthenon and the Great Wall of China. Whilst all these structures are deeply embedded in the itinerary of tourism, the everyday world of domesticity, leisure and work also stimulate the tourist imagination providing as they do a window through which to gaze upon other ways of living and being human. Attractions that speak of 'the way we were' are interesting because they illustrate one of the ways in which architecture *works* generally and in relation to tourism. Architecture exposes the network of relationships that reflect and shape, guide and control, liberate and prescribe individual and collective behaviour.

Capital cities and urban environments are a testament to the social, political and or ideological perspectives within and through which they were designed and built. Through an analysis of the relationship between architecture, power and national identity, Vale (1992) argues that throughout history governments have manipulated architecture and civic space for political gain. The resulting structures, whether civic or domestic significantly influence lived experience. High-rise apartment tower blocks for example, separate individuals from the ground where the major aspects of life, work and leisure take place. High-rise living may be one way of dealing with large populations but it offers a strange sort of life in limbo, up in the air gazing down upon the lives of others. Whereas public buildings, such as museums and government offices, grandly proclaim authority and power both individual and collective. This authority can be in terms of the acquisition, interpretation and display of knowledge or the power to devise, legalise and enact the rules by which a particular society should be governed.

The architectural grandeur and spectacle of many public buildings turns them into structures of enchantment where the whole can be grasped from the specific. Given the relationship between art and architecture, the idea of architecture as enchantment aligns with Gell's argument that works of art are part of a wider system of technological enchantment designed to support and reproduce the structures of relations that underpin a particular society, 'the *technology of enchantment* is founded on the *enchantment of technology* . . . the power that technical processes have of casting a spell over us so that we see the real world in an enchanted form' (1992a: 44, original emphasis). Tourism has also been referred to in this way, with Selwyn (2007) arguing that the tourism sector depends upon processes of enchantment to attract potential tourists and these processes are located within wider political and economic contexts. As such, the concept of enchantment is not something that can be confined to the superstitions of times past; it is in large part the defining condition of modern life (Bennett 2001).

The concept of enchantment helps to explain how and why the architecture of other places and people has the power to attract tourists. It offers an enchanted view of the basis upon which particular societies see themselves and of how they wish to be seen by others. As Benjamin (1999) argues in relation to the Parisian shopping arcades of the late nineteenth century, architecture is the most important testimony to a society's latent mythology. For Benjamin, the symbolic stories or myths upon which the fundamental character of French society is based are present in the structure of its public buildings, buildings such as the Arcades. Whilst these myths may be hidden beneath the surface of the building, they can be read and interpreted through its architecture. The Arcadian myths relate to the growth of consumerism, which at the time seemed to offer a fantastical world of luxury and excess, a world where desire and want had triumphed over need (Benjamin 1999). Tourism is a testament to the success of consumerism because its existence and economic significance is a flag of victory in terms of desire versus need, at least for large parts of the world's population.

In this respect architecture is the outer skin of a society, but it is an enchanted skin. Enchanted in terms of the techniques and aesthetics of building and interior design and in terms of the opportunity it gives to glimpse what lies beneath the skin, a society's fundamental beliefs and values. The buildings and structures used by tourists, the hotels, shopping arcades, gardens and attractions provide opportunities for encountering the social and economic relationships that structure the wider society. According to

Jameson (1984), John Portman, architect of the Westin Bonaventure Hotel in Los Angeles, provided a structure where the internal and external spaces both reflect and repel the capitalist credentials of the city within which it is located. A city accessible from the hotel lobby where the external elevators 'shoot' people 'up through the ceiling and outside, along one of the four symmetrical towers, with the referent, Los Angeles itself, spread out breathtakingly and even alarmingly before us' (1984: 83).

A similar point is made by Barthes (1979) in relation to the Eiffel Tower, which he argues enables a tourist to see the whole of Paris from its summit, and to imagine how the present-day structure of the city has evolved over time. In this way the Tower 'gives us the world to *read*. . . ' by exposing the structural relationships that connect history, people and place (1979: 9, original emphasis). The Pompidou Centre in Paris was designed with the building's skeleton of pipework, services and walkways on the outside of the building. Colour was employed to distinguish conduit and circulation channels for people, electricity, air conditioning and water and this mass of external ducting and pipes is there for all to see rather than hidden way within the internal walls of the structure. The exposed skeleton can be read as a monument to technology, where accepted ideas are turned on their head in relation to what a building should look like and what it is for.

The network of relationships exposed by architecture can connect or disconnect people to particular places. These relationships reveal the social, political and economic forces directing lives and livelihoods. The architecture of tourism provides numerous examples of the relationships that support and supported the rewriting of people and place, being and dwelling through political regimes and military activities such as colonialism and communism (Light 2000; Henderson 2004; McLaren 2006; Shannon 2009). Such relationships continue to draw tourists to particular sites and attractions. Elmina Castle on the Ghanaian coast for example, speaks of the economic and political forces that supported colonialism and the transatlantic slave trade. Now an established part of a roots tourism itinerary, the medieval architecture of the castle provides a visible reminder of the history, people and events that initiated an African diaspora. This is architecture as both a symbolic and tangible reminder of the origins of an African self-identity. As Finley argues, for roots tourists' sites like Elmina are one of:

> the few places where material evidence of the legacy of slavery still stands before their eyes and is available to be touched, walked through, and experienced with all of their senses and with the movement of their bodies through time and space.
>
> (2004: 114)

What this example illustrates is the symbiotic relationship between architecture and the embodiment of being. In this sense architecture offers a tangible experience of what Chapter 2 refers to as sensuous dwelling, an experience, which, for some tourists is deeply felt.

The relationships and forces driving war and conflict are also revealed through the architecture of terror; the ruins and memorials of past wars and ideological conflicts now incorporated into the itinerary of tourism. Checkpoint Charlie in Germany, the post-World War II border between West Berlin and the Communist-held East Berlin is one of the city's tourist attractions (Visit Berlin 2017). The German bunkers built along the French coast during World War II are also established tourist attractions. Virilio described these bunkers as concrete altars to the art of warfare '[a]bandoned on the sand of the littoral like the skin of a species that has disappeared' (1994: 46). As evocative as this description is, the cultural significance of a building is determined by more than the materiality of its construction. Chartres cathedral in France is both a place of worship and a tourist attraction, but Geertz argues that in order to understand Chartres as an expression of human existence, it is necessary to look beyond the proportions of glass and stone used in its construction:

> Chartres is . . . not just stone and glass; it is a cathedral, and not only a cathedral, but a particular cathedral built at a particular time by certain members of a particular society. To understand what it means, to perceive it for what it is, you need to know rather more than the generic properties of stone and glass . . . You need to understand also – and in my opinion, most critically – the specific concepts of the relations among God, man, and architecture that, since they have governed its creation, it consequently embodies.
>
> (1973: 50–51)

Looking beyond in order to understand rather succinctly describes my intention with regard to airports as it illustrates the need to look as well as to think beyond the physical materiality of airport structures as a way of uncovering wider truths about the relationship between people, environment and cosmos; what Heidegger refers to as the fourfold of mortals, sky, earth and divinities. As Harries (1993: 51) argues, the dwelling world brought forth through architecture should reflect a wider cosmological ordering whereby time and space are 'revealed in such a way that human beings are given their dwelling place, their ethos'. In this sense architecture allows something hidden to become visible.

Airport ethos

Of course, airports are highly visible structures organised within a landscape comprising: parking areas, terminals, runways, walkways, waiting, shopping and boarding spaces, check-in, baggage and immigration spaces, food and beverage outlets. Encircling all such spaces are the airplanes decked out in their distinctive corporate livery, '[t]he planes, plugged umbilically into the buildings or standing in solitary splendour just outside, are as much a part of the airport's architecture as' the retail outlets inside the terminal building (Pearman 2004: 16). An airport is built in much the same way as Heidegger's German farmhouse through a process of architectural ordering that brings humans into conversation with the surrounding environment. It is this relational conversation that is made visible and what is both heard and seen through airport architecture is the underlying ethos of human social relations.

The ethos of an airport is influenced by the dwelling characteristics brought forth through the principles and practices of architecture, which, as argued earlier, are concerned with structure and order, classifying and controlling, language and meaning. Interestingly, the exercise of control through architecture is not straightforward as it is not limited to the ways in which movement and behaviour are managed through design. This is because architecture and hence architectural dwelling is part of the network of global capitalism that finances the building of major projects such as airports. The huge cost of such projects means that global capital markets effectively control movement and mobility through the financing of large-scale transport networks (Chaplin and Holding 1998; Urry 2009; Kesselring 2009). In terms of tourism, for destinations within the global south, this can translate into control by airlines and other transnational tourism organisations of tourist numbers and hence income from tourism (Bianchi 2014).

Whilst this is certainly true, my interest and focus here is not on the political economy of airport architecture but on the cultural meanings embedded in and communicated by airport architecture. Of course, the political in one form or another permeates all aspects of life but then so too do the economic, the biological, the technological, and so on, and ultimately all such aspects speak of and through culture. Nevertheless, at this point in time my focus puts culture as philosophical ethos centre stage. Whilst airport culture can be interrogated through a variety of disciplinary lenses, for example Adey's (2008) architectural geography of the contextual practices and experiences associated with airport terminals, my questions are anthropological. Specifically, what does airport architecture tells us about being human through dwelling? What does it make visible?

In exploring these questions it is not my intention to present an overview of the socio-cultural, political or architectural history of airports and air travel, such aspects are extensively covered elsewhere (Pearman 2004; Gordon 2008; Cwerner et al 2009; Adey 2010a; Harley 2011; van Uffelen 2012). In addition, I do not intend to focus on a specific airport but on airports in general. This is because, despite the huge variety of airports that exist throughout the world from small local terminals to regional hubs and grand international gateways, they all serve the same fundamental purpose to move people from ground to air and then through the air from one place to the next. In addition, they all offer a similar range of experiences or services such as shopping, eating and drinking. These may not always be to the same scale; there are of course huge differences between what is offered at an international airport and what is available at an airport consisting of one runway and a hut for a terminal. Despite such differences, checking in, boarding, departing and arriving are what all airports do. Whilst airports and hence airport architecture may share the same *raison d'etre*, people are not passive recipients of architecture; they shape and endow buildings with history, emotion and identity through use.

In terms of airports 'people' usually refers to passengers or airport workers, but these are not the only people to be found at an airport. 'People' encompasses those individuals who find themselves stranded in airport space for reasons such as visa irregularities that turn them into stateless representatives of the global networks and forces that define the prevailing economic order (Lloyd 2002). Interestingly, 'people' can also include other types of 'beings' such as the supernatural. Ferguson's (2014) ethnography of Bangkok's Suvarnabhumi airport and Myanmar's Yangon International Airport provides a fascinating extension of airport users to include ghosts, spirits and other supernatural entities. In both airports Theravada Buddhist workers experience their respective work places as haunted environments, haunted by the ghosts and spirits to which they are cosmologically attached. These ghosts and spirits are not only embedded within the architectural fabric of the airport, they also own, operate and at times interfere with aviation logistics. In order to appease and pacify potentially malevolent spirits, the workers draw upon Buddhist practices and spirit folklore to ensure their safety at work and a safe outcome for their future travels.

Interestingly, Ferguson employs his ethnography to challenge and critique Augé's theory of the non-place, places that are transient and ephemeral such as airports, railway stations, supermarkets and hotels, any 'space that cannot be defined as relational, or historical, or concerned with identity will be a non-place' (2008: 63). For Augé, non-places lack a common understanding of the social bond between people; they are not places where people live out their lives as a group or community. They are places that people move through rather than move to, places that lack an embedded history of previous inhabitants. However, as Ferguson demonstrates, airports such as Suvarnabhumi and Yangon do have an embedded history and they are inhabited in the sense that they are haunted by the spirits that occupy them. Spirits that live in and through the architecture of the building and as such they cannot be described as non-places just because the permanent inhabitants are spirits.

Similarly, I argue that in relation to tourism, airports are places where a common understanding of the social bond between people does exist because tourists recognise other tourists as fellow travellers. They recognise each other as tourists and as being part of an internationally recognised community with a shared experience of the mechanics of travel – tour operators, airlines, hotels and such like – and in terms of airports a shared understanding of the comforts and discomforts associated with air travel. Airports are also places where individuals can engage with the sort of activities that define a distinctive way of life, for example many airports include a chapel or prayer room where religious observances can be maintained. Indeed, Kraftl and Adey argue that the architecture of such spaces actively encourages passengers to 'dwell spiritually' (2008: 222). As the Airport Chaplain at Liverpool's John Lennon airport states, 'to feel at home here, and relaxed, it's just what we want . . . that's a wonderful feeling' (cited in Kraftl and Adey 2008: 223).

I understand Augé's point and how he chooses to distinguish non-place from anthropological place, but to my mind airports are anthropological places. Indeed, Lloyd argues that non-places can be positive as they provide a home for marginalised individuals such that 'the nonplace may be the only home to be had' (2003: 98). Individuals do not, therefore, just live out their lives in villages, towns or cities; they also live through the activities and places wherein life takes place, activities such as work, faith and leisure. The places and locations associated with these activities are also anthropological because people and the social relations that are of such interest to anthropologists are to be found there. After watching what went on at Heathrow's Terminal 5 and talking to employees and passengers, Alain de Botton (2009: 45) states, '[m]y notebooks grew thick with anecdotes of loss, desire and expectation, snapshots of traveller's souls on their way to the skies'.

Airport architecture is designed to create a unique sense of place that articulates a relationship between people and culture such as the gardens at Israel's Ben Gurion airport and the lacework mosaic terminal for the Saudi Royal Family at Jeddah International airport (Weiss 2010; van Uffelen 2012). An important component in the creation of a sense of place is the way structures nurture a social life for people; people such as plane spotters. Plane spotters consider airports to be places where they can meet and engage in a shared activity that creates a social bond between fellow plane spotters. This bond continues beyond the physicality of the terminal via websites and social media, '[d]espite the anonymity and potential placelessness of the airport, architects have demonstrated that the built milieu can still create a sense of place with all of its social consequences' (Gottdiener 2001: 79–80). Similarly, Adey (2008) demonstrates how the airport viewing platform or balcony encourages watching activities such as sightseeing, people and plane spotting undertaken in companionable proximity to other interested individuals. Such places are anthropological because watching occurs 'simultaneously with others and, thus, there is a general sense of community and identity associated with the airport and the aircraft people came to watch' (2008: 40).

A sense of identity is also fostered by design as branding in relation to the logos and livery of airlines, individual airplanes and of course the distinctive uniforms worn by the air and cabin crews. The colour and style of cabin crew clothing not only reflect specific corporate and or national identities, they are also highly visible displays of particular social and cultural attitudes and beliefs. The role of women in society and ideas about female employment are an integral part of the history of aviation, serving to reflect and define wider understandings of gender relations and identities (Lovegrove 2000; Duffy et al 2017).

The above discussion demonstrates that airports do have an embedded history, they are relational, they do foster a social life and they are concerned with place and identity/ies. So, although this was not his intention, Augé's argument that there is anthropological place and non-place implies that human distinctiveness is located in one type of place. The result of which is an artificial ordering of where an anthropological gaze should focus its attention. This is unfortunate because it confines anthropology to the ground, as a means of looking down rather than up and as Fuller and Harley (2004) argue in relation to airports, life in the air changes everything on the ground.

An indication of the significance of this change is provided by Hannah Arendt's (1958) discussion of the invention of the telescope. According to Arendt, the telescope's significance was due to the fact that it provided a radically different view of the world that changed how people understood the relationship between man, heaven and earth. This is because the telescope enabled people to see that it was the sun that moved round the earth, not the earth that moved round the sun. In effect Arendt is arguing that technology, as represented by the telescope, freed individuals from an earth-bound existence defined by the burden of work because it provided a way to explore what lay beyond the earth – namely the sky and by implication the relationship between humans and God. Turning the telescope like the airplane into a means of escape.

Suspended being

The ability of life in the air to influence life on the ground is illustrated by Pearman's comment that, '[a]ll airport terminals are designed to handle people in a state of suspended being' (2008: 71). This state of suspension reaches its climax when passengers are in flight, when they are on board what Serres (1995) evocatively refers to as the angels of steel, which like God's angels serve as message bearers. However, the messages they bring speak of earthly matters; they speak of the relations between people, place and culture. The role of architecture in preparing people for the experience of suspended being in the air has yet to be fully explored.

Airports are, of course only one means of travel and Pearman's description can be applied to other forms of transport. However, I do think airports are a special case because the sense of 'suspended being' associated with them is not just in terms of the suspension in time resulting from the waiting, queuing, arriving and departing that is associated with nearly all forms of travel. It is because air travel means that individuals are actually suspended in the air. They leave *terra firma* physically and emotionally to travel in and through the air and this opens up an understanding of what it is to be human that is different to other forms of transport. As Logan's (2012) evocative exploration of air illustrates, air, which he refers to as 'the theatre of the world', has no borders or boundaries, it stretches from the earth to the heavens. It can be wet or dry, hot or cold, thick and thin, rise and fall but most importantly, '[b]reath turns a place into a habitat. If you can breathe there, you can live there' (2012: 301). Technology may enable us to survive, up to a point, in the air but other forms of transport do not separate us from that which enables us to live.

Moreover, a precursor to the suspension of being that occurs in the air is the suspension of being that occurs on the ground. At the airport we can pretend to be who we want to be because we are for the most part among strangers and this enables individuals to create a different version of the self, such that '[w]e can invent a new personal history on the spot. Short-lived, like x-rays or fireworks, these identities need only serve us for as long as we lounge before the boarding call is broadcast' (Gottdiener 2001: 38–39). The reinvention of 'who we are' occurs in relation to the time-space suspension that airports create and as such dwelling as suspended time has existential possibilities (Bishop 2013).

For passengers, the suspension of time is experienced as a disruption to the rhythm and flow of daily life. Sleep patterns can be disrupted by night flights and travel plans may mean crossing the invisible line of different time and date zones, both of which may cause people to feel physically, emotionally and psychologically disorientated. Being out of our time also disrupts bodily rhythms that dictate when we eat, what we wear and how we orientate the self in relation to place. Crossing over international date lines is a form of time travel as losing or gaining a day causes us to go back or forward in time. The disruption of time in this way not only affects the natural rhythms of the body, it also provides spaces of ambiguity that challenge who we are in relation to where and when we are. It is no wonder, therefore, that some individuals feel liberated from the norms of their existence and choose to suspend 'who I am' to play around with alternative versions of the self, versions that may be very different to those of home (see Selänniemi 2003).

Although the opportunity to be who we want to be is associated with travelling in general, not all forms of travel are the same. For example, sea cruising also offers fascinating possibilities for thinking through the idea of suspended being, as Andreu notes 'airspace resembles the ocean that links and separates at the same time' (1999: 59). Nevertheless, the ocean remains physically attached to the earth and as such travel by sea is not the same as travel by air:

> on the ocean one sees the water and the waves . . . one recognises one's place in a microcosm with a daily round of events, on a voyage that

> makes no pretence of instantaneity. Flying intimates that there is no journey, only trajectory.
>
> (Rosler 1997: 93)

In flight we see our separation from the earth, separation from that which defines us as humans; we are dwellers on, not above, the earth. Airport architecture prepares people for these moments of separation by providing them with time to adjust to what is to come. Time that can be spent in a myriad of ways such as waiting and queuing, shopping and sleeping, eating and drinking, talking and thinking, reading and listening. All such activities are but distractions that delay the inevitability of what is to come, the body's movement through time and space. In this sense airport architecture provides time-space intervals of distraction that gradually accustom an individual to the experience of being out of place.

The suspension of time that is associated with waiting and queuing at an airport is of a different order to that which occurs with other types of travel; different because of what happens at the end of the wait, departure from the solidity of the earth to the ethereal world of the air. In this sense airports provide a doorway between one world and the next and in crossing the threshold at departures we are making a decision to engage with what lies beyond, even if this decision is unconsciously made. The airport as threshold is a useful way of thinking through the symbolic as opposed to the functional purpose of an airport because a threshold is both a tangible and intangible crossing point betwixt and between one type of space and the next.

Mugerauer's (1993) discussion of the domestic porch in the American Midwest provides a good illustration of what I mean here through its ability to mediate between the inside and the outside, between the private space of the home and the public space of the street or neighbourhood. The porch is a place for gathering and lingering before making a transitional shift between one relationship and the next, '[t[he shift is from "the rest of the world" to another place or manner of being. *The Porch joins different worlds*' (Mugerauer 1993: 119). Worlds here refers to different ways or experiences of being human, the being that is part of a family or the being that is a member of civic society, both of which illustrate the type of relationships that define the human condition. The threshold of porch or airport marks the boundary between one relationship and another, as Mugerauer again argues '[i]n a continuous but changing manner, architecture gives what sustains us: sites for the establishment and cultivation of human worlds' (1993: 126).

As with the porch, the lingering and gathering that occurs at an airport takes place through the time-space intervals referred to above. Drawing from the work of Victor Turner, Lloyd (2003) argues that the architectural provision of liminal spaces of distraction and consumption can make waiting and lingering at an airport a pleasurable experience. Shopping as consumerism is defined in large part by the purchase of superfluous goods because we frequently buy on impulse that which we later regret. However, airport shopping is an exaggerated form of superfluous shopping because the items for sale are bought to pass the time. They are not bought because I am shopping but because I am waiting, waiting for what is to come. The 'what is to come' involves leaving the ground, leaving the environmental conditions that support human life for ones that endanger life in a very real sense. Ships have lifeboats, planes do not and so departing the land requires a different form of mental preparation; as the architect Paul Andreu (1999: 59) argues, airports are good examples of different types of borders and crossing between the land and the air and back again is 'an updated retelling of the myth of Icarus'.

This is significant because it links flying with death both as a physical and imaginary possibility, which in turn provides an opportunity to rethink the function of shopping in the context of an airport. Airport shopping is the magic cloak that individuals put on to avoid having to contemplate the possible consequences of what they are about to do. It is a good luck talisman to ward off the evil spirits that might disrupt my journey or even endanger my life, evil spirits that range from delays caused by a technological fault to the consequences of terrorism. However, shopping provides a false sense of security because it lulls people into thinking that the day they fly is just like any other day. As de Botton (2009) argues, airport shopping puts people in the right frame of mind to meet their maker, it helps them to maintain dignity in the face of death. Yet shopping can only do so much and the thought of what is to come is the invisible passenger accompanying every flight.

Conclusion

Anthropologically, then, airports mark the physical and mental boundary between one way of being and another. There are boundaries of the mind to be crossed, such as a fear of flying, which is often accompanied by thoughts of personal mortality. There are the political borders of a particular nation-state controlled by passport officers, immigration desks and customs officials regulating who and what are allowed to enter and depart. Whilst these technologies of control are highly visible manifestations of an earthly experience, they mask the wider significance of airports as structures of human cosmology. A cosmology made visible in the borderland of airport space, wherein lie the crossing points, the thresholds of arrival and departure that move individuals between land and air, earth and sky.

Crossing between one type of space and another provides an opportunity to reflect upon what happens in the in-between space of arriving and departing. As such, being human-in-an-airport is dwelling as liminal pause, the pause in-between leaving and arriving, the pause that occurs as passengers wait to cross the threshold between home and away, between the earth and the sky, between being on the ground and being in the air. In one sense, then, an airport is a protective shield separating the individual from the dangers associated with what lies beyond, which in terms of air travel is the possibility of death. As de Botton (2009) remarks, the apparent mundanity of flying is so indelibly linked with the momentous themes of existence that thoughts of the divine, the eternal and the significant accompany people covertly on to the airplane, haunting communication of the safety instructions, the weather announcements and the view through the window of the earth below.

The cosmological language of architecture discussed here builds the tangible and intangible structures that define and reflect human dwelling as a relationship between people, place and cosmos. As tourists encounter, move through and occupy architectural forms, they are engaging in a conversation with what this language reveals. Airport architecture creates the spaces, structures and experiences that confront individuals with thoughts of their own mortality. This is architecture as boundary marker, and as numerous ethnographies demonstrate, boundaries highlight the distinctiveness of human thinking and being (Barth 1969; Cohen 1982; Okely 1983). This distinctiveness is illustrated by Heidegger's (1971: 152) argument that a boundary should be seen not so much as a point of departure but as the point at which something *begins its presencing*. In terms of an airport, that which *begins its presencing*, that which is made visible is the absolute certainty that one day I will die and that the flight I am about to take could be the *presencing* of my death.

Airports mark this boundary between life and death, a boundary that provides an opportunity to reflect on who I am, what I have achieved, what I value and believe. In effect to contemplate what makes *me* human. So airports, like the Zafimaniry house, the Foi longhouse or Chartres cathedral, illustrate Geertz's point that architecture makes visible the specific concepts of the relations between God and man, what Heidegger refers to as the fourfold of heaven and earth, gods and human mortality. More specifically, airport architecture builds places for encountering not just a suspension of being but an end to being itself. Hence, airports are significant structures of cosmological thought.

Whilst architecture builds an enormous variety of buildings and structures, airports are particularly important because the gestures they create are ones that signal the limits of human existence. The vast expanse of glass that frames the view from the terminal to the runway focuses attention on the very means by which an end to life may be brought about, the airplane. The architectural ordering of airport space produces activities and experiences designed to distract passengers from this truth, activities such as shopping. Drawing on Gell, shopping is a technology of enchantment and the spell it casts is intended to cloud the eyes and the mind as to the implications of crossing the threshold between the land and the air, between the earth and the sky.

In this sense airports are sacred buildings because, like churches, temples and mosques, they are physical manifestations of the border between life and death. Whilst sacred architecture designs buildings where acts of worship support adherence to a set of beliefs that speak of a common destiny, airport architecture creates buildings that speak of a common fate. A fate that defies culture and politics because in the end no matter who we are, where we live or what we believe, one day each of us will succumb to the inevitability of human mortality. One function of architecture is the creation of structures and experiences that confront individuals with spaces in which to contemplate personal and collective mortality. In this sense human creativity as expressed through architecture brings forth structures, places and landscapes that shape, organise and support fundamental truths of human existence.

Through architecture people find their place and purpose in the world, they see and experience the relationship between people, place and belief, a relationship that establishes ways of being and ways of experiencing human existence, including the limits of this existence. As such, airports resemble what Pint has referred to as a shamanistic membrane between one world and the next:

> this membrane no longer functions as a gateway to some kind of spirit world but rather serves as a material interface that allows us to interact with immaterial things such as the fantasies and collective dream-images that surround us as an invisible but influential force field.
>
> (2013: 126)

Ultimately, architectural dwelling is a way of being human in relation to measurements, calculations, dimensions, and equations; materials, lines and patterns, corners and angles, balance and imbalance, joining and moulding, inside and outside; thinking and imagining, precision and tolerance, creativity and flair. These 'techniques' are ways of making who we are, ways of connecting people, place and belief. In this sense the techniques of airport architecture reveal how cosmology creates human worlds

In arguing that airports have cosmological significance, I do not mean that the particularities of cosmology are the same, as each airport will reflect and embody aspects of the culture within which it is located. So what I have set out here are a set of arguments that can be applied, amended and/or expanded in relation to other cultural and philosophical ways of thinking and being through architecture.

5 Earthly dwelling

Introduction

The previous chapters focused on singular aspects of being and dwelling through tourism. With this chapter I adopt a more holistic approach to argue that the senses, the body, materiality and architecture are part of a wider dwelling relationship resulting from being on the earth, a relationship I refer to as earthly dwelling. In Chapter 4 I argued that because air travel and being in the air separates us from the earth, it causes us to reflect upon a defining characteristic of human existence by revealing that which we are not. We are dwellers on not above the earth. In saying this I am not arguing that earthly dwelling is only about a relationship with the ground, as clearly the sky, the air, the weather and so forth are inseparable from the lifeworld of human activity and experience. Indeed, as humans, we live, work, play and hence engage in tourism in relation to the earth because that is where tourism occurs. Despite the technological drive to develop space tourism, this does not change the fact that our bodies are conditioned for life on the earth. In addition, space tourism is a misnomer because it is not tourism, but a means of transport and as such it is no more a form of tourism than is air travel.

My use of 'earthly' is a way of emphasising my argument that being human is a being in relation to the earth, and as such earthly dwelling describes what Jackson (2007) refers to as the vital, significant and reciprocal relationship that exists between human subjects and the earth. The distinction between *on* the earth and *in relation to* the earth is an important one to make because earthly dwelling concerns the relational totality of being human-in-the-world, whether this is in the air, on the land, at sea, or in relation to nature and the natural world. This relational totality is evident in the ways in which individuals and groups think about and relate to the earth. For example, Western modes of thinking dominated by science, objectivity and rationality encourage a subject-object, human-earth relationship. Whereas animist thinking based around anthropomorphic metaphors of the earth as a living, breathing, moving entity encourages a subject-subject, human-earth relationship (Jackson 2007).

However, animist thinking like rational thinking is not a coherent, stable whole and Willerslev (2007) provides a good illustration of this point through his ethnography of hunting practices among the Siberian Yukaghirs. These practices demonstrate that the categories human, animal and nonhuman are interchangeable; animals can be both persons and prey and humans can be both persons and animals. When nonhumans are in their own habitats, they are referred to as 'reindeer people', 'elk people' or 'fox people', but when they roam the forest or swim in the lakes they become prey and can be hunted. Likewise, the Yukaghir hunter imitates the movements, behaviour and smells of the hunted in order to trick the prey into getting caught. As a result, for the Yukaghirs, animism 'is a particular way of perceiving animals and the environment that is brought into play in specific contexts of practical activities' (Willerslev 2007: 116).

Despite such complexities, earthly dwelling is inseparable from the nonhuman environment since being human is very much a being deeply embedded in a world shaped by such as animals, plants, and spirits, leading one anthropologist to argue for an anthropology of beyond human (Kohn 2013). Trees are interesting in this respect, whether individual or as part of a forest or orchard, because they breathe, they are 'alive' and as such they not only share life with humans they are able to sustain life. They achieve this through the production of food in the form of fruit, by providing shelter through the use of wood to make houses, and as the previous chapter's discussion of Bloch's Zafimaniry house showed, by transforming into 'bones' that support generational continuity. This life-sustaining function of trees influences how we think about and understand who we are in relation to what we eat and how we live (Jones and Cloke 2002; Macnaghten and Urry 2000). How trees are used and the role they play in social and economic systems tells us much about the basis upon which a particular society operates, leading Bloch (2005) to argue that trees are good to think with.

The human-earth relationship is embedded within the ways in which people live their lives; it is not something separate to or that stands apart from daily life. It is the physical union that defines how we dwell as humans in the world; that defines our earthly dwelling. As Bender argues in relation to landscape, the 'context-dependency of people's being-in-the-world is a physical context' (2002: S104). Moreover, as Chapter 2 argued, this physical union, this relational totality is not only experienced in terms of the materiality of the earth; it is also experienced as an embodied, multisensory human-earth relationship. Although the manner of our earthly dwelling manifests itself in many ways, I do not intend to discuss specific examples of the differences and similarities that exist, as these can be found in the vast body of ethnographic work that has already been published focusing on aspects such as myth, kinship, magic, cosmology and so on. My intention with this chapter is to argue that humans engage with and relate to their earthly surroundings as a means of locating and being a self in the world.

Clearly, individuals do not engage with the earth world as a whole; they engage with the places, locations, people and practices – including the non-human 'world' of nature, animals and so forth – that comprise their everyday existence. This engagement has profound implications for the relationship between people, earth and world because it brings together all that humans are, what they feel and how they think into contact with the environing world. Tilley and Cameron-Daum's (2017: 20) ethnography of an English heathland provides a good illustration of what I mean here when they argue that landscapes 'gather topographies, geologies, plants and animals, persons and their biographies, social and political relationships, material things and monuments, dreams and emotions, discourses and representations'. All such aspects weave through the experience of landscape as a particular world.

In addition to landscape there are numerous other smaller worlds such as a house – the immediate familiar world of kith and kin – then there are the worlds associated with the wider community, the street, town, city and country. Anthropologists talk about my world, your world, their world, the world of work and that of everyday life. Radiating out from the everyday are the wider connections and relationships that also serve to locate the self in the world, such as those cultural, ethnic or religious ties that cut across borders and boundaries. Within the relational totality of the earth world, therefore, there are numerous *worlds* being lived in, visited, shared, fought over or avoided. Hence, in a lifetime the self stays, lingers, and moves back and forth in and out through a number of familiar and unfamiliar worlds, including the world of tourism, which, as argued throughout this book, is one of the defining activities whereby the relationship between self and world is constructed, negotiated and challenged. As Selwyn (2010: 212) demonstrates through his interrogation of postcards and travel brochures, tourism images provide 'a 'grammar' of engagement of self with the world'.

The 'self' I am referring to here is not a psychologically dissected self, but what Jackson refers to as the experience of being a social person in the world since '[n]o human being comes to a knowledge of himself or herself except through others' (1995: 118). The activity of tourism is inherently a social activity geared towards an engagement with other people, places and things on the basis of those aspects of 'otherness' deemed to represent self and world. Theme parks, heritage attractions, museums and castles; eco-tourism and adventure tourism; beach holidays and weekends away all take the self into the wider world and back again. The relationship between self and world is, therefore, reciprocal in that it entails a response, such that understandings of self and world are continually being made and remade in light of experience. This is not to say that responses to encounters between people are cosy, equal and mutually beneficial, clearly they are not. Indeed, the large amount of literature on the political economy of tourism is testament to the power dynamics that control the relationship between the self of the tourist and the self of the visited (Britton 1982; Bianchi 2014; Stein 2008). Furthermore, the transformation of the tourist self promised by the discourse of tourism rarely occurs, as many encounters between people merely confirm stereotypes and fail to challenge prejudice (Adams 1984; Bruner 1991; Palmer and Lester 2007).

The fourfold of earthly dwelling

In order to explore the human-earth relationship in terms of locating and being a self in the world, I intend to focus on some of the primary meaning-making referents through which this relationship is understood, experienced and reproduced namely, time, place, history and memory. These four interrelated elements of earthly dwelling are ways of classifying, explaining and knowing the world and as such they are of significant interest to anthropologists, geographers, historians and so on (see Halbwachs 1992; Hirsch and O'Hanlon 1995; Ingold 2011b; Bender 2002; Schama 2004; Casey 2009; Macdonald 2013). These four referents are not, however, meant to be exclusive, for example nature, animals and the natural world are clearly significant aspects of earthly dwelling as are myth making and mythical thinking. Likewise, there are relational links between myth and history, between myth, people and place and so on (Levi-Strauss 1986; Calder 1991; Bell 2003).

Nevertheless, what interests me is the collective significance of these four in terms of understanding earthly dwelling as a way of locating and being a self in the world. To borrow from Lund and Jóhannesson (2016), these four are the early substances that entangle the human and the nonhuman in a poetic making of self and world. Furthermore, these four are also woven into the experience and activity of tourism. In effect, they are the defining characteristics of tourism because to engage in and with tourism is to engage with particular configurations of time, place, history and memory; configurations experienced in the places, people, buildings, souvenirs, landscapes, activities and so forth that are part of what tourists do.

In focusing on these four I am not arguing that everyone has the same understanding of and relationship with them, as clearly they do not. Within anthropology debates exists over how time has been used by anthropologists to construct a primitive Other through the 'glorification of distance based on a denial of the conditions of shared Time' (Fabian 2014: 65). This critique notwithstanding, numerous ethnographies and linguistic studies demonstrate that the concept and experience of time is understood in different ways. In addition to clock time, there is sacred time, social and monumental time demonstrating that time is a way of organising human activity and human lifeworlds (Herzfeld 1991; Eliade 1959; Gell 1992b; Munn 1992; James and Mills 2005).

For example, the Amazonian Tupi language and culture Amondawa does not include words or phrases associated with a linear understanding of time, such as 'month', 'next week' or 'last year'. Life is organised as divisions of night and day, rainy or dry season and in relation to life stage and position within society (Sinha, C. et al 2011; Sinha et al 2012). Likewise, in the language and thinking of the Yolngu people of northern Australia, time is subordinate to place. 'Time was created through the transformation of ancestral beings into place . . . Whatever events happened at the place, whatever sequence they occurred in, whatever intervals existed between them, all became subordinate to their representation in space' (Morphy 1995: 188).

Understandings of time are not always linked to the objects of time such as clocks, calendars and watches, as Birth's discussion of how the time needed to accomplish the responsibilities of daily life in rural Trinidad illustrates. Here, the determination of time is not always brought to mind by clocks or watches but by sound and by touch. The sound:

> of route taxis coming and going allows one to time when to seek transportation . . . the toughness of bull grass during the heat of the day determines the optimum time to cut it; the sound of school children walking by the road signals the opportune moment to open shops; and the fact that the tropical downpours can be heard before they arrive provides a signal for when to seek shelter or to cover drying cocoa.
>
> (2012: 106–107)

References to sound and touch highlight the embodiment of time, which of course means that time is gendered as the female reproductive cycle clearly illustrates. Here, the passage of time is brought to mind through the body such that time is a physical and emotional experience for women, and also for men. Bodies age and decay, and as they do so men and women are reminded of their past body and the life it has led.

As with time, place, history and memory are conceived, expressed and experienced in diverse ways and this has resulted in some fascinating discussions of the relationship between them and of the role they play in shaping ways of knowing and being human in the world (see Comaroff and Comaroff 1992; Fentress 1992; Halbwachs 1992; Schama 2004; Casey 2009). There are also numerous debates about the concept of space and the relationship between space and place, including the circumstances in which the binary space/place division is not only unhelpful but also misleading (Kuper 1972; Tuan 1977; Lefebvre 1991; Massey 2005; Bawaka Country et al 2016). Is space empty and lifeless? How does space become place? What do we mean by a sense of place? Why is it even necessary to distinguish between place/space? Ultimately I agree with Ingold that space is too abstract a concept to adequately describe how life is both talked about and lived because life is not lived in space but in relation to somewhere in particular, a somewhere that includes people and what they do:

> Farmers plant their crops in the *earth*, not in space, and harvest them from *fields*, not from space. Their animals graze *pastures*, not space . . . Painters set up their easels in the *landscape*, not in space. When we are

> at home, we are *indoors*, not in space . . . Casting our eyes upwards we see the *sky*, not space, and on a windy day we feel the *air*, not space. Space is nothing, and because it is nothing it cannot be truly inhabited at all.
>
> (2011a: 145, original emphasis)

Whilst accepting that debates about time, place, history and memory are both inevitable and productive, I do not intend to engage in lengthy discussions of each one because unpicking each from the other ignores their collective significance as constitutive elements of earthly dwelling. For example, although the tensions between history and memory have been highlighted by such as Nora, he nonetheless acknowledges the fundamental ties that bind the two together by referring to 'the tree of memory and the bark of history' (1989: 10).

Likewise, being human is inextricably tied to how people understand and relate to a particular place and the sense of belonging or alienation associated with it. In this sense memory can anchor individuals to place in a physical geographic sense as well as emotionally in terms of knowing my place in the world. Of course a phrase such as 'know your place' illustrates that place is a sociological marker of status and class such that to be 'out of place' can indicate that some social code or boundary has been traversed. Human beings are social beings and the ability to locate and to place the self in relation to a particular group, whether this is an ethnic, family or kinship group, a work or leisure group is one of the ways in which identity and belonging is understood and experienced. Finding my place in the world means that the past and the memories associated with that place or particular group resonate, they mean something to the individual. As Said argues in relation to the late twentieth century, during periods of rapid societal change people look to memory 'especially in its collective forms, to give themselves a coherent identity, a national narrative, a place in the world' (2000: 179).

Thus, ties to place are often linked to questions of identity or to feelings and emotions that coalesce into what is frequently referred to as a sense of place. Interestingly Jackson (1994) argues that when traced back to its Latin origins, *genius loci*, sense of place referred to the spiritual or divine guardian who watched over particular locations. The location acquired a special status, for which the inhabitants cared and to which visitors returned time and again as a form of ritual recognition of the location's significance. Jackson maintains that this ritual return to the divine spirit of place remains even though contemporary usage has done away with the divine and defines sense of place in relation to atmosphere or the quality of the environment:

> we recognize that certain localities have an attraction which gives us a certain indefinable sense of wellbeing and which we want to return to, time and again. So, that original notion of ritual, of repeated celebration or reverence is still inherent in the phrase. It is not a temporary

> response, for it persists and brings us back, reminding us of previous visits.
>
> (1994: 158)

Tourist destinations and attractions strive to create and communicate a sense of place that is unique in some way in order to attract new and repeat business and by doing so *genius loci* is the commercialisation of memory and emotion as place.

Although ties to place can bind or release, attract or deter, enchant or disturb, places that are contested or from which individuals and groups are excluded or driven away are still reference points for locating the self in relation to world. Individuals, families and groups who leave an ancestral homeland through voluntary social mobility or are forced to do so as a result of war, conflict and persecution can retain strong political, cultural and religious affiliations to the places left behind (Vertovec 2004; Sheffer 2006 Basu 2007).

Understanding self and world draws from ancestors and events that have gone before, which are then used to interpret the present, influence and imagine the future. This is so even for cultures where the concept of and even the word history is understood differently, is expressed as myth or is not part of the language (Levi-Strauss 1986, 1995). Being human is also a being in relation to the rhythm and flow of human and nonhuman activity that marks the passage of time. Circulating around, in and through experiences of time, place and history, is memory, which provides a trigger for how people connect to or disconnect from the world around them. As Bender notes, '[a] place inflected with memory serves to draw people towards it or to keep them away, permits the assertion or denial of knowledge claims, becomes a nexus of contested meaning' (2002: S104). Hence, memory is at best partial and at worst false; it involves forgetting, can be misleading and is definitely open to political appropriation (Douglas 1995; Winter 2007; Macdonald 2013)

The inseparability of time, place, history and memory is exemplified by relationships to place. Place can be many things, an individual home, a neighbourhood, a municipal park, somewhere to meet, a city or village, a forest or farm. Furthermore, place and places are both tangible and intangible. We physically live, visit or fleetingly pass through particular places and we imagine, remember and even reconstruct the experiences, attachments and connections embedded in a place. But no matter how a particular place is configured, it carries within it layers of time and the history of the people and events that have gone before and this is most strikingly evident through relationships with the land and with landscape. Jackson (1994) illustrates how time and history are made visible in New Mexico as a result of the hot, dry climate, which has preserved the physical evidence of previous generations long after the people have migrated to a more comfortable existence. The buildings and ruins and the visible impact on the land of both human and nonhuman activity enables the past to occupy the present. In effect the past is never past in the sense of being over, it merely continues into the present as physical remnant or as memories passed on from one generation to the next. In this sense history and memory are softly spoken whispers that accompany us on the path between life and death.

Basso (1996) provides a further illustration of the inseparability of the four referents of earthly dwelling in his ethnography of the tribal landscape of the Western Apache people of Arizona. Here time, place, history and memory coalesce as acquired wisdom, wisdom acquired through the lessons to be learnt from memories presented as stories handed down from father to son, mother to daughter, grandparent to grandchild. Stories of the events that occurred on hunting trips, of what took place close to a particular mountain or of the consequences of not heeding the landscape when out gathering firewood:

> The trail of wisdom – that is what I'm going to talk about. I'm going to speak as the old people do, as my grandmother spoke to me. . . 'Do you want a long life?' she said. 'Well you will need to have wisdom'. Wisdom sits in places. It's like water that never dries up. You need to drink water to stay alive, don't you? Well you also need to drink from places.
> (cited in Basso 1996: 70)

This gradual acquisition of wisdom rather nicely illustrates an argument made by Ingold (2011a) that knowledge should be seen as something that people grow into rather than something that is literally handed down to them.

As mentioned in Chapter 1, Basso's thinking is influenced by Heidegger's philosophy of dwelling, which Basso argues assigns importance to the ways in which people consciously perceive and understand the world through their lived engagement with the immediate environment. This argument aligns with Ingold's (1993) comment that an anthropologically informed dwelling perspective privileges the understandings people derive from their everyday, active involvement in the world. Hence, being and dwelling is anchored in the associations brought to mind, or sensed as Basso refers to it, through the self-conscious, active relationship between people and place. 'Sensing places, men and women become sharply aware of the complex attachments that link them to features of the physical world. Sensing places, they dwell, as it were, on aspects of dwelling' (Basso 1996: 54–55).

What individuals are sensing here are the attachments and associations evoked in the coming together of time, place, history and memory. Hence, my argument that these four belong to one another, they are intertwined and inseparable because each one carries within it the presence of the other three. As Heidegger argues in relation to the fourfold of earth, sky, divinities and mortals, '[e]ach of the four mirrors in its own way the presence of the others' (2001: 177). What is of interest here is Heidegger's use of the fourfold concept to illustrate the relational totality of human existence where being and dwelling is characterised as a merging of self and world. Hence, I am not interested in what each element of my 'fourfold' may or may not mean but in their inseparability. As Rose (2012) states, the bulk of the analysis of Heidegger's fourfold is restricted to defining the individual elements when what really matters here is Heidegger's overarching point that they belong together.

In belonging together by virtue of the fact that each is a mirror reflection of the other, the four become one, become self and world united. 'This appropriating mirror-play of the simple onefold of earth and sky, divinities and mortals, we call the world' (Heidegger 2001: 177). The merging of self and world as earthly dwelling is based on the inseparability of the relationship between time, place, history and memory. It is through the everyday and frequently taken-for-granted encounters with the fourfold of earthly dwelling that individuals acquire the knowledge needed to sustain and reproduce what it is to dwell as humans, in effect to continually reproduce and reaffirm the foundations of the relationship between self and world. Tourism is one of the taken-for-granted activities through which humans engage with and relate to their earthly surroundings, providing as it does a myriad of opportunities for locating and being a self in the world.

Tourism and the dwelling fourfold

I have already argued that time, place, history and memory are woven into the experience and activity of tourism. In terms of place the whole point of tourism is to visit somewhere that has been identified as a place worth visiting. Whether this is in relation to a person or a group of people whose achievements or way of life maybe very different to those of the tourist or because particular configurations of nature and geography mark out places where culture and nature can be experienced as wilderness, the picturesque or the sublime (Short 1991; Ousby 2002; Vannini and Vannini 2016). The places of tourism maybe local or far away, and in this way place provides a way of understanding where and who we are in relation to the particularities of other places; particularities that include the people who live there, the natural world of animals, plants, topography and also climate (Gómez-Martín 2005; Markwell 2015). In effect visiting the familiar and unfamiliar places of self and other enables an individual to locate her/himself in time and space and hence there is a strong connection between the places of tourism and understandings of identity and belonging (Palmer 2005; Pretes 2003).

Like place, time in tourism can be understood and experienced in various ways. Given the association of tourism with notions of escape, freedom and relaxation, going on holiday is not just about having 'the time of our lives, but time *for* our lives' (Ryan 1997: 203, original emphasis). There is the bounded so-called sacred time of a two-week holiday, meaning that tourists are frequently preoccupied with how long it takes to get where they are going relative to the length of the holiday. Time is also drawn upon to explain the holiday experience illustrated by questions such as 'did you have a good time?' Time organises and controls behaviour via the arrival and departure times associated with specific forms of transport and the checking in and out of apartments and hotel accommodation or the timed entry tickets to attractions and theme park rides. Tourists can also exercise control over time by choosing to slow down as a way to experience a more meaningful relationship with both the self and the environment. Long-term self-drive travellers in Australia deliberately chose a slower pace of travel, resulting in periods of self-reflection in relation to the landscape (Small 2016).

Time within tourism is frequently linked to price, which in turn is indicative of class, power and status so that the more you pay the quicker you can navigate the challenges associated with certain forms of transport. For example, check-in and waiting times at airports differ depending upon the type of ticket and the flight category, charter or scheduled. British Airways First offers fast track check-in, security and arrivals whereas charter flights do not. Certain activities such as skiing and sunbathing are time-season specific and as Chapter 4 argued, air travel is a form of time travel as passengers cross international date and time configurations. Similarly time, specifically linear time, is inextricably linked to the concept of heritage and its association with inheritance where things, values, events or skills are handed down from one generation to the next, as Howard notes the Western 'concept of heritage requires, a past, a present, and a future, *in that order*' (1994: 9, original emphasis). Heritage time is not the only constructed category of tourist time. The Etches Collection of prehistoric marine fossils in Dorset, England offers visitors an experience of Deep Time, which like heritage time seeks to highlight the unbroken link between the past, the present and the future, as Steve Etches states 'I love to see kids engaging with the past. It's all about their future' (Tourist Brochure 2017).

Time is also experienced on and through the places visited. Places, people and landscapes are promoted as unchanging and timeless representations of a supposedly more authentic past. The rise of movements such as Citta'slow or Slow City and the emergence of Slow Tourism illustrate how place is produced in relation to time as local foods, skills and crafts associated with the values and traditions of the past are preferred over those linked to the global homogenising forces of present-day modernity (Pink 2008). On the surface Slow Tourism, the child of Citta'slow, is marketed as an alternative to mass tourism and as a more sustainable and environmentally friendly form of tourism (Dickinson and Lumsdon 2010; Caffyn 2012; Timms and Conway 2012). However, Slow Tourism is really about the packaging of time where time becomes the product, or more specifically the experience of time in relation to place. Time-place in Slow Tourism is an experience in opposition to that associated with the rigid controlling ethos of clock time characteristic of daily life, it is about 'stepping off the treadmill, seeking work-life balance or refusing the dominant logic of speed' (Fullagar et al 2012: 1). Through a focus on time, this form of tourism seeks to encourage a different understanding of and relationship with self, place and people.

The connectivity of time and place in tourism is also evident in repeat visits to the same location, which reveal the passage of time in intricate ways such as trees planted or hedges removed, new buildings replacing the old, roads where fields used to be, tunnels through mountains that once separated places and people. However, recognition of changes such as these is not meant to imply a detached association with time. Time is not, as Ingold (1993) argues, something to be observed at a distance since the passage referred to is in fact our own journey as part of the business of dwelling. In this sense time in relation to tourism is but a gathering together of experiences as a means of locating individual and collective life histories. The experience of time passing is an experience of history in the making.

Time, place and memory are also made visible through sites of historic significance as illustrated in Chapter 3. These three may be experienced through the cloak of nostalgia that surrounds much of what is labelled heritage tourism, and also through appeals to the macabre associated with so-called dark tourism, visits to sites where death, atrocity or disaster have left an indelible imprint (Lennon and Foley 2000; MacDonald 2013). Indeed, Lennon and Mitchell (2007: 177) argue that '[t]he importance psychologically of *place* in confronting and memorialising death, whether of an individual or of thousands of disenfranchised people, is a main driver of dark tourism'. The places of dark tourism are inseparable from the histories and memories of the events associated with them, which all too often haunt the present and the future. Ultimately, no matter how it is configured, tourism is a way of linking the past, the present and the future and in this sense history as time, people and event is inseparable from the experience of tourism; within tourism it is the companion that walks with, behind and alongside time, place and memory.

In terms of memory a significant part of tourism is the collection of experiences, objects and memorabilia as ways of remembering where I went and what I did. More specifically, the photographic practices of many tourists have been referred to as 'memory work' because they create the stories that are used to compile an individual's life-narrative (Bærenholdt et al 2004). Online sites such as TripAdvisor and Oyster.com are repositories for such memory work, whether positive or negative, demonstrating the value attached to the supposedly sacred non-work time of tourism. Holiday memories are knowledge banks from which decisions are made about where to go and where to avoid, with whom to fly, in which hotel to stay and the type of activities in which to engage whilst away. The memories of away are embedded in the souvenirs, images and photographs collected, and in the stories told of the places, people and experiences encountered. Such memories are brought back to the familiar world of home to be displayed, shared and talked over with family, friends and social network groups. What is being shared here are the recently acquired remembered experiences of a time and a place. These experiences then become part of an individual's travel biography or history of going on holiday, a history that may be recalled time and again over the course of a life. In sharing the objects, stories and experiences of travel, the connectivity of time, place, history and memory is made visible and it is this connectivity that defines our earthly dwelling.

The concept of earthly dwelling then is a way of understanding how the activities that shape and explain behaviour, activities such as tourism, occur within the same time and space as part of a relational totality. Not literally at the same time, or in the same place or part of the same kinship group and certainly not in a state of harmonious accord, but in relation to the chronologies, histories, places and memories of other people and other ways of being human. Engaging in tourism is, therefore, an engagement with time, place, history and memory. These four are the building blocks of tourism and it is through appeals made to particular configurations of the tourism fourfold, configurations marketed as dark tourism, as cultural tourism, heritage tourism, adventure tourism and so on, that individuals are encouraged to become tourists. The gathering together of the tourism fourfold into recognisable tourism products is not just about the creation of appealing destinations, attractions and experiences. Ultimately, it is about how tourism *works* to make and remake the relationship between self and world. A relationship described by Selwyn (2013) as the self in the world and the world in the self.

Displaying self and world

Whilst the above discussion provides a useful starting point, as with previous chapters I intend to narrow down my focus to more effectively illustrate the overall argument. The focus I have chosen is the museum. The museum not only represents a particularly fascinating example of the human-earth relationship characterised as earthly dwelling but in the form of an ethnographic museum, it is deeply embedded in the history of anthropology both as a practice and as a discipline (Stocking 1987; Clifford 1988; Ames 1992; Levell 2000; Henare 2005; Shelton 2011).

Given the fact that the museum label can encompass a multitude of types and claims to ownership, it would be impossible to include the entire range of museums in this discussion. As Hooper-Greenhill notes, by the early 1990s, understandings of the role, purpose and even the appearance of a museum had so fundamentally changed, that 'almost anything may turn out to be a museum, and museums can be found in farms, boats, coal mines, warehouses, prisons, castles, or cottages' (1992: 1). Similarly, there are museums that speak to local or international audiences; there are community museums and museums with public access restrictions such as Harvard University's *Herbariar*. So, although I can only draw on a limited number of examples, my argument is applicable to all museums, to what has been referred to as the idea of the museum in general (Preziosi and Farago 2004a).

Having said this, I am not intending to discuss how specific museum objects are assembled, displayed or interpreted, as there is already a huge body of knowledge focusing on these aspects within disciplines such as anthropology and archaeology and in fields such as material culture studies and museum studies (see Pearce 1994; Knell 2007; Dudley et al 2012; Harrison et al 2013; Karp and Kratz 2014). My interest in the museum lies in the fact that it gathers together those elements of time, place, history and memory considered to be the most significant for locating not only the self in the world, but also the group, community or nation to which a particular self feels allegiance. As Preziosi and Farago argue:

> The beliefs that have constituted the core of 'modernity' rest upon certain assumptions about the nature of meaningful relationships between subjects and objects, between individuals and communities and the worlds they weave about themselves . . . the institution of the museum has for some time been essential to the fabrication and sustenance of this system of beliefs.
>
> (2004b: 1)

Museums represent numerous human-world relationships, not merely those that occur between people. Museums devoted to the natural world, to science and technology such as the *Boston Science Museum*, the *American Museum of Natural History*, London's *Natural History Museum* and the *Beijing Museum of Natural History* speak of the relational ties between humans, animals, nature and the environment. These ties not only reveal how each one is influenced by the other three, they also reveal the underlying forces that construct particular understandings of earthly dwelling. Forces such as the social, cultural, economic, political and technological circumstances that shape the worlds in which people live.

Museum exhibitions that focus on the solar system or human space exploration document how the human search for meaning extends beyond the boundaries of the earth world. Interestingly, space exploration of the solar cosmos serves to shrink the distance between the known and the unknown through a process of familiarisation that presents the vastness of space as if it were just next door. As illustrated by the Boston *Museum of Science's* 'Explore' series which offers virtual tours to '[e]xplore our beautiful solar system and its thousands of varied worlds – the Sun, planets, moons, and newly discovered objects that are changing the way we view our neighborhood in space' (Museum of Science 2015). Time and space are similarly collapsed in the 2015 multi-media installation 'From the Big Bang to Today' at the Museum für Naturkunde in Berlin. Such museums display how human understandings of time, place, history and memory shape and are shaped by events beyond the boundaries of the earth world.

In returning to the earth a focus on museums is also instructive because as Kirshenblatt-Gimblett (1998) argues, the purpose of tourism is to turn places into destinations and given the imperative for museums to make money, one way in which they can do this is to present themselves as part of a tourist itinerary where the ultimate in situ installation is the lifeworld as a museum of itself; a form of self-fashioning that resonates with what Clifford (1988 216) has referred to as 'collecting ourselves'. The construction and display of self and world that occurs through the collecting or gathering together of time, place, history and memory as a museum exhibit illustrates the relationships, systems and processes that shape how the world was, is and how we might like it to be, which helps to explain the appeal of museums within the context of tourism. Through encounters with the people, practices, things and events of previous and current generations, they provide opportunities for visitors to think through who I am, who we are and who we might become.

An interesting example is the 2014–15 Disobedient Objects exhibition held at the *Victoria and Albert* museum of art and design in London. Objects as diverse as 'finely woven banners; defaced currency; changing designs for barricades and blockades; political video games; an inflatable general assembly to facilitate consensus decision-making; experimental activist-bicycles; and textiles bearing witness to political murders' illustrate the role of objects in bringing about social and political change (Victoria and Albert Museum 2016). Objects such as these are inextricably tied to the times, places, histories and memories of the people and events with which they are associated. Here, the tourism fourfold is put to work as tool-objects of resistance, protest and rebellion. As tools they speak of the ways in which individuals and groups experience and challenge the boundaries between conformity and conflict and how the tensions between these forces shape experiences of earthly dwelling.

Similarly, museums focus on how developments in transport technology effectively shrink the tangible and intangible barriers between people, places and ideas. The *London Transport Museum*, for example, tells the story of London through its transport system and its influence on the physical and cultural evolution of London society and by extension that of urban transport globally. As their website explains the collections encompass:

> a wide spectrum of materials and media, including vehicles, rolling stock, posters and original artworks, signs, uniforms, photographs, ephemera, maps and engineering drawings. Together, they make up the most comprehensive record of urban mass transit in the world.
>
> By conserving and explaining the Capital city's transport heritage, London Transport Museum offers people an understanding of the Capital's past development and engages them in the debate about its future.
>
> (London Transport Museum 2016)

Whether the museum in question focuses on art and design, archaeological remains, transport or warfare; whether it displays the history of scientific or technological innovation, the history of theatre or of media forms such as film, photography or television, all museums display the fabric from which humankind has constructed a meaningful life. However, the fabric of human being and becoming presented in a museum is only one perspective, that of the individuals and the organising principles that decide what should be assembled and how it should be interpreted and displayed. Museum exhibitions seeking to explain the relationship between human beings and the cosmos or between humans and the natural world are framed from within a particular worldview. Understandings of time, place, history and memory are therefore reflective of a particular cosmological understanding of how these elements frame such relationships. Two extremes here would be a relational understanding based on scientism as opposed to animism.

The *British Museum's* former director, Neil MacGregor, provided a fascinating interpretation of how human beings make themselves and their world in a series of radio programmes for the BBC broadcast in 2010 – recounting a history of the world in one hundred objects. The programmes were subsequently reproduced as a book. Despite the fact that someone else might choose a different set of objects, choice is after all coloured by time, motivation and perspective, both the book and the radio series demonstrate the inseparability of time, place, history and memory. Through objects such as the mummy of Hornedjitef, the Ain Sakhri lovers figurine – believed to be the first representation of a couple having sex – a jade axe, an Arabian bronze hand, the Persian Oxus chariot model, a painting by David Hockney and a solar powered lamp, MacGregor argues that:

> we travel back in time and across the globe, to see how we humans have shaped our world and been shaped by it over the past two million years . . . to tell a history of the world . . . by deciphering the messages which objects communicate across time – messages about peoples and places, environments and interactions, about different moments in history and about our own time as we reflect upon it.
>
> (2012: xv)

Clearly, time, place and history are made visible in and through the objects chosen and what is revealed are some of the transformative moments in the evolution of the earthly dwelling of human beings. The Ain Sakhri lover's figurine speaks of our changing relationship with the natural world as humans moved from being hunter gatherers to a more domesticated form of existence based around farming, understandings of home and the role of human sexuality. The figurine thus embodies and communicates a time when humans began to conceive of 'a different way of thinking about ourselves' (MacGregor 2012: 37). Likewise, the Oxus chariot model with its differently sized driver and passenger depicts the emergence of systems that defined and organised the geographic and social relationships between one group and another; systems that in contemporary times are referred to as politics, statesmanship and the power relations of a globalised world. Finally, the nineteenth-century marine chronometer from the naval ship HMS Beagle provided an accurate way to chart the oceans such that huge distances could be travelled by sea as well as by land. 'The chronometer for the first time allowed absolutely accurate charting of the oceans, with all that implied for establishing safe and rapid shipping routes' (MacGregor 2012: 505).

Yet how does memory sit within MacGregor's objects or in any museum for that matter? Whilst memory, history and time are closely intertwined within the context of a museum (Crane 2000, 2011a, 2011b), it is memory and history that are frequently viewed as the pre-eminent partnership. Indeed museums, along with libraries and archives, have been referred to as memory institutions (Dempsey 2000; Trant 2009; Robinson 2009), and in terms of tourism, museum professionals use memory as exhibit to attract visitors, turning museums into what Samuel (1994) has referred to as 'theatres of memory'. These exhibits can trigger the personal and collective memories of those who visit. Memories of not only the times, histories and places associated with a particular exhibit but also in terms of creating memories of the museum experience.

Clearly, museum objects, collections and exhibitions may be far removed from personal experiences of time, place and history. I, like most people do not have personal memories of ancient Persia or of owning a Hockney painting but to say this is to miss the point about memory in relation to the worlds gathered together and displayed in a museum. The display of ourselves triggers memories of how we came to be who we are and where we are in relation to our own individual life story. Museum collections present individuals with opportunities to make imaginative links that trace and connect the personal history of *me* with the collective history of *we* and of *you*; with all the conflicts, contradictions, triumphs and tragedies revealed along the way. This is memory as thread, the thread that connects, ruptures, mends and reworks the times, places and histories of human being and becoming. This thread may not be continuous because memory is selective, partial and incomplete, yet in visiting a museum people are offered the opportunity to make real or imagined connections with some of the constitutive elements of individual and collective being human-in-the-world.

However, as indicated earlier a note of caution is needed here because when museum professionals talk of 'world', whose world do they mean? Inevitably it is a view of world reflective of a particular understanding of to what and to whom 'we' and 'our' relate. Even when significant museums such as the *British Museum*, the *Metropolitan Museum* in New York and the *Louvre* in Paris aim to 'subvert the hierarchies of the past, there remains a risk that, like 'World Art' and 'World Music', 'World Culture' actually refers to those 'cultures' that can be most readily accommodated into the long established paradigms of the West' (Harris and O'Hanlon 2013: 9). Interestingly, Neil MacGregor used an appeal to universal values to justify the *British Museum*'s ownership of the *Elgin Marbles*, the acquisition of which is still disputed by Greece '[l]ike Shakespeare or Beethoven, the art of Greece belongs to us all' (2004: 7). Consequently, a history of the world in one hundred objects depends upon the cosmological framing of both history and world. A framing underpinned by certain cultural assumptions about how these two relate to understandings of time, place and memory.

Such arguments notwithstanding, cultural museums are appealing because they provide an easily accessible understanding of and encounter with self and other. This encounter between me, we and you is established through the objects and artefacts, images and stories on display. For example, an exhibition of wedding dresses at London's *Victoria and Albert Museum* traced the history and evolution of the fashionable white wedding dress between 1775 and 2014. The dresses and accessories, the design and construction process, the lives and stories, letters and photographs of the wearers whether private or public figures provided a fascinating picture of changing fashions, design and construction techniques. However, the exhibition's significance went beyond fabric and fashion as what was displayed for all to see were the societal rules and conventions within which the dresses were produced; conventions reflecting a predominantly Judeo Christian perspective. The symbolic significance of accessories such as the veil and orange blossom and the association of white with youth, purity and virginity all communicate the fundamental principles upon which the relationship between the self and a particular world are constructed and maintained.

Whilst the stories, events and dresses illustrate the changing role and status of women in society, notions of sexuality and the relationship between men and women at any given time, there is a more subtle underlying message in such an exhibition. In gathering together time, history and memory as a wedding dress, the museum as place displays the socially sanctioned circumstances in which human reproduction is supposed to occur. Circumstances that privilege heterosexuality as the founding principle of human relationships (Ingraham 2008). Challenges to these circumstances and conventions certainly abound. A bride may choose to wear red or black instead of white. She may select a design that pushes the boundaries of what is considered to be 'traditional'. The bride to be may already be pregnant, there may be a male bride or two brides as in ceremonies between same sex couples. Nevertheless, although attitudes and conventions may change over time the fundamental principles behind them remain, serving as a set of moral and aesthetic codes for judging human behaviour. As Nash (2013) demonstrates through her research into the pregnancy bride, despite the fact that contemporary Western marriages are associated with individual choice and negotiation, the availability and visibility of maternity bridal wear reinforces normative ideals of femininity and the role of marriage within society.

Museums do not, however, merely reveal the self-world relationship; they also seek to document, explain and interpret; lay claim to, challenge and subvert; they may also distort and hide depending upon the motivation and intentions of the individuals in charge (Ames 1992; Willett 1994; MacDonald 1998; Crane 2011a). In some cases they may also alienate the very people they claim to speak for as occurred with South Africa's post-apartheid *Red Location* museum in the District Six area of Cape Town. Built on the site of the corrugated iron homes of the township that played a defining part in the struggle against apartheid, the museum was designed as a community-based initiative to tell the stories of local residents forcibly removed from the city centre; stories that a more traditional museum may have marginalised (Msila 2013). However, despite the good intentions of those individuals and groups behind the museum project, it proved to be controversial and the museum was closed for a period of time as a result of community protests highlighting the disparity between their living conditions and the money spent building the museum (news24 2014).

Despite the closure of the museum, Rassool's (2006) discussion of the rationale for its creation illustrates not only the inseparability of time, place history and memory, but also and more specifically the role of memory in the recreation of people and place. Memory workshops were organised with ex-residents who brought in artefacts such as photographs, street signs, documents, memorabilia and household objects, which later became part of the museum. The museum used the material remnants of District Six to reconstruct the landscape of District Six, turning the museum into what Rassool refers to as 'an archaeology of memory' (2006: 13). The materiality of District Six served as memory maps detailing where people had been forcibly removed from and in doing so provided the evidence to support land restitution claims (Cassidy 2012). As such, the museum did not merely use memory objects to recreate District Six as a specific place, it also put memory to work by calling for the restitution of land rights for the dispossessed community. This is interesting because it demonstrates how time, place, history and memory work in the present to (re)build community out of conflict and in so doing contribute to the evolution of the relationships that construct one community's experience of earthly dwelling.

I argued earlier that museums gather together time, place, history and memory as reflections of human-world relationships. However, it is clearly not the museum itself that does this, but rather the individuals and groups that set out to collect, interpret and display aspects of earthly dwelling in the first place. A museum is merely the most suitable structural configuration for the organised classification, interpretation and display of human knowledge and experience at a given point in time. As Kirshenblatt-Gimblett notes museums are 'exhibits of those who make them' (1998: 2) and in this sense a museum is a repository of the significant relationships that shape human societies and cultures. However, the relationships displayed have been selected for a specific purpose and as such the motivations behind the process of selection cannot be ignored because notions of objectivity, credibility, and authority are invested in the very idea of a museum.

In this sense the museum is not a benign entity, given its roots in the politics of power, nationalism and social status whereby rich and powerful individuals, nations and groups asserted their economic and cultural dominance through the purchase, appropriation and ostentatious display of goods and artefacts (Hooper-Greenhill 1992; Rosman and Rubel 1998; Henare 2005). Moreover, Horne argues that during the nineteenth century one of the unintended functions of European museums and galleries 'was to put most people in their place' (1984: 16). This is an interesting perspective because putting someone in his or her place, and by extension other peoples, nations and groups, is an assertion of authority whereby certain beliefs and values, certain ways of thinking and being are privileged.

The association of museums with cultural and economic supremacy is not the only rationale behind the idea of a museum. The desire to collect as a means of documenting and maintaining what is deemed significant and distinctive about the human-world relationship is also a fundamental part of the role and purpose of a museum. What and how to collect is of course influenced by culture in its broadest sense and by specific domains such as politics, religion, technology and so forth (Elsner and Cardinal 1994; Macdonald 2011). Nevertheless, the desire to collect tells us something about the attitudes and values of the social world in which it takes places. In this sense the collection and display of culture, nature, ways of thinking and being reflects particular configurations of time, place, history and memory. Configurations that speak of the values invested in that which is deemed worth collecting. As Clifford (1988) argues the Western fascination with collecting the culture and art of other places and people is based upon the fact that such artefacts embody sought after expectations of wholeness, continuity and essence.

Collecting is, therefore, a means of confirming human existence in relation to the past and to the people and events that coalesce to produce multiple understandings of collective memory. Whether these memories are based on oral histories or on tangible objects or monuments of materiality, the role of the museum is to provide a place in which they can be encountered and experienced. As such, museums play a significant part in constructing and explaining human-world relationships and in so doing make visible the building blocks of self and group identity (Walsh 1992; Kaplan 1994, 2011); which helps to explain why they are so implicated in not just the politics of value but also the politics of identity, including what Stokes-Rees (2013) refers to as the politics of cultural citizenship.

Whilst museum exhibits reveal the cultural and economic power relations that structure the human-world relationship, they also reveal how time, place, history and memory are employed as stories reflective of a particular worldview. In this sense Bal (2004) argues that collecting is not a process but a narrative; this is interesting because it highlights what has already been referred to and that is the storytelling function of a museum. All stories draw on various combinations of time, place, history and memory to reinforce the underlying cosmology of the world in which they are located and as such they may change over time in response to the prevailing ideology. For example, Crane (2011b) illustrates that time, history and memory can be manipulated to both hide and reveal how the past should be interpreted in the present. After World War II, Japan's first museums of atomic power, the *Hiroshima Peace Museum* and the *Nagasaki Atomic Bomb Museum* obscured the country's recent past by focusing almost exclusively on honouring the dead and decrying the future use of atomic weapons. In so doing the Japanese were kept largely in ignorance of their wartime history, learning nothing until victims chose to speak out about atrocities:

> of wartime biological experiments in China, of sexual slavery as so-called "comfort women" from Korea in particular . . . No museums had included these memories or any other that challenged the official national narrative of victimhood and peace advocacy. Time had been allowed to follow its natural, destructive flow.
>
> (Crane 2011b: 106)

This quote illustrates how the same event can produce conflicting stories in response to different experiences of a particular time. Such stories draw on memories that reveal contested interpretations of past events and places, thereby producing alternative understandings of what was once considered to be accepted history. These alternative experiences and understandings of history draw attention to the consequences of how time and history are employed in the museum context (Crane 2011b). Reworked understandings and interpretations of time, place, history and memory resulting from reactions to these Japanese museums generate multiple collective memories of the past, memories which in turn shape how future generations experience their earthly dwelling in relation to past events.

Conclusion

This chapter has highlighted the significance of the human-earth relationship for understanding not just what makes us human but also *how* we are made human in relation to the earth as world. A relationship characterised here as earthly dwelling. This making is not, however, imposed on or passively received by individuals as people actively participate in, challenge and remake individual and collective experiences of being human. In this sense earthly dwelling is a dwelling that is always in flux, a constant negotiation of the relationship between people and world. This relationship is constructed through the interplay of the dwelling fourfold namely, time, place, history and memory. The significance and implications of the dwelling fourfold as inseparable elements is yet to be fully explored, particularly within tourism studies.

Although I have focused on Western understandings of earthly dwelling, there is enormous scope for exploring non-Western experiences of the fourfold. Such perspectives are important because, as argued earlier, understandings of the four elements are not only culturally determined but may also be manipulated to serve the needs of the state. In this sense, museums, and by association tourism, illustrate how being and dwelling is influenced by particular configurations of time, place, history and memory. Configurations that speak of the diverse ways in which human subjects come to make and remake who they are in the world. In this sense, museums are highly visible expressions of particular understandings, or perhaps more precisely particular moments, of earthly dwelling.

As with Heidegger, my dwelling fourfold is interlinked and interrelated, they belong together with each being a mirror reflection of the other. Locating and being a self in the world is shaped by everyday encounters with these four. In this respect my focus on the museum illustrates how these four operate to construct and explain the worlds of self and other. The connective ties between the four may be loose or tight, strong or weak, clear or opaque but they are always there. Indeed, at any given time an element of the dwelling fourfold may be more or less significant in encouraging someone to engage in tourism or to take part in certain activities such as visiting a museum or destination. Hence, history maybe the *raison d'être* of heritage tourism but the people and events associated with a particular attraction cannot be separated from the timeframes, places or memories associated with the attraction. In this sense my focus on museums illustrates how the dwelling fourfold works to construct and communicate the worldview of the society within which it is located. A worldview that shapes the relationship between self and world, producing particular understandings of how the world is and should be.

In many ways museums bring order to our earthly dwelling by taking charge of the human and nonhuman relationships that are part and parcel of being human-in-the- world, and in terms of post conflict museums they seek to bring order out of chaos and death by exercising control over the documents, monuments and materiality of conflict. The ordering function of a museum aligns with Franklin's (2004, 2007) description of tourism as a form of sociological ordering whereby the architects of tourism, such as Thomas Cook, created the processes by which tourism was 'made to happen'. Once brought into being tourism went on to order and thereby to organise people as tourists, places as destinations or sites to be visited; objects as souvenirs, transportation networks as mobility enablers and so on. However, tourism as ordering privileges process over experience, and although process is important its association with structure, with the mechanics of the tourism-world relationship ignores the essential messiness of that relationship. Tourism as ordering is devoid of the flesh and blood nuances and contradictions, the ebb and flow of life as it is lived. It is an illustration of what Comaroff and Comaroff (1992: 6) described in Chapter 1 as 'our own rationalizing cosmology posing as science, our culture posing as historical causality'.

Drawing from his research with the Iatmul people of Papua New Guinea, Moutu (2007) argues that collections and hence collecting are not always the result of knowledge-based classificatory practices but rather a way of being grounded in and through the social relationships that govern everyday life – contrary to Elsner and Cardinal's perspective, Moutu maintains that classification is not always 'an epistemological midwife at the call of order, management and control' (2007: 98). Iatmul collect on the basis of analogy rather than classification; on the basis of clan, tribe, family, group, nations or different identities. Here collecting is not the result of a classificatory way of thinking but an enactment of social relations that generate and structure the everyday lifeworld of the Iatmul.

As such, the sense of order that emerges as a result of collecting, cataloguing, describing and displaying the contents of a museum is a mirage. This is because all exhibits are inevitably divorced from their context and from the people, places and messiness of the social life in which they originally existed. The contents have effectively been removed from the times, places, histories and memories that made them, that imprinted them with cultural value, that marked them as worth keeping and hence worthy of display. Whilst this removal could be criticised for representing a loss in the sense of continuity between the past and the present that museum collections frequently strive to communicate, this is not always the case. An exhibition at the *Victoria and Albert Museum* in London (2016–17) entitled *Undressed: A brief history of underwear* demonstrates that concerns about body image and body consciousness are not confined to the present-day. Indeed, conventions influencing the underwear people choose to hide or reveal can be read as morality tales of each generation's attitudes towards understandings of intimacy, sexuality and gender.

Moreover, Moutu (2007) argues that loss has an integral part to play in collection practices because it heightens the temporal threads linking people to memories of places and events. He illustrates his argument through a discussion of the loss of life associated with the objects included in the exhibition at the National Museum of Papua New Guinea commemorating the tsunami that hit the region in 1998, concluding that collecting is an artificial act of 'piecing together temporal moments, and in doing so it contrives a sense of continuity that is predicated on a sense of loss. Loss, therefore, has a productive role in the temporal constitution of collections' (Moutu 2007: 109). Through such exhibitions that which is deemed important is defined in relation to loss, which highlights the role of loss in defining the human-earth relationship. By unpicking the threads of earthly dwelling exemplified by the fourfold of time, place, history and memory, it is possible to uncover not only what people, events and things are valued but also how value is determined and what consequences may ensue as a result.

Furthermore, within many museums the form of ordering that occurs is one where the dwelling fourfold has been tamed and reassembled to present a particular understanding of *world*. This is not meant to deny the significance of museums or to ignore the fact that visiting a museum is a hugely enjoyable activity, even if challenging at times. But rather to emphasise that the worldmaking function of a museum is partial and incomplete because it is based on what is known and knowable at any point in time. The knowledge that is created by the collection and display of time, place, history and memory as museum exhibit raises many questions. Not least of which is what this knowledge may reveal about the triumphs and tragedies, the conflicts and contradictions of being human in relation to world, of being part of the wider human-world relationship of earthly dwelling.

6 Being, dwelling and thinking

Introduction

When I set out on this journey, my intention was to construct a way of thinking about tourism that went beyond particularities such as visuality, identity, mobility, performance and so on by weaving together arguments drawn from anthropology and philosophy. In doing so I distanced myself from any attempt at abstract philosophising, arguing that although this may well contribute towards a theoretical understanding of tourism, it will not help to explain how tourism *works* as a felt experience of the self-world relationship. Whether this experience is that of a tourist or of tourist workers or that of the places and communities visited by tourists. Uncovering how and why tourism *works* sheds light on aspects of the human condition. Given this focus, my aim has been to avoid the kind of conceptual abstraction that acts as a barrier to understanding lived experience by using philosophy to illustrate how everyday life inspires thinking, feeling and doing. Specifically, in this instance thinking about what dwelling through tourism might mean as well as feel like, thereby uncovering how being human shapes and is shaped by doing tourism. With this argument philosophy does not make action, action makes philosophy, as Jackson states:

> the separation of the vita contemplative from the vita activa is not only false; it is utopian, which is to say it can be achieved nowhere. It is an illusion, akin to the alienation that follows the separation of product from process, text from context, capital from labor.
>
> (2009: 236)

The inseparable link between living and thinking aligns with Ingold's (1992) understanding of anthropology as philosophy with the people firmly embedded within it. Taking Ingold's definition as a guiding ethos, each chapter has demonstrated how philosophical concepts can help to explain how tourism works to make and remake the experience of being human. Or more precisely experience in the plural as there is no singular experience but a myriad of experiences from the individual to the collective. However, whether singular or plural, experience is ultimately an expression of what it is to dwell as a human being. Where dwelling is that which precedes and emerges from a practical everyday engagement with our surroundings.

By focusing on specific tourist activities such as walking and sightseeing, visiting heritage attractions, experiencing airport architecture and visits to museums, philosophy is put to work. Whilst these activities are not the only examples of the relationship between being, dwelling and tourism, they are significant because, as argued in Chapter 1, they illustrate the core foundations of this relationship namely: the body, things, the built environment and the four interrelated elements of earthly dwelling – time, place, history and memory. As a result, this chapter needs to be read as a pause in the argument rather than as a point of closure. Nevertheless, a pause still requires a pulling together of the threads that have been unravelled so far.

In this respect being human-in-the-world through tourism entails travelling to the familiar and unfamiliar places and worlds gathered together by the local-global forces of contemporary capitalism. These forces are hugely significant and tourism does not sit outside issues such as inequality and discrimination that beset many work-leisure environments. As I have noted elsewhere, the gathering of land and resources to make golf courses has a detrimental effect on the lives and livelihoods of communities (Palmer 2004). However, politics and economics alone cannot explain how and why tourism *works* as an expression of the being and dwelling of human existence. They certainly have a significant influence, but they cannot be separated from the ideas, imagination and culturally derived assumptions of individual tourists that ascribe significance to tourism and so explain why it *works*. Going outside of ourselves to visit other ways of being human provides opportunities to think about what we know, and the means by which we know. This does not mean all tourists will think about or question their understanding of so-called received wisdom, as Sir Walter Raleigh once wrote 'it is not truth, but opinion, that can travel the world without a passport' (cited in Lowenthal 1961: 260), but the possibility for doing so is there nonetheless. Herein lies the significance of tourism. It is, as argued in Chapter 2, an embodied experience because thinking cannot be separated from doing and tourism entails both thinking and doing. This brings me to the relationship between being, dwelling and thinking.

The title of this chapter deliberately mirrors Heidegger's essay that inspired the approach set forth in this book, because thinking is central to dwelling and to being human and tourism provides an opportunity for individuals to think about their place in the world. Engaging in or doing tourism presupposes a period of thinking about tourism beforehand. This thinking through of what needs to be done to make tourism happen entails consideration of how to get there and of the time to be set aside in being away for a day or a few weeks. In thinking about being away we think about the people, places and activities we are likely to encounter and make decisions based on what constitutes an enjoyable trip in terms of aspects such as acceptable clothing, the type of accommodation or the sort of food and drink provided. In effect thinking about what is a comfortable balance between the familiar and the unfamiliar, a balance that is of course subjective.

Moutu (2007) illustrates the importance of thinking through in his discussion of the activity of collecting, in this instance collecting not just objects but also stories. Specifically, he argues that the sequence of events whereby a graduate student returns to college to collect her bicycle keys or the Iatmul women of Papua New Guinea prepare to empty rain water from their canoes before setting out to collect the fish caught in their nets necessitates a thinking through of what needs to be done to fulfil such tasks. This thinking through, he argues, requires a purposeful engagement with the world illustrative of a Heideggerian sense of being-in-the-world, 'the ordinary aspects of human existence – such as collecting keys, or food from a shop or lagoon – provide an immediate entry into thinking about how one's sense of being-in-the-world unfolds through daily existential chores and concerns' (Moutu 2007: 103).

Although tourism is a leisure activity rather than a daily chore and except for those individuals who work in tourism, it is not a routine part of daily life. Nevertheless, it is something that many people encounter within the everyday even if they do not give it their full attention. For example, the plethora of advertising on television and on advertising boards, in newspapers and magazines, on the internet and through social media; the use if not lure of tourism as a prize in competitions or as part of a work-related bonus package means that tourism is here and now in some form or another. Even momentary encounters with one or more of the above can stimulate memories of where I have been, the experiences I have had and also ideas about the trips I might like to take, the places I would like to see. Such 'encounters', no matter how fleeting they may be, are ways of engaging *in* and with the world. In this sense tourism serves a similar function to the student's bicycle keys and the Iatmul canoe; it is a way into imagining how one's sense of being human-in-the-world unfolds through encounters with what for many people is a taken-for-granted activity. As Moutu goes onto state:

> The keys and canoes reveal our entanglement with a world of equipment, and it is these kinds of contexts – such as a missing key or a wet canoe – that the nature of one's being-in-the-world becomes expressed as a concerned orientation with equipment.
>
> (2007: 103)

Whilst tourism may not strike many people as a piece of equipment akin to keys and canoes, it is a kind of equipment, or more precisely an instrument for engaging with and bringing the world *ready-to-hand* – to borrow a phrase from Heidegger. In this sense, tourism has more in common with what in Greek philosophy is referred to as *techne* – a technique or equipment of everyday life. Desjarlais provides a useful example of what I mean here drawn from his photographs of Nepalese children at play:

> In Gulphubanyang boys and girls played with small, tubular wheels which, while running alongside them, they rounded along level ground with an ingenious steering device. In photographing their efforts it struck me that, through their skilled play, the children were learning how to apply *techne* in the world.
>
> (2015: 217, original emphasis)

Tourism as *techne* provides knowledge and skills for thinking about and engaging with the world, a know-how of travelling and of being a tourist that, like the keys and the canoe, reveal our entanglement with the world. In this sense tourism as *techne* helps to construct what Ingold (2008) has referred to as a zone of entanglement, an admixture or intermingling of person and world. As Ingold argues, '[l]ife is lived in a zone in which earthly substances and aerial media are brought together in the constitution of beings which, in their activity, participate in weaving the textures of the land' (2008: 1796).

This point aligns with my argument in Chapter 5 that the activity of tourism is an important ingredient in the constitution of human experience; in doing tourism individuals help to create the texture and feel of their earthly dwelling that defines the human condition. Interestingly, tourism provides numerous zones of entanglement in which encounters between people, places and things provide opportunities to experience life and living in different ways. These experiences may not always be pleasant, for either the tourist or the visited community, but they do provide the knowledge and skills required to be a tourist and to understand, and hopefully to manage the effects of tourism. In this sense being and dwelling through tourism focuses attention on the relationship between people wherever it may occur and on the ways in which the nonhuman shapes and is shaped by this relationship.

Being and dwelling

As the previous chapters demonstrate, the intermingling of being, dwelling and tourism occurs in the everydayness of life, in visits to museums or in bodily reactions to particular activities or through the architectural structuring of the tourist experience. However, it would be a mistake to read being or dwelling as implying fixed states, as points of arrival rather than as points of departure. Indeed, as argued in Chapter 1, criticisms of the dwelling perspective – including those of Ingold himself – are based on the association of dwelling with a particular type of place, a place that is cosy and warm and where the individual can feel at home in the world. However, to my mind dwelling is not a static living in one place but involves moving about, coming and going, getting lost, being found; being warm or cold, brave or afraid. Dwelling through tourism can be disorderly as well orderly and is in fact frequently unsettling. Transport via buses, trains, airplanes and so on is often disrupted, or subject to cancellation. Crime is not something that only happens at home, and holidays can be disrupted by politics, conflict and terrorism.

In 2015 tourists were evacuated from Egypt following a suspected terrorist attack that brought down a Russian airplane returning from the Red Sea resort of Sharm el-Sheikh and British holidaymakers to the Gambia had to be evacuated in 2017 when a state of emergency was announced in the aftermath of a presidential election. All too many people suffer the consequences of insecurity and conflict on a daily basis, and tourists and tourism do not exist outside of the forces that feed and create instability in the world, despite the escapist message underpinning most travel advertising. The dwelling experience that comes through tourism can be joyful or not, it can be violently disruptive or a welcome interlude in the madness of life. Whether good or bad, all travel experiences are part of the admixture resulting from the intermingling of person and world referred to above by Ingold, and all such experiences illustrate some of the ways in which dwelling through tourism influences the experience of being human whether positive or negative.

As an expression of human experience, tourism enables us to build the multiple ways in which we come to know who we are and to express who we are through the choices we make in life. Despite the fact that choice is not something all individuals enjoy, going on holiday, packing a suitcase, climbing the steps to the Parthenon, buying a postcard, taking a photograph, sharing 'my holiday' experiences on social media are all ways of dwelling through tourism. Hence, tourism as an expression of the human condition illustrates the multiple ways in which the experience of being human is constructed as life is lived. In this sense dwelling is the journey taken through life – not the final destination, and it is the journey that shapes individual and collective experiences of being human, '[t]he path, not the place, is the primary condition of being, or rather of becoming' (Ingold 2008: 1808).

Chapter 1 argued that the privileging of becoming over being is reflective of the argument that discussions of being human should be replaced by discussions of becoming human because life is composed of paths of experience, what Ingold (2011a, 2015) refers to as multiple trails or lines of becoming. However, to my mind being and becoming are not an either or way of understanding how tourism works to influence who I am or who we are, because being a tourist and becoming a tourist are two sides of the same coin. Hence, I do not ascribe to the view that being a tourist implies a finished state, whereas becoming a tourist is an altogether more appealing journey of discovery (see Obrador-Pons 2003; Scarles 2012) since the being of a tourist is just as fluid, risky and open to possibilities. As Jackson argues, being is unstable and precarious, it has its ups and downs, it can be understood as a being on the move or being creative; however, it is never an either/or but is 'in continual flux, waxing and waning according to a person's situation' (2005: x). Through tourism I may choose to become someone else for a while by pretending, or by acting out an alternative self to strangers. However, when I return home I return to being me, even if that me has been altered by the experience of tourism. In becoming a tourist, we reveal ways of being who we are or who we might like to be and in this sense becoming is an integral part of being.

In the coming together of being and becoming through tourism, the individual is an active participant in making a meaningful world and, as Chapter 2 argued, this participation is predicated on an embodied engagement with the world. The body of the tourist brings forth the world through embodied perception. Here the individual is not a passive receiver of representations whether symbolic or experiential but actively creates her/his own understanding of the world through engagement with what the world has to offer. This engagement occurs through the intimacy of being that results from the relationship between mind, body and the senses such that walking and sightseeing body forth ways of being a tourist, based on the enactment of practices that define and identify the doing of tourism.

Engagement with what the world has to offer also occurs through material dwelling, the gathering of objects and things in tourist attractions such as Hever Castle. As Chapter 3 demonstrates, the gathering of materiality at the castle produces a particular understanding of Englishness drawn from the historic events of the Tudor period, events reconstructed as heritage tourism. More specifically, dwelling through heritage is a dwelling through constructed time, and heritage time demonstrates the human need to make connections between the self and the wider temporalities of other people, places and events. In effect to establish, maintain and perpetuate the lineage of human existence.

The principles, techniques and practices of architecture that bring structure and order to the world, referred to in Chapter 4 as architectural dwelling, are a further example of the engagement between self and world. Here, airport architecture creates the spaces, structures and experiences that confront individuals with thoughts of their own mortality. Finally, Chapter 5 argued that engagement in the world is a holistic experience based on the coming together of time, place, history and memory, what I referred to as the dwelling fourfold. My focus on museums illustrates how the dwelling fourfold works to construct and communicate the worldview of the society within which it is located. A worldview based upon particular understandings of how the world is or how it should be.

Thinking as experience

The examples discussed in the previous chapters demonstrate the importance of thinking for understanding how being and dwelling are shaped through engagement with tourism. How and what someone thinks about tourism not only defines their relationship with the world around them, it also highlights the significance of the choices a person makes in life in terms of when and how to travel, where to visit and the activities engaged in that collectively create individual understandings of what an enjoyable holiday should look and feel like. Thinking within tourism can take many forms from the quiet contemplative reverie of a particular moment or experience to the thinking out loud of the various options before a decision can be made. Thinking in relation to tourism is reflective of a preoccupation with desire and curiosity. The desire to see and a curiosity about not just other people and other ways of living, but also about myself, my life, and my past weaves through the complex and hard to pin down reasons why people travel.

The desire, if not the unwritten law of tourism, concerns the need to collect evidence of having been there, of having seen and experienced something as if that in some way validates who I am, that I am someone in the world; ultimately that I exist. Through visits to heritage attractions and museums, through walking and sightseeing, through the purchase of souvenirs, the taking of photographs and indeed through travel itself lies a desire to have and to possess experiences. I own the experience and here is the souvenir to prove it. I may not be able to own the Eiffel Tower, but I can possess it in miniature and use it as a mnemonic device for sharing my experiences with others. A sharing that now occurs virtually as well as physically (see Molz 2004, 2012).

Indeed, travel blogs and posts on Facebook pages are also souvenirs or more precisely souvenir-stories. However, unlike tangible souvenirs such as key rings and fridge magnets, they can be shared with a much wider audience and in the sharing they may be expanded upon, altered or embellished in response to the posts of family and friends. Souvenirs not only evidence experience, they also construct who I am or how I would like to be seen by others, based upon the choices made about what to buy; choices that become tangible reflections of aspects such as class, status, values and beliefs; aspects that are rooted in being a tourist and engaging with tourism. The choices we make are also the ways in which we build individual understandings of what it is to be human, and the activity of tourism provides multiple opportunities to build different versions of me through particular travel experiences.

In a sense this is the fundamental cosmology of tourism, it is a cosmology of the self, understood as the freedom to use tourism to make and remake the self through engagement with the lifeworld of others. Through engagement with the activities, things, people and places that are part of what being a tourist is all about. No matter how imperfect, fleeting and partial this engagement might be, it enables an individual to form an understanding of how she/he does or does not *fit* with or in the world. Being and dwelling through tourism is a way of negotiating the foundations of this cosmology of the self, and this is why a dwelling perspective resonates with me. It resonates because it does not privilege one concept or paradigm for understanding tourism over another, it does not argue that tourism is all about mobility or performance or gazing and so on.

Indeed, we are frequently reminded that mobility is ubiquitous, that it is a vital and fundamental concept for explaining how the world is and how it came to be out of the past, such that '[w]ithout mobility we could not live' (Adey 2010b: 1). Certainly, tourism and travel would not be possible without movement, whether as transport or as bodies walking, climbing, sitting and standing. Likewise, mobility underpins, influences and makes possible what are for many people the taken for granted activities of daily life. For example, money is moved physically and electronically across the globe in and out of bank accounts and share portfolios. Food is driven, flown and shipped from one continent to the next. Even our thoughts, ideas and opinions 'move' huge distances via communication technologies that are themselves constantly on the move through innovation into ever more sophisticated and updated versions. However, to state that we live in, are made by or are dependent upon mobility has always seemed to me to be a self-evident truth, what Ingold (2011a) refers to as the primacy of movement. However, movement and mobility are not the same.

People have always been mobile, either through choice, obligation or sheer necessity. Mobility is evident in tilling the soil to grow crops, going on a pilgrimage, setting out to wage war on neighbouring tribes. Over the centuries, and sadly still today, mobility has re-shaped the geography of whole populations as conflict, starvation and disease force communities to migrate in order to survive. So for me, the significance of a 'mobility turn' (Cresswell 2006) or a 'new mobilities paradigm' (Sheller and Urry 2006) is that it opens up to critical scrutiny the many ways in which mobility (including immobility) and the imperative to be mobile has shaped and continues to shape the world around us. My issue is that a mobilities paradigm in tourism scholarship privileges moving over feeling and thinking, which does not mean that the body is not a central part of a mobile world, as Elliott and Urry argue, '[t]he body especially senses as it *moves*' (2010: 16, original emphasis). It senses through hands on the steering wheel or feet on the pavement, and as it moves so the body works to reshape cities, towns and the countryside. However, the body not only moves and senses, it also *thinks* and how and what it thinks is ultimately what reshapes cities, towns and the countryside; shapes relationships between people and place.

Furthermore, as previously argued, moving is one of the ways (albeit an important one) in which the conditions of human dwelling are revealed, yet a tendency to privilege movement and mobility runs the risk of drowning out other, just as important aspects. Aspects such as emotion, beauty, love, fear and so on are also important elements in shaping how humans dwell through tourism. Perhaps my concern is essentially one of epistemology. As

Franquesa rather succinctly puts it in relation to her ethnographic research into tourism in Majorca, 'the reification of mobility rests on an understanding of social reality where things, ideas, and people flow across a seemingly neutral space, ultimately reinforcing the "old positivism" that the mobility turn pretends to overcome' (2011: 1012–13).

The reification of mobility also ignores the collective significance of time, place, history and memory as constitutive elements of our individual and collective being human-in-the-world. Of course, questions of mobility can be asked of these referents individually and collectively, but my point is that it is the *relationship* between them that is important. A relationship that Chapter 4 argued is inseparable because it influences how individuals locate themselves in the world and how they think about, understand and experience the world. All of which involve thinking. Thinking about myself in relation to the people, places, things and events that influence my involvement in the world around me.

This argument is again nicely illustrated by one of the participants in Franquesa's research, referred to above. The need to re-orientate Majorca's model of mass tourism in order to reverse the decline in tourist numbers resulted in the gentrification of Palma's historic landscape. The only residents allowed to live in the historic city centre were those able to promote the unique historic character needed to attract tourists. One such resident was the baker, Miguel. The gentrification policy not only attracted tourists but also non-Spanish 'gentrifiers' able to afford a second home in the historic centre, gentrifiers such as Ingrid – a Swedish national mobilised by her ability to pay. Franquesa's analysis of an encounter between Miguel and Ingrid demonstrates that his inability to move out of the old centre was not caused by her mobility but by his relationship to her. A relationship forced upon him by the tourism sector's need to promote the centre to tourists as being uniquely 'old' in some way. Leading Franquesa to argue that '[i]t is not mobility that opposes the world of fixed forms of positivism criticized by the mobility turn, it is relationality, a dialectical way of understanding things in the world as nexuses of multiple determinations' (2011: 1029).

To reiterate, then, dwelling as a holistic way of understanding what being human means resonates with me because it highlights the relational foundations that make and remake self and other, self and world. These relationships, how and what we *think* about them is the key to understanding the human experience. Thinking through the relationship between being and dwelling *and* tourism focuses attention on what Ingold refers to as the tangle of relationships in and through which life is continually made and remade, and as he argues, '[t]his tangle is the texture of the world' (2011: 71). Tourism is part of the tangle that provides texture to the world and being and dwelling highlights the tangle of relationships that bring individuals into the world *through* tourism. In effect, tourism is one of the threads from which the fabric of human dwelling is built, and what is built is a way of thinking about what being human means in relation to all that tourism has to offer. Thinking through, about and in relation to tourism illustrates the argument made by Jackson (2009) that thinking is the key to understanding what it is to be human. In this sense, tourism is an example of how thought is anchored in, rather than abstracted from, human experience, because tourism encourages thinking about the self and how the self is understood in relation to other people, places and events.

In this sense, dwelling as a way of being in, thinking about and relating to the world occurs through engaging in and with things, with other people, with ourselves and with the myriad of experiences made possible by the activity of tourism. First and foremost dwelling through tourism encourages a sensuous engagement with the world based on how we use our body through, for example, walking and sightseeing, the two most identifiable activities in terms of what tourists do. Both these activities not only identify someone as a tourist, they are also ways of relating to the world, in effect walking and sightseeing are ways of creating and sustaining relationships with people and with places. Of course, walking and seeing – whether sightseeing, gazing or looking – also happen in daily life not just on holiday. Individuals walk to work or to the shops, they walk to the church or to the mosque and walking occurs on protest marches. People gaze into shop windows or out of the window of a bus; they sit in coffee shops and watch the passers-by. However, this does not mean that our engagement with and involvement in the world is the same. The walking and sightseeing of tourism encourage a particular orientation to the world that identifies the individual as a tourist and as someone who is on holiday. Walking like a tourist is not the same as walking like a mother taking the children to school. Sightseeing is not the same kind of seeing that occurs as we watch our children in the park.

This is an important distinction because it demonstrates how the roles and activities that define us to ourselves and to others are made visible through the ways in which our bodies are used; a use, which is of course, socially and culturally conditioned. As illustrated by Young's (1980) research, referred to in Chapter 2, highlighting how culture and in particular patriarchal culture teaches girls to move in different ways to boys, to throw, sit and walk like a girl. The culture of tourism teaches individuals to walk, see and move like a tourist and in so doing they make themselves visible and identifiable as tourists; tourists who stand out from the crowd of people who live *here*. In being identified as a tourist through how we use our bodies the relationship we have with the world, including the relationship with ourselves, is that of a stranger. I do not mean a stranger in the usual sense of someone in unfamiliar cultural or geographic surroundings, although travel (both domestic and overseas) does takes people to places with which they are unfamiliar. Furthermore, the tourist as stranger is not a new or uncontested idea (Machlis and Burch 1983; Knight 1995). Nevertheless, the label tourist does make strangers of people in the sense of feeling out of place, and thereby not quite sure of themselves because a stranger can feel like a fish out of water. Someone who has to find a way to re-orientate her/himself, who has to think in a different way. As Schutz (1944) noted, for the stranger, thinking as usual is not an option.

Being a stranger in this sense is more about being unsure of *myself*. Of not quite knowing how I fit in or even if I want to fit in. It is in such moments of displacement, what Andrews (2009) refers to as disruption, that questions of identity come to the fore. Yet as previously argued, I am using identity in the wider sense of what identifies me, you, and us as human beings rather than in terms of the various identities that may be attached to us by ourselves and others; identifiers such as nationality, occupation, gender, religion and so on. Dwelling through tourism brings about a disruption in habitual patterns of thinking and being; it is a temporary or permanent displacement of the self, and as such, being human-in-the world is not always a comfortable place to be.

This displacement occurs in a similar way to Heidegger's (2001) bridge, which not only supports life by enabling people to get from one place to the next, it transforms the land around it into a location by gathering the earth as landscape around the stream below. Tourism also supports life in terms of creating and defining what a good life should look and feel like. It does this through processes of ordering or worldmaking (Franklin 2004; Hollinshead 2007), whereby tour operators, marketing agencies and transport networks enable tourism to happen. Tourism happens by transforming the 'land', by gathering places, people and historic events into destinations and attractions.

However, tourism ordering and worldmaking, or tourism as performance or as a way of seeing are pieces in a kaleidoscope of shapes, patterns and colours that cohere as reference points for a particular moment in time. They are certainly important pieces, but they are pieces nonetheless. By focusing on the body, on the materiality of things and buildings and on the relationship between time, place, history and memory, I am highlighting the fixings that enable these pieces to come together in the here and now. These fixings are however soft rather than hard, temporary rather than permanent, fluid rather than rigid. This is because all social and cultural fixings are inherently unstable; they come unstuck, they move and reform over time in response to the ongoing interplay of the human and the nonhuman environment. In a sense these fixings work in a similar way to Ingold's lines and knots:

> every line overtakes the knot in which it is tied. Its end is always loose, somewhere beyond the knot, where it is groping towards an entanglement with other lines, in other knots. What is life, indeed, but a proliferation of loose ends!
>
> (2013: 132)

Intermission

My purpose in writing this book is to bring these fixings to the forefront of how we think about and think through tourism, but in saying this I am fully aware that the arguments I make here are incomplete. They are in effect loose ends. This is necessarily so as the thinking upon which they are based is ongoing, and this is because thinking is never finished. It weaves about, stops and starts and gets stuck down numerous blind alleys in its unravelling of the relationship between being, dwelling and tourism. Nevertheless, thinking is important because it opens us up to other ways of understanding what tourism does and why it matters. As this book demonstrates, a philosophical approach is one that highlights the role and importance of thinking as a way to unravel the experience of being human. Being for me is and always will be about being human; it is not an existential search for some form of authentic self, which in any case does not exist. Hence, my interest in how we, individually and collectively, create a meaningful life through the activities, practices, and things we engage with as life is lived, activities such as tourism.

In saying this, I am fully conscious of the fact that going on holiday is not an activity open to all, and that not all tourism-related work leads to what might be described as job satisfaction. Nevertheless, looking beneath the surface of our individual and collective engagement in and with the world through tourism is no different to thinking through other aspects of life such as shopping, the desire to collect, hunting for food or living in a village. Indeed, Ingold (2011b) argues that thinking is inseparable from doing, which it is, but doing can encompass many things and I would include the imagination here since this is also an activity.

Although the imagination is important, the constitution of beings through tourism is more effectively understood in relation to anticipation. I do not mean anticipation in terms of a tourist's expectations of what will be provided or anticipation in relation to the imagination of desire. Both of which are, of course, significant for understanding motivations to travel and for managing discrepancies between expectation and actual experience (see Skinner and Theodossopoulos 2011). In referring to anticipation I am highlighting the meeting ground between freedom (tourism) and restraint (obligations of daily life). People work out life and living as they go and part of doing so entails coping mechanisms for dealing with what comes their way. Individuals manage or cope with the restraints imposed by societal rules and obligations through a constant and delicate negotiation of the balance between what I am able to do with what I would like to do. Every society has ways of balancing freedom and constrain and for many societies tourism is a tool or mechanism for doing so. Being and dwelling through tourism illustrates one of the ways in which this balance is achieved however imperfect the result may be in reality.

At this point it is important to acknowledge that my thinking is necessarily influenced by the social particularities of my worldview, and as Winter

(2009) argues, tourism research needs a wider lens, a lens that goes beyond European and North American understandings and experiences. In this vein, future research centred on being and dwelling through tourism should look far and wide to acknowledge other cultures and other ways of seeing, thinking and doing. Research should focus on Africa and the Middle East, on Asia, China and Russia, on cold climates as well as hot climates, on virtual worlds and gaming worlds, on cities and rural communities, on those displaced by tourism or those for whom tourism is a means of escape from the grind of the everyday. It should focus on different forms of tourism such as slow tourism, volunteering and cruise tourism, and on natural phenomena such as the weather and the sea.

A dwelling approach seeks a deeper engagement with current thinking that goes beyond the search for more case study examples of say media-induced tourism or tourism impacts. Going deeper means exploring what lies beneath the superficial rush to label events from the past as dark tourism or to package a range of experiences as wellness tourism. I am never quite sure what wellness *means* other than the obvious connection to health, and I find myself wanting to ask, to whom does it speak, why and particularly why now?

In addition to material dwelling and earthly dwelling, I could add community dwelling as a way of exploring what community means, how it is defined, by whom and for what purpose. A focus on being and dwelling as community might also unpack the whole notion of community participation in tourism development by exploring the ideological basis of such approaches (see the chapters in Singh 2012 for a critique of the community participation agenda). Indeed, being and dwelling through tourism is as much political as it is cultural, and whilst this book has not focused on significant aspects such as globalisation and economics, or on issues such as power, authority and surveillance or on inequality or labour practices, all of these could and should be part of a being and dwelling approach to tourism. An approach inspired by the coming together of anthropology and philosophy, because both these disciplines open up our minds to the type of questions that need to be asked and how we might respond to them as we focus on life as it is lived, experienced, felt, imagined, resisted, remembered and forgotten.

Heidegger's role here has been to set my thinking in motion. I accept that I have drawn from him selectively and that in doing so my use of his concepts and his thinking are necessarily divorced from their original context, but Heidegger is and has been useful to me. This does not mean that the tangled threads of our individual and collective being and dwelling always have to be unravelled in relation to Heidegger; as I noted in Chapter 1, Heidegger should not be allowed to straightjacket thinking, he offers a starting point for thinking and a means by which to open up thinking. However, dwelling as a way of understanding how tourism influences what being human might look and feel like requires a more experiential approach than that provided by Heidegger's rather obscure philosophical language. What matters is how concepts help to illuminate lived experience by focusing on the practices and activities that are part and parcel of this experience. I accept that what I have set in motion here is more a way of thinking about lived experience than empirically derived descriptions or narratives of lived experience, Chapter 3 excepted. Future explorations of being and dwelling through tourism should seek to address this gap.

Nevertheless, dwelling as a way of being human has opened up a rich seam of possibilities when applied to tourism because, as I have argued, tourism is one of the ways in which the experience of being human is continually made and remade. As such, dwelling as a way of being human-in-the-world is a particularly useful way of thinking through tourism because it enables tourism to be located within the totality of life and of living. Criticisms of Heidegger's concept of dwelling as romantic and nostalgic are certainly well made and Ingold has criticised his own dwelling perspective for conjuring up images of a cosy, warm and comfortable existence. Yet for me dwelling is an overarching concept, not a place in which to stay put and as such I would like to liberate dwelling from its 'aura of snug, well-wrapped localism' (Ingold 2011a: 12). Dwelling can reveal a harsh and unyielding experience of being human-in-the-world in much the same way as a home can be both a place of refuge and a place to be feared.

As noted previously, this chapter represents a pause in my thinking rather than a neat and final point of closure. For Ingold (2011a), his anthropological mission is to restore life to anthropology; my more humble endeavour is to argue that we should pay more attention to how the activity of tourism can shed light on the experience of being human. Ultimately, tourism is a way of being alive and more attention needs to be given to how tourism shapes and reshapes the condition of life and living.

Bibliography

Ablett, P. G. and Dyer, P. K. (2009) Heritage and Hermeneutics: Towards a Broader Interpretation of Interpretation. *Current Issues in Tourism*, 12 (3): 209–233.

Abramson, A. and Holbraad, M. (2014) Introduction: The Cosmological Frame in Anthropology, in *Framing Cosmologies: The Anthropology of Worlds*, edited by A. Abramson and M. Holbraad. Manchester: Manchester University Press, pp. 1–28.

Adams, K. (1984) Come to Tana Toraja, "Land of the Heavenly Kings": Travel Agents as Brokers of Ethnicity. *Annals of Tourism Research*, 11 (3): 469–485.

Adey, P. (2008) Architectural Geographies of the Airport Balcony: Mobility, Sensations and the Theatre of Flight. *Geografiska Annaler: Series B, Human Geography*, 90 (1): 29–47.

Adey, P. (2010a) *Aerial Life: Spaces, Mobilities, Affects*. Chichester: Wiley-Blackwell.

———. (2010b) *Mobility*. London: Routledge.

Al-Mohammad, H. (2011) Less Methodology More Epistemology Please: The Body, Metaphysics and 'Certainty'. *Critique of Anthropology*, 31 (2): 121–138.

Ames, M. (1992) *Cannibal Tours and Glass Boxes: The Anthropology of Museum*, 2nd ed. Vancouver: University of British Columbia Press.

Amsinck, P. (1810) *Tunbridge Wells and Neighbourhood*. London: William Miller.

Anderson, B. (1991) *Imagined Communities*, 2nd ed. London: Verso.

Anderson, T. (2011) Complicating Heidegger and the Truth of Architecture, in *The Aesthetics of Architecture: Philosophical Investigations into the Art of Building*, edited by D. Goldblatt and R. Paden. Chichester: Wiley-Blackwell, pp. 69–79.

Andreu, P. (1999) Borders and Borderers, trans. G. Walker, in *Architecture of the Borderlands*, edited by T. Cruz and A. Boddington. Chichester: Academy Editions, Wiley-Blackwell, pp. 56–61.

Andrews, H. (2005) Feeling at Home: Embodying Britishness in a Spanish Charter Tourism Resort. *Tourist Studies*, 5 (3): 247–266.

———. (2009) Tourism as a 'Moment of Being'. *Suomen Antropologi: Journal of the Finnish Anthropological Society*, 34 (2): 5–21.

———. (2011) *The British on Holiday: Charter Tourism, Identity and Consumption*. Bristol: Channel View publications.

Appadurai, A. (ed) (1986) *The Social Life of Things: Commodities in Cultural Perspective*. Cambridge: Cambridge University Press.

Arbid, M. (2015) Toward a Neuroscience of the Design Process, in *Mind in Architecture: Neuroscience, Embodiment, and the Future of Design*, edited by S. Robinson and J. Pallasmaa. Cambridge, MA: The MIT Press, pp. 75–98.

Arendt, H. (1958) *The Human Condition*. New York: Doubleday Anchor Books.
Asad, T. (ed) (1973) *Anthropology and the Colonial Encounter*. London: Ithaca Press.
Aslet, C. (1997) *Anyone for England? A Search for British Identity*. London: Little & Brown.
Augé, M. (2008) *Non-Places: An Introduction to Supermodernity*, 2nd ed. London: Verson.
Aziz, H. (2001) The Journey: An Overview of Tourism and Travel in the Arab/Islamic Context, in *Tourism and the Less Developed World: Issues and Case Studies*, edited by D. Harrison. Wallingford: Channel View, pp. 151–159.
Bachelard, G. (1994 [1958]) *The Poetics of Space*, trans. M. Jolas. Boston, MA: Beacon Press.
Bærenholdt, J., Haldrup, M., Larsen, J. and Urry, J. (2004) *Performing Tourist Places*. Farnham: Ashgate.
Bal, M. (2004) Telling Objects: A Narrative Perspective on Collecting, in *Grasping the World: The Idea of the Museum*, edited by D. Preziosi and C. Farago. Aldershot: Ashgate, pp. 84–102.
Barth, F. (1969) Introduction, in *Ethnic Groups and Boundaries: The Social Organization of Culture Difference*, edited by F. Barth. London: Allen and Unwin, pp. 9–38.
Barthes, R. (1979) *The Eiffel Tower and Other Mythologies*. New York: Hill and Wang.
Basso, K. (1996) Wisdom Sits in Places: Notes on a Western Apache Landscape, in *Senses of Place*, edited by S. Feld and K. Basso. Santa Fe: School of American Research Press, pp. 53–90.
Basu, P. (2007) *Highland Homecoming: Genealogy and Heritage Tourism in the Scottish Diaspora*. Abingdon, Oxon: Routledge.
Bauby, J-D. (1998) *The Diving-Bell and the Butterfly*, trans. J. Leggatt. London: Fourth Estate.
Bawaka Country, Wright, S., Suchet-Pearson, S., Lloyd, K., Burarrwanga, L., Ganambarr, R., Ganambarr-Stubbs, M., Ganambarr, B., Maymuru, D. and Sweeney, J. (2016) Co-Becoming Bawaka: Towards a Relational Understanding of Place/Space. *Progress in Human Geography*, 40 (4): 455–475.
Behr, R. (2010) An Englishman's Home Is His Castle, If He Can Get One. *The Guardian* [online], 3rd January. Available at: www.theguardian.com/commentisfree/2010/jan/03/property-prices-house-building [accessed 30th June 2014].
Bell, D. (2003) Mythscapes: Memory, Mythology, and National Identity. *British Journal of Sociology*, 54 (1): 63–81.
Ben-David, R. (2013) Hunting the Wild 'Other' to Become a Man: Wildlife Tourism and the Modern Identity Crisis in Israel Safaris to East Africa, in *Living Beings: Perspectives on Interspecies Engagements*, edited by P. Dransart. London: Bloomsbury, pp. 125–144.
Ben-Ze'ev, E. (2004) The Politics of Taste and Smell: Palestinian Rites of Return, in *The Politics of Food*, edited by M. E. Lien and B. Nerlich. Oxford: Berg, pp. 141–160.
Bender, B. (2002) Time and Landscape. *Current Anthropology*, 43 (Supplement): S103–S112.
Benjamin, W. (1973) *Charles Baudelaire: A Lyric Poet in the Era of High Capitalism*, trans. H. Zohn. London: New Left Books.

———. (1999) *The Arcades Project*, trans. H. Eiland and K. McLaughlin. Cambridge, MA: Belknap/Harvard University Press.

Bennett, J. (2001) *The Enchantment of Modern life: Attachments, Crossings, and Ethics*. Princeton: Princeton University Press.

Bianchi, R. (2014) Towards a New Political Economy of Global Tourism Revisited, in *Tourism and Development: Concepts and Issues*, 2nd ed, edited by R. Sharpley and D. Telfer. Bristol: Channel View Publications, pp. 287–331.

Bird, G. (2011) *Tourism, Remembrance and the Landscape of War*. Unpublished PhD Thesis, University of Brighton.

Birth, K. (2012) *Objects of Time: How Things Shape Temporality*. New York: Palgrave MacMillan.

Bishop, P. (2013) Surveying 'The Waiting Room'. *Architectural Theory Review*, 18 (2): 135–149.

Blencowe, R. W. (1858) Cowden and Its Neighbourhood. *Archaeologica Cantiana*, 1: 111–123.

Bloch, M. (1991) Language, Anthropology and Cognitive Science. *Man (N.S.)*, 26 (2): 183–198.

———. (1995) The Resurrection of the House Amongst the Zafimaniry, in *About the House: Levi-Strauss and Beyond*, edited by J. Carsten and S. Hugh-Jones. Cambridge: Cambridge University Press, pp. 69–83.

———. (2005) *Essays on Cultural Transmission*. Oxford: Berg.

Bloomer, K. C. and Moore, C. W. (1977) *Body, Memory, and Architecture*. London: Yale University Press.

Boissevain, J. (1977) Tourism and Development in Malta. *Development and Change*, 8: 523–538.

Boivin, N., Brumm, A., Lewis, H., Robinson, D. and Korisettar, R. (2007) Sensual, Material, and Technological Understanding: Exploring Prehistoric Soundscapes in South India. *Journal of the Royal Anthropological Institute (N.S.)*, 13 (2): 267–294.

Botton, A. de. (2002) *The Art of Travel*. London: Hamish Hamilton.

———. (2007) *The Architecture of Happiness*. London: Penguin.

———. (2009) *A Week at the Airport: A Heathrow Diary*. London: Profile Books.

Bourdieu, P. (1977) *Outline of a Theory of Practice*. Cambridge: Cambridge University Press.

———. (1979) *Algeria 1960: The Disenchantment of the World*. Cambridge: Cambridge University Press.

———. (1990) *The Logic of Practice*. Cambridge: Polity Press.

———. (1991) *The Political Ontology of Martin Heidegger*, New ed. Stanford: Stanford University Press.

Brace, C. (2003) Rural Mappings, in *Country Visions*, edited by P. Cloke. Harlow: Pearson, Prentice Hall, pp. 47–72.

Britton, S. G. (1982) The Political Economy of Tourism in the Third World. *Annals of Tourism Research*, 9 (3): 331–358.

Bruner, E. (1991) Transformation of Self in Tourism. *Annals of Tourism Research*, 18 (2): 238–250.

Buchli, V. (2013) *An Anthropology of Architecture*. London: Bloomsbury.

Burdea, G. C. and Coiffet, P. (2003) *Virtual Reality Technology*, 2nd ed. Hoboken, NJ: Wiley.

Buttimer, A. (1976) Grasping the Dynamism of Lifeworld. *Annals of the Association of American Geographers*, 66 (2): 277–292.

Byng-Hall, J. (1990) The Power of Family Myths, in *The Myths We Live By*, edited by R. Samuel and P. Thompson. London: Routledge, pp. 216–224.

Caffyn, A. (2012) Advocating and Implementing Slow Tourism. *Tourism Recreation Research*, 37 (1): 77–80.

Calder, A. (1991) *The Myth of the Blitz*. London: Pimlico.

Campo, A.R.R. and Turbay, S. (2015) The Silence of the Kogi in Front of Tourists. *Annals of Tourism Research*, 52: 44–59.

Cannon, W. (1963) *The Wisdom of the Body*, revised and enlarged ed. New York: Norton.

Carsten, J. and Hugh-Jones, S. (eds) (1995) *About the House: Levi-Strauss and Beyond*. Cambridge: Cambridge University Press.

Casey, E. (2009) *Getting Back into Place: Toward a Renewed Understanding of the Place-World*, 2nd ed. Bloomington, IN: Indiana University Press.

Cassidy, L. (2012) Salford 7/District Six: The Use of Participatory Mapping and Material Artefacts, in *Cultural Memory Projects, in Mapping Cultures: Place, Practice, Performance*, edited by L. Roberts. New York: Palgrave Macmillan, pp. 181–198.

Casson, L. (1994) *Travel in the Ancient World*. Maryland: The John Hopkins University Press.

Certeau, M. de. (1988) *The Practice of Everyday Life*, trans. S. Rendell. Berkley: University of California Press.

Chaplin, S. and Holding, E. (1998) Consuming Architecture, in *Consuming Architecture*, edited by S. Chaplin and E. Holding. London: Architectural Design, pp. 7–9.

Childs, P. (2017) Places and Peoples: Nation and Region, in *British Cultural Identities*, 5th ed, edited by M. Storry and P. Childs. Abingdon, Oxon: Routledge, pp. 37–76.

Chronis, A. (2006) Heritage of the Senses: Collective Remembering as an Embodied Praxis. *Tourist Studies*, 6 (3): 267–296.

Church, A. and Coles, T. (eds) (2007) *Tourism, Power and Space*. Abingdon, Oxon: Routledge.

Clarke, T. (2002) *Martin Heidegger*. London: Routledge.

Classen, C. (1993) *Worlds of Sense: Exploring the Senses in History and Across Cultures*. London: Routledge.

Clifford, J. (1997) *Routes: Travel and Translation in the Late Twentieth Century*. Cambridge, MA: Harvard University Press.

———. (1988) *The Predicament of Culture: Twentieth-Century Ethnography, Literature, and Art*. Cambridge, MA: Harvard University Press.

Cloke, P. and Jones, O. (2001) Dwelling, Place, and Landscape: An Orchard in Somerset. *Environment and Planning A*, 33: 649–666.

Cohen, A. (ed) (1982) Belonging: The Experience of Culture, in *Belonging. Identity and Social Organisation in British Rural Cultures*, edited by A. P. Cohen. Manchester: Manchester University Press, pp. 1–17.

Cohen, E. (2012) Authenticity in Tourism Studies, in *Critical Debates in Tourism*, edited by V. Singh. Bristol: Channel View Publications, pp. 250–260.

Comaroff, J. and Comaroff, J. (1992) *Ethnography and the Historical Imagination*. Boulder, CO: Westview Press.

Cone, C. (1995) Crafting Selves: The Lives of Two Mayan Women. *Annals of Tourism Research*, 22 (2): 314–327.
Connerton, P. (1989) *How Societies Remember*. Cambridge: Cambridge University Press.
Connor, W. (1993) Beyond Reason: The Nature of the Ethnonational Bond. *Ethnic and Racial Studies*, 16 (3): 373–389.
Copertino, D. (2014) The Tools of the Trade: The Materiality of Architecture in the Patrimonialization of 'Arab Houses' in Damascus. *Journal of Material Culture*, 19 (3): 327–351.
Corbin, A. (1986) *The Foul and the Fragrant: Odor and the French Social Imagination*, trans. M. Kochan, R. Porter and C. Pendergast. Leamington Spa: Berg.
Cosgrove, D. (1997) Inhabiting Modern Landscape. *Archaeological Dialogues*, 4 (1): 23–28.
Costas, J. and Grey, C. (2016) *Secrecy at Work: The Hidden Architecture of Organizational Life*. Stanford: Stanford University Press.
Crane, S. (ed) (2000) *Museums and Memory*. Stanford: Stanford University Press.
———. (2011a) Memory, Distortion, and History in the Museum, in *Museum Studies: An Anthology of Contexts*, edited by B. Carbonell, 2nd ed. Oxford: Wiley-Blackwell, pp. 303–316.
———. (2011b) The Conundrum of Ephemerality: Time, Memory, and Museums, in *A Companion to Museum Studies*, edited by S. Macdonald. Chichester: Wiley-Blackwell, pp. 98–109.
Cresswell, T. (2006) *On the Move: Mobility in the Modern Western World*. Abingdon, Oxon: Routledge.
Crick, M. (1994) *Resplendent Sites, Discordant Voices: Sri Lankans and International Tourism*. Chur, Switzerland: Harwood.
Crossley, N. (2001) *The Social Body: Habit, Identity and Desire*. London: Sage.
Crouch, D. (2000) Places Around Us: Embodied Lay Geographies in Leisure and Tourism. *Leisure Studies*, 19 (2): 63–76.
———. (2010) *Flirting With Space: Journeys and Creativity*. Farnham: Ashgate.
Crouch, D. and Desforges, L. (2003) The Sensuous in the Tourist Encounter. Introduction: The Power of the Body in Tourist Studies. *Tourist Studies*, 3 (1): 5–22.
Csordas, T. J. (1990) Embodiment as a Paradigm for Anthropology. *Ethos*, 18 (1): 5–47.
———. (ed) (1994) *Embodiment and Experience: The Existential Ground of Culture and Self*. Cambridge: Cambridge University Press.
———. (1999) Embodiment and Cultural Phenomenology, in *Perspectives on Embodiment: The Intersections of Nature and Culture*, edited by G. Weiss and H. Haber. New York: Routledge, pp. 143–162.
Culler, J. (1981) Semiotics of Tourism. *American Journal of Semiotics*, 1: 127–140.
Cwerner, S., Kesselring, S. and Urry, J. (eds) (2009) *Aeromobilities*. London: Routledge.
Damasio, A. (2010) *Self Comes to Mind: Constructing the Conscious Brain*. New York: Pantheon Books.
Dann, G. (1996) *The Language of Tourism*. Wallingford: CABI.
Dann, E. and Dann, G. (2011) *Sightseeing for the Sightless and Soundless: Tourism Experiences of the Dual Sensory Impaired*: International Centre for Research and Study on Tourism. Available at: www.ciret-tourism.com/.

Davies, N. (1999) *The Isles: A History*. London: Palgrave MacMillan.
Day, C. (2002) *Spirit & Place: Healing Our Environment: Healing Environment.* Oxford: Architectural.
———. (2004) *Places of the Soul: Architecture and Environmental Design as a Healing Art*, 2nd ed. Oxford: Elsevier.
Dempsey, L. (2000) Scientific, Industrial, and Cultural Heritage: A Shared Approach. *Ariadne*, 22. Available at: www.ariadne.ac.uk/issue22/dempsey [accessed 3rd June 2016].
Desjarlais, R. (2015) Seared With Reality: Phenomenology Through Photography in Nepal, in *Phenomenology in Anthropology: A Sense of Perspective*, edited by K. Ram and C. Huston. Bloomington, IN: Indiana University Press, pp. 197–223.
Devereux, C. and Carnegie, E. (2006) Pilgrimage: Journeying Beyond Self. *Tourism Recreation Research*, 31 (1): 47–56.
Dewey, J. (1958) *Experience and Nature*. New York: Dover Publications.
Dickinson, J. and Lumsdon, L. (2010) *Slow Travel and Tourism*. London: Earthscan.
Din, K. (1989) Islam and Tourism: Patterns, Issues, and Options. *Annals of Tourism Research*, 16 (4): 542–563.
Dodds, G. and Tavernor, R. (eds) (2002) *Body and Building: Essays on the Changing Relations of Body and Architecture*. Cambridge, MA: MIT Press.
Douglas, M. (1995) Forgotten Knowledge, in *Shifting Contexts: Transformations in Anthropological Knowledge*, edited by M. Strathern. London: Routledge, pp. 13–29.
———. (1996) *Natural Symbols*, 2nd ed. London: Routledge.
Dreyfus, D. L. (1991) *Being-in-the-World: A Commentary on Heidegger's Being and Time, Division I*. Cambridge, MA: MIT Press.
Dreyfus, H. L. and Spinosa, C. (1997) *Highway Bridges and Feasts: Heidegger and Borgmann on How to Affirm Technology*. After Postmodernism Conference, Chicago: University of Chicago Press, 14–16th November 1997. Available at: www.focusing.org/apm_papers/ dreyfus.html [accessed 14th November 2011].
Dudley, S., Barnes, A., Binnie J., Petrov, J. and Walklate, J. (eds) (2012) *Narrating Objects, Collecting Stories*. Abingdon, Oxon: Routledge.
Dudzinski, D. (2001) The Diving Bell Meets the Butterfly: On Identity Lost and Re-Membered. *Theoretical Medicine and Bioethics*, 22 (1): 33–46.
Duffy, K., Hancock, P. and Tyler, M. (2017) Still Red Hot? Postfeminism and Gender Subjectivity in the Airline Industry. *Gender, Work and Organization*, 24 (3): 260–273.
Easthope, A. (1992) *What a Man's Gotta Do. The Masculine Myth in Popular Culture*. New York: Routledge.
Eberhard, J. P. (2015) Architecture and Neuroscience: A Double Helix, in *Mind in Architecture: Neuroscience, Embodiment, and the Future of Design*, edited by S. Robinson and J. Pallasmaa. Cambridge, MA: The MIT Press, pp. 123–136.
Edensor, T. (1998) *Tourists at the Taj: Performance and Meaning at a Symbolic Site*. London: Routledge.
———. (2002) *National Identity, Popular Culture and Everyday Life*. Oxford: Berg.
———. (2008) Walking Through Ruins, in *Ways of Walking*, edited by T. Ingold and J. L. Vergunst Farnham: Ashgate, pp. 123–141.
———. (2010) Walking in Rhythms: Place, Regulation, Style, and the Flow of Experience. *Visual Studies*, 25 (1): 69–79.

Edwards, P. (1989) Heidegger's Quest for Being. *Philosophy*, 64 (250): 437–470.

Edwards, S. (1998) The body as object *versus* the body as subject: the case of disability. *Medicine. Health Care, and Philosophy*, 1: 47–56.

Elastic City. (2017) Available at: www.elastic-city.org/thumbs-up [accessed 16th June 2017].

Eliade, M. (1959) *The Sacred and the Profane: The Nature of Religion*, trans. W. R. Trask. New York: Harcourt, Brace & World Inc.

Elliott, A. and Urry, J. (2010) *Mobile Lives*. Abingdon, Oxon: Routledge.

Elsner, J. and Cardinal, R. (1994) *The Cultures of Collecting*. London: Reaktion.

Elton, G. R. (1974) *England under the Tudors*, 2nd ed. London: Methuen.

The Enchanted Forest. (2017) Available at: www.enchantedforest.org.uk/about-us/about [accessed 16th June 2017].

Eriksen, T. H. (2004) *What is Anthropology?* London: Pluto Press.

Erzen, J. (2011) Reading Mosques: Meaning and Architecture in Islam, in *The Aesthetics of Architecture: Philosophical Investigations into the Art of Building*, edited by D. Goldblatt and R. Paden. Chichester: Wiley-Blackwell, The American Society for Aesthetics, pp. 125–131.

The Etches Collection. (2017) Tourist Brochure.

Fabian, J. (2014 [1983]) *Time and the Other: How Anthropology Makes its Object*, forward by M. Bunzl. New York: Columbia University Press.

Fees, C. (1996) Tourism and the Politics of Authenticity in a North Cotswold Town, in *The Tourist Image: Myths and Myth Making in Tourism*, edited by T. Selwyn. Chichester: Wiley-Blackwell, pp. 121–146.

Fentress, J. (1992) *Social Memory*. Oxford: Blackwell.

Ferguson, J. M. (2014) Terminally Haunted: Aviation Ghosts, Hybrid Buddhist Practices, and Disaster Aversion Strategies Amongst Airport Workers in Myanmar and Thailand. *The Asia Pacific Journal of Anthropology*, 15 (1): 47–64.

Finley, C. (2004) Authenticating Dungeons, Whitewashing Castles: The Former Sites of the Slave Trade on the Ghanaian Coast, in *Architecture and Tourism: Perception, Place and Performance*, edited by D. M. Lasansky and B. McLaren. Oxford: Berg, pp. 109–126.

Foucault, M. (1977) *Discipline and Punish: The Birth of the Prison*. London: Penguin.

Franklin, A. (2004) Tourism as Ordering: Towards a New Ontology of Tourism. *Tourist Studies*, 4 (3): 277–301.

———. (2007) The Problem With Tourism Theory, in *The Critical Turn in Tourism Studies: Innovative Research Methodologies*, edited by I. Ateljevic, A. Pritchard and N. Morgan. Oxford: Elsevier, pp. 131–148.

Franquesa, J. (2011) "We've Lost Our Bearings": Place, Tourism, and the Limits of the "Mobility Turn". *Antipode*, 43 (4): 1012–1033.

Fullagar, S., Wilson, E. and Markwell, K. (2012) Starting Slow: Thinking Through Slow Mobilities and Experiences, in *Slow Tourism: Experiences and Mobilities*, edited by S. Fullagar, K. Markwell and E. Wilson. Bristol: Channel View Publications, pp. 1–8.

Fuller, G. and Harley, R. (2004) *Aviopolis: A Book About Airports*. London: Black Dog Publishing.

Geertz, C. (1973) *The Interpretation of Cultures*. New York: basic Books.

Gell, A. (1992a) The Technology of Enchantment and the Enchantment of Technology, in *Anthropology, Art and Aesthetics*, edited by J. Coote and A. Sheldon. Oxford: Oxford University Press, pp. 40–63.

———. (1992b) *The Anthropology of Time: Cultural Constructions of Temporal Maps and Images*. Oxford: Berg.
Geurts, K. L. (2002) *Culture and the Senses: Bodily Ways of Knowing in an African Community*. Berkeley: University of California Press.
Gieryn, T. (2002) What Buildings Do. *Theory and Society*, 31: 35–74.
Goffman, E. (1969) *The Presentation of Self in Everyday Life*. London: Penguin.
Goldblatt, D. and Paden, R. (eds) (2011) *The Aesthetics of Architecture: Philosophical Investigations into the Art of Building*. Chichester: Wiley-Blackwell.
Gómez-Martín, M. B. (2005) Weather, Climate and Tourism: A Geographical Perspective. *Annals of Tourism Research*, 32 (3): 571–591.
Gordon, A. (2008) *Naked Airport: A Cultural History of the World's Most Revolutionary Structure*. Chicago: University of Chicago Press.
Gottdiener, M. (2001) *Life in the Air: Surviving the New Culture of Air Travel*. Lanham: Rowman & Littlefield.
Graburn, N.H.H. (ed) (1976) *Ethnic and Tourist Arts: Cultural Expressions From the Fourth World*. Berkeley: University of California Press.
———. (1983) The Anthropology of Tourism. *Annals of Tourism Research*, 10: 9–33.
Grange, J. (2000) Place, Body, Situation, in *Dwelling, Place and Environment: Towards a Phenomenology of Person and World*, edited by D. Seamon and R. Mugerauer. Malabar, FL: Krierger Publishing, pp. 71–84.
Gray, J. (1999) Open Spaces and Dewing Places: Being at Home on Hill Farms in the Scottish Border. *American Ethnologist*, 26 (2): 440–460.
Gros, F. (2014) *A Philosophy of Walking*, trans. J. Howe. London: Verso.
Guichard-Anguis, S. and Moon, O. (eds) (2009) *Japanese Tourism and Travel Culture*. London: Routledge, Taylor and Francis.
Hagen, J. (2010) Architecture, Symbolism, and Function: The Nazi Party's 'Forum of the Movement'. *Environment and Planning D: Society and Space*, 28: 397–424.
Haigh, C. (1987) The Recent Historiography of the English Reformation, in *The English Reformation Revised*, edited by C. Haig. Cambridge: Cambridge University Press, pp. 19–33.
———. (1993) *English Reformations: Religion, Politics and Society Under the Tudors*. Oxford: Oxford University Press.
Halbwachs, M. (1992) *On Collective Memory*, ed. and trans. L. Coser. Chicago: University of Chicago Press.
Haldrup, M. and Larsen, J. (2006) Material Cultures of Tourism. *Leisure Studies*, 25 (3): 275–289.
———. (2010) *Tourism, Performance and the Everyday, Consuming the Orient*. Abingdon, Oxon: Routledge.
Hall, S. (1996) Introduction, Who Needs 'Identity?' in *Questions of Cultural Identity*, edited by S. Hall and P. du Guy. London: Sage, pp. 1–17.
Halliburton, D. (1981) *Poetic Thinking: An Approach to Heidegger*. Chicago: University of Chicago Press.
Harkin, M. (1995) Modernist Anthropology and Tourism of the Authentic. *Annals of Tourism Research*, 22 (3): 650–670.
Harley, R. (2011) Airportals: The Functional Significance of Stillness in the Junkspace of Airports, in *Stillness in a Mobile World*, edited by D. Bissell and G. Fuller. Abingdon, Oxon: Routledge, pp. 38–50.

Harries, K. (1993) Thoughts on a Non-Arbitrary Architecture, in *Dwelling, Seeing, and Designing*, edited by D. Seamon. Albany: State University of New York Press, pp. 41–59.

———. (1997) *The Ethical Function of Architecture*. Cambridge, MA: Massachusetts Institute of Technology.

———. (2011) Fantastic Architecture: Lessons of Laputa and the Unbearable lightness of our Architecture, in *The Aesthetics of Architecture: Philosophical Investigations into the Art of Building*, edited by D. Goldblatt and R. Paden. Chichester: Wiley-Blackwell, pp. 51–160.

Harris, C. and O'Hanlon, M. (2013) The Future of the Ethnographic Museum. *Anthropology Today*, 29 (1): 8–12.

Harrison, J. (2003) *Being a Tourist: Finding Meaning in Pleasure Travel*. Vancouver: UBC Press.

Harrison, P. (2007) The Space Between Us: Opening Remarks on the Concept of Dwelling. *Environment and Planning D*, 25 (4): 625–647.

Harrison, R., Byrne, S. and Clarke, A. (eds) (2013) *Reassembling the Collection: Ethnographic Museums and Indigenous Agency*. Santa Fe, New Mexico: SAR Press.

Haseler, S. (1996) *The English Tribe: Identity, Nation and Europe*. London: Palgrave MacMillan.

Headrick, D. R. (1981) *The Tools of Empire: Technology and European Imperialism in the Nineteenth Century*. Oxford: Oxford University Press.

Heidegger, M. (1962) *Being and Time*, trans. J. Macquarrie and E. Robinson. Oxford: Blackwell.

———. (1982) *On the Way to Language*. New York: Harper & Row.

———. (2001 [1971]) *Poetry, Language, Thought*, trans. A. Hofstadter. New York: Harper Perennial Modern Classic.

———. (2008) *Towards a Definition of Philosophy*, trans. T. Sadler. London: Continuum.

Henare, A., Holbraad, M. and Wastell, S. (2007) Introduction: Thinking Through Things, in *Thinking Through Things: Theorising Artefacts Ethnographically*, edited by A. Henare, M. Holbraad and S. Wastell. Abingdon, Oxon: Routledge, pp. 1–31.

Henare, M. (2005) *Museums, Anthropology and Imperial Exchange*. Cambridge: Cambridge University Press. Henderson, J. C. (2004) Tourism and British Colonial Heritage in Malaysia and Singapore, in *Tourism and Postcolonialism: Contested Discourses, Identities and Representations*, edited by C. M. Hall and H. Tucker. London: Routledge, pp. 113–125.

———. (2010) Islam and Tourism: Brunei, Indonesia, Malaysia and Singapore, in *Tourism in the Muslim World*, vol. 2, edited by N. Scott and J. Jafari. Bingley: Emerald Publishing, pp. 75–90.

Herzfeld, M. (1991) *A Place in History: Social and Monumental Time in a Cretan Town*. Princeton: Princeton University Press.

———. (2001) *Anthropology: Theoretical Practice in Culture and Society*. Oxford: Blackwell.

Hever Castle and Gardens. (1966) *Tourist Guide*. The Times Publishing Company.

———. (1972) *Tourist Guide*. Norwich: Jarrold & Sons.

———. (1995) *Tourist Guide*. Edenbridge.

———. (2008) *Tourist Guide*. Edenbridge: Hever Castle Ltd.

———. (2012) *Tourist Guide*: Hever Castle and Jigsaw Design and Publishing.
———. (2015) News Section. Available at: www.hevercastle.co.uk/news/hever-castle-unveils-two-new-tudor-treasures/ [accessed 16th May 2017].
Hill, J. (2012) *Weather Architecture*. London: Routledge.
Hirsch, E. and O'Hanlon, M. (eds) (1995) *The Anthropology of Landscape: Perspectives on Place and Space*. Oxford: Clarendon Press.
Hoelscher, S. (2011) Heritage, in *A Companion to Museum Studies*, edited by S. Macdonald. Chichester: Wiley-Blackwell, pp. 198–218.
Hollinshead, K. (2007) 'Worldmaking' and the Transformation of Place and Culture: The Enlargement of Meethan's Analysis of Tourism and Global Change, in *The Critical Turn in Tourism Studies: Innovative Research Methodologies*, edited by I. Ateljevic, A. Pritchard and N. Morgan. Oxford: Elsevier, pp. 165–193.
Hollinshead, K., Ateljevic, I. and Ali, N. (2009) Worldmaking Agency – Worldmaking Authority: The Sovereign Constitutive Role of Tourism. *Tourism Geographies*, 11 (4): 427–443.
Hooper-Greenhill, E. (1992) *Museums and the Shaping of Knowledge*. London: Routledge.
Hornborg, A-C. (2006) Visiting the Six Worlds: Shamanistic Journeys in Canadian Mi'Kmaq Cosmology. *Journal of American Folklore*, 119 (473): 312–336.
Horne, D. (1984) *The Great Museum: The Re-Presentation of History*. London: Pluto Press.
Howard, P. J. (1994) The Nature of the Times Deceas'd. *International Journal of Heritage Studies*, 1 (1): 6–17.
Huberman, J. (2012) *Ambivalent Encounters: Childhood, Tourism, and Social Change in Banaras, India*. New Brunswick: Rutgers University Press.
Howes, D. (2005) Introduction: Empires of the Senses, in *Empire of the Senses*, edited by D. Howes. Oxford: Berg, 1–17.
Howes, D. and Classen, C. (2014) *Ways of Sensing: Understanding the Senses in Society*. Abingdon, Oxon: Routledge.
Husserl, E. (1970 [1936]) *The Crisis of European Sciences and Transcendental Phenomenology: An Introduction to Phenomenological Philosophy*, trans. D. Carr. Evanston, IL: Northwestern University Press.
Ingold, T. (1992) Editorial. *Man (N.S.)*, 27 (4): 693–696.
———. (1993) The Temporality of the Landscape. *World Archaeology*, 25 (2): 152–174.
———. (1995) Building, Dwelling, Living: How Animals and People Make Themselves at Home in the World, in *Shifting Contexts: Transformations in Anthropological Knowledge*, edited by M. Strathern. London: Routledge, pp. 57–80.
———. (2003) From the Perception of Archaeology to the Anthropology of Perception: An Interview With Tim Ingold. *Journal of Social Archaeology*, 3 (1): 5–22.
———. (2004) Culture on the Ground: The World Perceived Through the Feet. *Journal of Material Culture*, 9 (3): 315–340.
———. (2005) Epilogue: Towards a Politics of Dwelling. *Conservation & Society*, 3 (2): 501–508.
———. (2007) *Lines: A Brief History*. London: Routledge.
———. (2008) Bindings Against Boundaries: Entanglements of Life in an Open World. *Environment and Planning A*, 40: 1796–1810.
———. (2010) Ways of Mind-Walking: Reading, Writing, Painting. *Visual Studies*, 25 (1): 15–23.

———. (2011a) *Being Alive: Essays on Movement, Knowledge and Description.* Abingdon, Oxon: Sage.

———. (2011b [2000]) *The Perception of the Environment: Essays on Livelihood, Dwelling and Skill*, new preface ed. London: Routledge.

———. (2013) *Making: Anthropology, Archaeology, Art and Architecture.* Abingdon, Oxon: Routledge.

———. (2015) *Life of Lines.* London: Routledge.

Ingraham, C. (2008) *White Weddings: Romancing Heterosexuality in Popular Culture*, 2nd ed. London: Routledge.

Irving, A. (2005) Life Made Strange: An Essay on the Re-Inhabitation of Bodies and Landscapes, in *The Qualities of Time: Anthropological Approaches*, edited by W. James and D. Mills. Oxford: Berg, pp. 317–329.

———. (2013) Bridges: A New Sense of Scale. *The Senses and Society*, 8 (3): 290–313.

Ives, E. (2005) *The Life and Death of Anne Boleyn.* Oxford: Wiley-Blackwell.

Jackson, J. B. (1994) *A Sense of Place, a Sense of Time.* New Haven: Yale University Press.

Jackson, M. (1983) Knowledge of the Body. *Man (NS)*, 18 (2): 327–345.

———. (1989) *Paths Toward a Clearing: Radical Empiricism and Ethnographic Enquiry.* Bloomington, IN: Indiana University Press.

———. (1995) *At Home in the World.* Durham, NC: Duke University Press.

———. (2005) *Existential Anthropology, Events, Exigencies and Effects.* New York: Berghahn.

———. (2007) *Excursions.* Durham, NC: Duke University Press.

———. (2009) Where Thought Belongs: An Anthropological Critique of the Project of Philosophy. *Anthropological Theory*, 9 (3): 235–251.

Jamal, T. and Stronza, A. (2009) 'Dwelling' With Ecotourism in the Peruvian Amazon. *Tourist Studies*, 8 (3): 313–336.

James, W. and Mills, D. (eds) (2005) *The Qualities of Time: Anthropological Approaches.* Oxford: Berg.

Jameson, F. (1984) Postmodernism, or The Cultural Logic of Late Capitalism. *New Left Review*, 146 (July–August): 53–92.

Jones, N. (2001) *The English Reformation: Religion and Cultural Adaptation.* Oxford: Wiley-Blackwell.

Jones, O. and Cloke, P. (2002) *Tree Cultures.* Oxford: Berg.

Kadman, N. and Kabha, M. (2016) 'Home Tourism' Within a Conflict: Palestinian Visits to Houses and Villages Depopulated in 1948, in *Tourism and Memories of Home: Migrants, Displaced People, Exiles, and Diasporic Communities*, edited by S. Marschall. Bristol: Channel View Publications, pp. 88–112.

Kaplan, J. (2007) *When the Astors Owned New York.* London: Penguin.

Kaplan, F.E.S. (ed) (1994) *Museums and the Making of "Ourselves": The Role of Objects in National Identity.* London: Leicester University Press.

———. (2011) Making and Remaking National Identities, in *A Companion to Museum Studies*, edited by S. Macdonald. Chichester: Wiley-Blackwell, pp. 152–169.

Karp, I. and Kratz, C. (2014) Collecting, Exhibiting, and Interpreting: Museums as Midwives of Meaning. *Museum Anthropology*, 37 (1): 51–65.

Kavaler, L. (2000) *The Astors: A Family Chronicle of Pomp and Power.* London: iUniverse.

Keane, W. (1995) The Spoken House: Text, Act, and Object in Eastern Indonesia. *American Ethnologist*, 22 (1): 102–124.
Keesing, R. (1987) Anthropology as Interpretive Quest. *Current Anthropology*, 28 (2): 161–176.
Kensinger, K. (1995) *How Real People Ought to Live: The Cashinahua of Eastern Peru*. Prospect Heights, IL: Waveland Press.
Kershaw, S. W. (1880) *Famous Kentish Houses: Their History and Architecture*. Paper read to the Architectural Association of London. High Holborn: Batsford.
Kesselring, S. (2009) Global Transfer Points: The Making of Airports in the Mobile Risk Society, in *Aeromobilities*, edited by S. Cwerner, S. Kesselring and J. Urry. London: Routledge, pp. 39–59.
Kim, H. and Jamal, T. (2007) Touristic Quest for Existential Authenticity. *Annals of Tourism Research*, 34 (1): 181–201.
Kirshenblatt-Gimblett, B. (1998) *Destination Culture: Tourism, Museums and Heritage*. Berkley, Los Angeles: University of California Press.
Kissell, J. L. (2001) Embodiment: An Introduction. *Theoretical Medicine and Bioethics*, 22 (1): 1–4.
Knell, S. (ed) (2007) *Museums in the Material World*. Abingdon, Oxon: Routledge.
Knight, J. (1995) Tourist as Stranger? Explaining Tourism in Rural Japan. *Social Anthropology*, 3 (3): 219–234.
Kohn, E. (2013) *How Forests Think: Toward an Anthropology of Beyond Human*. Berkeley: University of California Press.
Kolas, A. (2008) *Tourism and Tibetan Culture in Transition: A Place Called Shangrila*. London: Routledge.
Kollewe, J. (2017) Inside the New Battersea Power Station. *The Guardian*, Saturday, 13th May. Available at: www.theguardian.com/business/2017/may/13/inside-the-new-battersea-power-station [accessed 26th June 2017].
Kraftl, P. and Adey, P. (2008) Architecture/Affect/Inhabitation: Geographies of Being-In Buildings. *Annals of the Association of American Geographers*, 98 (1): 213–231.
Kuper, H. (1972) The Language of Sites in the Politics of Space. *American Anthropologist*, 74 (3): 411–425.
Lagerkvist, A. (2007) Gazing at Pudong – "With a Drink in Your Hand": Time Travel, Mediation, and Multisensuous Immersion in the Future City of Shanghai. *Senses & Society*, 2 (2): 155–172.
Lakoff, G. and Johnson, M. (1980) *Metaphors We Live By*. Chicago: Chicago University Press.
———. (1999) *Philosophy in the Flesh: The Embodied Mind and Its Challenge to Western Thought*. New York: Basic Books.
Lambek, M. (1998) Body and Mind in Mind, Body and Mind in Body: Some Anthropological Interventions in a Long Conversation, in *Bodies and Persons: Comparative Perspectives From Africa and Melanesia*, edited by M. Lambek and A. Strathern. Cambridge: Cambridge University Press, pp. 103–124.
Lande, B. (2007) Breathing Like a Soldier: Culture Incarnate, in *Embodying Sociology: Retrospect, Progress and Prospects*, edited by C. Shilling. Oxford: Wiley-Blackwell, pp. 95–108.
Larsen, J. (2008) De-Exoticizing Tourist Travel: Everyday Life and Sociality on the Move. *Leisure Studies*, 27 (1): 21–34.
Larsen, J. and Urry, J. (2011) Gazing and Performing. *Environment and Planning D: Society and Space*, 29: 1110–1125.

Lau, R.W.J. (2010) Revisiting Authenticity. *Annals of Tourism Research*, 37 (2): 478–498.

Lazarin, M. (2008) Temporal Architecture: Poetic Dwelling in Japanese Buildings. *Architecture and Phenomenology*, (Autumn): 97–112.

Leach, N. (2000) Forget Heidegger. *Scroope: Cambridge Architecture Journal*, 12: 28–32.

Lefebvre, H. (1991) *The Production of Space*, trans. D. Nicolson-Smith. Oxford: Wiley-Blackwell.

Lennon, J. and Foley, M. (2000) *Dark Tourism: The Attraction of Death and Disaster*. London: Continuum.

Lennon, J. and Mitchell, M. (2007) Dark Tourism: The Role of Sites of Death in Tourism, in *Remember Me: Constructing Immortality: Beliefs on Immortality, Life and Death*, edited by M. Mitchell. London: Routledge, pp. 167–178.

Levell, N. (2000) *Oriental Visions: Exhibitions, Travel and Collecting in the Victorian Age*. London: Horniman Museum.

Levi-Strauss, C. (1972) *The Savage Mind*. London: Weidenfeld & Nicolson.

———. (1983) *The Way of the Masks*, trans. S. Modelski. London: Jonathan Cape.

———. (1986) *The Raw and the Cooked: Introduction to a Science of Mythology*, trans. J and D. Weightman. Harmondsworth: Penguin.

———. (1995) *Myth and Meaning. Cracking the Code of Culture*. New York: Schocken Books.

Light, D. (2000) Gazing on Communism: Heritage Tourism and Post-Communist Identities in Germany, Hungary and Romania. *Tourist Geographies*, 2 (2): 157–176.

Lloyd, J. (2002) Departing Sovereignty. *Borderlands e-Journal*, 1 (2): 1–11. Available at: http:/www.borderlands.net.au/vol1no2_2002/lloyd_departing.html [accessed 18th January 2015].

———. (2003) Dwelltime: Airport Technology, Travel, and Consumption. *Space & Culture*, 6 (2): 93–109.

Lloyd, G.E.R. (2011) Humanity Between Gods and Beasts? Ontologies in Question. *Journal of the Royal Anthropological Institute (NS)*, 17: 829–845.

Lobell, J. (1979) *Between Silence and Light: Spirit in the Architecture of Louis I. Kahn*. Boston, MA: Shambhala Publications.

Logan, W. (2012) *Air: The Restless Shaper of the World*. New York: W. W. Norton & Company.

London Transport Museum (2016) Available at: www.ltmuseum.co.uk/collections/museum-collection/collecting-policy [accessed 15th April 2016].

Lovegrove, K. (2000) *Airline: Identity, Design and Culture*. London: Laurence King Publishing.

Lowenthal, D. (1961) Geography, Experience, and Imagination: Towards a Geographical Epistemology. *Annals of the Association of American Geographers*, 51 (3): 241–260.

———. (1998) *The Heritage Crusade and the Spoils of History*. Cambridge: Cambridge University Press.

Lund, K. A. and Jóhannesson, G. T. (2016) Earthly Substances and Narrative Encounters: Poetics of Making a Tourism Destination. *Cultural Geographies*, 23 (4): 653–669.

Lury, C. (1997) The Objects of Travel, in *Touring Cultures: Transformations of Travel and Theory*, edited by C. Rojek and J. Urry. London: Routledge, pp. 75–95.

Lytton, U. (1989) Aspects of Dual Symbolic Classification: Right and Left in a Japanese Kyū-Dōjō. *Asian Folklore Studies*, 48: 277–291.
Macdonald, S. (ed) (1998) *The Politics of Display: Museums, Science and Culture*. London: Routledge.
———. (2006) Undesirable Heritage: Fascist Material Culture and Historical Consciousness in Nuremberg. *International Journal of Heritage Studies*, 12 (1): 9–28.
———. (2011) Collecting practices, in *A Companion to Museum Studies*, edited by S. Macdonald. Chichester: Wiley-Blackwell, pp. 81–97.
———. (2013) *Memorylands: Heritage and Identity in Europe Today*. Abingdon, Oxon: Routledge.
MacGregor, N. (2004) Oi, Hands Off Our Marbles! *The Sunday Times News Review*, 18th January, 7.
———. (2012) *A History of the World in 100 Objects*. London: Penguin.
Machlis, G. and Burch, W. (1983) Relations Between Strangers: Cycles of Structure and Meaning in Tourist Systems. *The Sociological Review*, 31 (4): 666–692.
Macleod, D. and Carrier, J. (eds) (2010) *Tourism, Power and Culture: Anthropological Insights*. Bristol: Channel View Publications.
Macnaghten, P. and Urry, J. (2000) Bodies in the Wood. *Body & Society*, 6 (3–4): 166–182.
MacPhee, G. (2002) *The Architecture of the Invisible: Technology and Urban Visual Culture*. London: Continuum.
Macpherson, H. (2009) Articulating Blind Touch: Thinking Through the Feet. *The Senses and Society*, 4 (2): 179–194.
Malkki, L. (1995) *Purity in Exile: Violence, Memory, and National Cosmology Among Hutu Refugees in Tanzania*. Chicago: University of Chicago Press.
Mallgrave, F. (2010) *The Architect's Brain: Neuroscience, Creativity and Architecture*. Chichester: Wiley-Blackwell.
Malpas, J. (2008) *Heidegger's Topology: Being, Place, World*. Cambridge, MA: Massachusetts Institute of Technology Press.
Markwell, K. (2015) Birds, Beats and Tourists: Human-Animal Relationships in Tourism, in *Animals and Tourism: Understanding Diverse Relationships*, edited by K. Markwell. Bristol: Channel View Publications, pp. 1–23.
Marsh, R. and Hudson, J. (2014) *Locked in: One Man's Miraculous Escape From the Terrifying Confines of Locked-in Syndrome*. London: Piatkus.
Martin, A. M. (2016) Introduction: The Sensory in Russian and Soviet History, in *Russian History Through the Senses: From 1700 to the Present*, edited by M. P. Romaniello and T. Starks. London: Bloomsbury, pp. 1–19.
Martin, E. (1992) The End of the Body? *American Ethnologist*, 19 (1): 121–129.
Massey, D. (2005) *For Space*. London: Sage.
Matless, D. (1998) *Landscape and Englishness*. London: Reaktion Books.
Matteucci, X. (2014) Forms of Body Usage in Tourists' Experiences of Flamenco. *Annals of Tourism Research*, 46: 29–43.
Mauss, M. (1979) *Sociology and Psychology: Essays by Marcel Mauss*. London: Routledge.
McLaren, B. (2006) *Architecture and Tourism in Italian Colonial Libya*. Seattle: University of Washington Press.
Medina, L. K. (2003) Commoditizing Culture: Tourism and Maya Identity. *Annals of Tourism Research*, 30 (2): 353–368.

Melhuish, C. (2005) Towards a Phenomenology of the Concrete Megastructure. *Journal of Material Culture*, 10 (1): 5–29.
Merchant, S. (2011) Negotiating Underwater Space: The Sensorium, the Body and the Practice of Scuba-Diving. *Tourist Studies*, 11 (3): 215–234.
Merleau-Ponty, M. (2002 [1945]) *Phenomenology of Perception*. London: Routledge.
Miller, D. (1998a) *A Theory of Shopping*. London: Sage.
———. (ed) (1998b) *Material Cultures: Why Some Things Matter*. London: Sage.
———. (2007) Stone Age or Plastic Age? *Archaeological Dialogues*, 14 (1): 23–27.
Molz, J. G. (2004) Playing Online and Between the Lines: Round-the-World Websites as Virtual Places to Play, in *Tourism Mobilities: Places to Play, Places in Play*, edited by M. Sheller and J. Urry. London: Routledge, pp. 169–180.
———. (2012) *Travel Connections: Tourism, Technology and Togetherness in a Mobile World*. Abingdon, Oxon: Routledge.
Morosan, C. and Fesenmaier, D. R. (2007) A Conceptual Framework of Persuasive Architecture of Tourism Websites: Propositions and Implications, in *Information and Communication Technologies in Tourism*. Proceedings of the International Conference in Ljubljana, Slovenia, edited by M. Sigala, L. Mich and J. Murphy. New York: Springer Ein, pp. 243–254. Available at: https://link.springer.com/book/10.1007/978-3-211-69566-1.
Morphy, H. (1995) Landscape and the Reproduction of the Ancestral Past, in *The Anthropology of Landscape: Perspectives on Place and Space*, edited by E. Hirsch and M. O'Hanlon. Oxford: Clarendon Press, pp. 184–209.
Morris, B. (1997) In Defence of Realism and Truth: Critical Reflections on the Anthropological Followers of Heidegger. *Critique of Anthropology*, 17 (3): 313–340.
Moutu, A. (2007) Collection as a Way of Being, in *Thinking Through Things: Theorising Artefacts Ethnographically*, edited by A. Henare, M. Holbraad and S. Wastell. Abingdon, Oxon: Routledge, pp. 93–112.
Msila, V. (2013) The Liberatory Function of a Museum: The Case of New Brighton's Red Location Museum. *Anthropologist*, 15 (2): 209–218.
Munn, N. (1992) A Cultural Anthropology of Time: A Critical Essay. *Annual Review of Anthropology*, 23: 91–123.
Mugerauer, R. (1993) Toward an Architectural Vocabulary: The Porch as Between, in *Dwelling, Seeing, and Designing: Toward a Phenomenological Ecology*, edited by D. Seamon. Albany: State University of New York Press, pp. 103–128.
Mukhopadhyay, B. (2006) Crossing the Howrah Bridge: Calcutta, Filth and Dwelling – Forms, Fragments, Phantasms. *Theory, Culture and Society*, 27 (7–8): 221–241.
Mullen, R. and Munson, J. (2009) *The Smell of the Continent*. London: Palgrave MacMillan.
Museum of Science, Boston (2015) Available at: www.mos.org/planetarium/explore-the-solar-system [accessed 22nd October 2015].
Myers, A. and Moshenska, G. (eds) (2011) *Archaeologies of Internment*. New York: Springer.
Nadel-Klein, J. (2003) *Fishing for Heritage: Modernity and Loss Along the Scottish Coast*. Oxford: Berg.
Nash, M. (2013) Brides N' Bumps: A Critical Look at Bridal Pregnancy Identities, Maternity Wedding Dresses, and Post-Feminism. *Feminist Media Studies*, 13 (4): 593–612.

Neuman, E. (2016) *Shoah Presence: Architectural Representations of the Holocaust*. Abingdon, Oxon: Routledge. Available at: news24: www.news24.com/SouthAfrica/News/PE-residents-force-anti-apartheid-museum-to-close-20140731 [accessed 8th April 2016].

Nielsen, N. K. (2003) New Year in . . . On Nationalism and Sensuous Holidays in Finland. *Tourist Studies*, 3 (1): 83–98.

Nora, P. (1989) Between Memory and History. *Les Lieux de Mémoire: Representations*, trans. M. Roudebush, 26: 7–24.

Norberg-Schulz, C. (1980) *Genius Loci: Towards a Phenomenology of Architecture*. London: Academy Editions.

Notar, B. (2007) *Displacing Desire: Travel and Popular Culture in China*. Honolulu: University of Hawaii Press.

Noy, C. (2004) This Trip Really Changed Me: Backpacker's Narratives of Self-Change. *Annals of Tourism Research*, 31 (1): 78–102.

Nunez, T. (1963) Tourism, Tradition and Acculturation: Weekendismo in a Mexican Village. *Ethnology*, 2 (3): 347–352.

Nyíri, P. (2006) *Scenic Spots: Chinese Tourism, the State, and Cultural Authority*. Seattle: University of Washington Press.

Obrador-Pons, P. (2003) Being-On-Holiday: Tourist Dwelling, Bodies and Place. *Tourist Studies*, 31 (1): 47–66.

———. (2007) A Haptic Geography of the Beach: Naked Bodies, Vision and Touch. *Social & Cultural Geography*, 8 (1): 123–141.

Okely, J. (1983) *Changing Cultures: The Traveller-Gypsies*. New York: Cambridge University Press.

Okhovat, H. (2010) A Study on Religious Tourism Industry Management Case Study: Islamic Republic of Iran. *International Journal of Academic Research*, 2 (5): 302–307. Available at: www.ijar.lit.az/.

O'Regan, M. (2016) A Backpacker Habitus: The Body and Dress, Embodiment and the Self. *Annals of Leisure Research*, 19 (3): 329–346.

O'Rourke, D. (Producer and Director) (1987) *Cannibal Tours* [Videotape]. Canberra: O'Rourke and Associates.

Østergaard, J. and Christensen, R. (2010) Walking Towards Oneself: The Authentication of Place and Self, in *Re-Investing Authenticity: Tourism, Place and Emotions*, edited by B. T. Knudsen and A. M. Waade. Bristol: Channel View, pp. 241–253.

Ousby, I. (2002) *The Englishman's England: Taste, Travel and the Rise of Tourism*. London: Pimlico.

Pallasmaa, J. (2005) *The Eyes of the Skin: Architecture and the Senses*. Chichester: Wiley-Blackwell.

———. (2012) *The Eyes of the Skin: Architecture and the Senses*, 3rd ed. Chichester: Wiley-Blackwell.

Palmer, C. (1994) Tourism and Colonialism: The Experience of the Bahamas. *Annals of Tourism Research*, 21 (4): 792–812.

———. (1998) *Heritage Tourism and English National Identity*. Unpublished PhD Thesis, University of North, London.

———. (2003) Touring Churchill's England: Rituals of Kinship and Belonging. *Annals of Tourism Research*, 30 (2): 426–445.

———. (2004) 'More Than Just a Game': The Consequences of Golf Tourism, in *Sport Tourism: Interrelationships, Impacts and Issues*, edited by B. W. Ritchie and D. Adair. Clevedon: Channel View publications, pp. 117–134.

———. (2005) An Ethnography of Englishness: Experiencing Identity Through Tourism. *Annals of Tourism Research*, 32: 7–27.

———. (2009) Reflections on the Practice of Ethnography in Heritage Tourism, in *Heritage Studies: Methods and Approaches*, edited by M-L. S. Sørensen and J. Carman. London: Routledge, pp. 123–139.

Palmer, C. and Lester, J. (2007) Stalking the Cannibals: Photographic Behaviour on the Sepik River. *Tourist Studies*, 7 (1): 83–106.

Palmer, C., Cooper, J. and Burns, P. (2010) Culture, Identity and Belonging in the Culinary Underbelly. *International Journal of Culture, Tourism and Hospitality Research*, 4 (4): 311–326.

Parker Pearson, M. and Richards, C. (eds) (1997) *Architecture and Order: Approaches to Social Space*. London: Routledge.

Pearman, H. (2004) *Airports: A Century of Architecture*. London: Laurence King Publishing.

———. (2008) The Onward Journey. *The Architectural Review*, 224 (1338): 70–73.

Pearce, S. (ed) (1994) *Interpreting Objects and Collections*. London: Routledge.

Pernecky, T. (2010) The Being of Tourism. *The Journal of Tourism and Peace Research*, 1 (1): 1–15.

Pernecky, T. and Jamal, T. (2010) (Hermeneutic) Phenomenology in Tourism Studies. *Annals of Tourism Research*, 37 (4): 1055–1075.

Philipse, H. (1998) *Heidegger's Philosophy of Being: A Critical Interpretation*. Princeton: Princeton University Press.

Picard, D. (2011) *Tourism, Magic and Modernity: Cultivating the Human Garden*: New York and Oxford: Berghahn.

Picard, D. and Di Giovine, M. (2014) Introduction: Through Other Worlds, in *Tourism and the Power of Otherness: Seductions of Difference*, edited by D. Picard and M. Di Giovine. Bristol: Channel View publications, pp. 1–28.

Picard, D. and Robinson, M. (eds) (2012) *Emotion in Motion: Tourism, Affect and Transformation*. Abingdon, Oxon: Routledge.

Picken, F. (2010) Tourism, Design and Controversy: Calling on Non-Humans to Explain Ourselves. *Tourist Studies*, 10 (3): 245–263.

Pink, S. (2008) Sense and Sensibility: The Case of the Slow City Movement. *Local Environment*, 13 (2): 95–106.

Pint, K. (2013) If These Walls Could Walk: Architecture as a Deformative Scenography of the Past, in *Performing Memory in Art and Popular Culture*, edited by L. Plate and A. Smelik. Abingdon, Oxon: Routledge, pp. 123–134.

Polt, R. (1999) *Heidegger: An Introduction*. Abingdon, Oxon: Routledge.

Powles, J. (2005) Embodied Memories: Displacements in Time and Space, in *The Qualities of Time: Anthropological Approaches*, edited by W. James and D. Mills. Oxford: Berg, pp. 331–347.

Pretes, M. (2003) Tourism and Nationalism. *Annals of Tourism Research*, 30 (1): 125–142.

Preziosi, D. and Farago, C. (eds) (2004a) *Grasping the World: The Idea of the Museum*. Aldershot: Ashgate.

———. (eds) (2004b) General Introduction: What Are Museums For? in *Grasping the World: The Idea of the Museum*, edited by D. Preziosi and C. Farago. Aldershot: Ashgate, pp. 1–9.

Pritchard, A. and Morgan, N. (2006) Hotel Babylon? Exploring Hotels as Liminal Sites of Transition and Transgression. *Tourism Management*, 27: 762–772.

Prussin, L. (1995) *African Nomadic Architecture: Space, Place and Gender*. Washington, DC: Smithsonian Institution Press.

Rabinow, P. (2008) *Marking Time: On the Anthropology of the Contemporary*. Princeton: Princeton University Press.

Rakić, T. and Chambers, D. (2012) Rethinking the Consumption of Places. *Annals of Tourism Research*, 39 (3): 1612–1633.

Rassool, C. (2006) Making the District Six Museum in Cape Town. *Museum International*, 58 (1–2): 9–18.

Reisinger, Y. and Steiner, C. J. (2006) Reconceptualizing Object Authenticity. *Annals of Tourism Research*, 33: 65–86.

Ren, C. (2011) Non-Human Agency, Radical Ontology and Tourism Realities. *Annals of Tourism Research*, 38 (3): 858–881.

Richards, V., Pritchard, A. and Morgan, N. (2010) (Re)envisioning Tourism and Visual Impairment. *Annals of Tourism Research*, 37 (4): 1097–1116.

Richardson, M. (1982) Being-in-the-Market Versus Being-in-the-Plaza: Material Culture and the Construction of Social Reality in Spanish America. *American Ethnologist*, 9 (2): 421–436.

Rickley-Boyd, J. M., Knudsen, D. C., Braverman, L. C. and Metro-Roland, M. M. (2014) *Tourism, Performance, and Place: A Geographic Perspective*. Farnham: Ashgate.

Robinson, H. (2009) Digital Heritage: Remembering Things Differently: Museums, Libraries and Archives as Memory Institutions and the Implications for Convergence. *Museum Management and Curatorship*, 27 (4): 431–429.

Robinson, M. and Phipps, A. (2003) Editorial. Worlds Passing by: Journeys of Culture and Cultural Journeys. *Journal of Tourism and Cultural Change*, 1 (1): 1–10.

Rodaway, P. (1994) *Sensuous Geographies: body, sense and place*. London: Routledge.

Rodger, J. (2015) *The Hero Building: An Architecture of Scottish National Identity*. Farnham: Ashgate.

Romaniello, M. P. and Starks, T. (eds) (2016) *Russian History Through the Senses: From 1700 to the Present*. London: Bloomsbury.

Rose, M. (2012) Dwelling as Marking and Claiming. *Environment and Planning D: Society and Space*, 30: 757–771.

Rosler, M. (1997) In the Place of the Public: Observations of a Frequent Flyer, in *Airport: The Most Important Buildings of the Twentieth-Century*, edited by S. Bode and J. Millar. London: The Photographer's Gallery, pp. 89–109.

Rosman, A. and Rubel, P. (1998) Why They Collected: The History of Artifact Collecting in New Ireland. *Museum Anthropology*, 22 (2): 35–49.

Rovelli, C. (2015) *Seven Brief Lessons on Physics*, trans. S. Carnell and E. Segre. London: Penguin.

Ryan, C. (1997) 'The Time of Our Lives' or Time for Our Lives: An Examination of Time in Holidaying, in *The Tourist Experience: A New Introduction*, edited by C. Ryan. London: Cassell, pp. 194–205.

Ryan, C. and Crotts, J. (1997) Carving and Tourism: A Maori Perspective. *Annals of Tourism Research*, 24 (4): 898–918.

Ryan, C. and Huimin, G. (eds) (2009) *Tourism in China, Destination, Cultures and Communities*. New York: Routledge.

Said, E. (2000) Invention, Memory and Place. *Critical Inquiry*, 26: 175–192.

Saldaña, J. (2006) This Is Not a Performance Text. *Qualitative Inquiry*, 12 (6): 1091–1098.
Samuel, R. (1994) *Theatres of Memory*. London: Verso.
Sanad, H., Kassem, A. and Scott, N. (2010) Tourism and Islamic Law, in *Tourism in the Muslim World*, vol. 2, edited by N. Scott and J. Jafari. Bingley: Emerald Publishing, pp. 17–30.
Sandström, K. (2007) The Lived Body – Experiences From Adults With Cerebral Palsy. *Clinical Rehabilitation*, 21: 432–441.
Scannell, P. (2014) *Television and the Meaning of Life*. Cambridge: Polity Press.
Scarles, C. (2009) Becoming Tourist: Renegotiating the Visual in the Tourist Experience. *Environment and Planning D: Society and Space*, 27: 465–488.
———. (2012) Eliciting Embodied Knowledge and Response: Respondent-Led Photography and Autoethnography, in *An Introduction to Visual Research Methods in Tourism*, edited by T. Rakić and D. Chambers. Abingdon, Oxon: Routledge, pp. 70–91.
Schama, S. (2004) *Landscape and Memory*. London: Harper Perennial.
Scheper-Hughes, N. and Lock, M. (1987) The Mindful Body: A Prolegomenon to Future Work in Medical Anthropology. *Medical Anthropology Quarterly (NS)*, 1 (1): 6–41.
Schrock, D. and Boyd, E. (2006) Reflexive Transembodiment, in *Body/Embodiment: Symbolic Interaction and the Sociology of the body*, edited by D. Waskul and P. Vannini. Abingdon, Oxon: Ashgate, Routledge, pp. 51–66.
Schutz, A. (1944) The Stranger: An Essay in Social Psychology. *American Journal of Sociology*, 49 (6): 499–507.
Schwarz, O. (2013) What Should Nature Sound Like? Techniques of Engagement With Nature Sites and Sonic Preferences of Israeli Visitors. *Annals of Tourism Research*, 42: 382–401.
Scott, J. and Selwyn, T. (2010) Introduction: Thinking Through Tourism – Framing the Volume, in *Thinking Through Tourism*, edited by J. Scott and T. Selwyn. Oxford: Berg, pp. 1–25.
Seamon, D. (1979) *A Geography of the Lifeworld*. London: Croom Helm.
———. (2000) A Way of Seeing People and Place: Phenomenology in Environment-Behavior Research, in *Theoretical Perspectives in Environment-Behavior Research*, edited by S. Wapner, J. Demick, T. Yamamoto and H. Minami. New York: Kluwer Academic, Plenum Publishers, pp. 157–178.
Selänniemi, T. (2003) On Holiday in the Liminoid Playground: Place, Time, and Self, in *Sex and Tourism: Journeys of Romance, Love, and Lust*, edited by T. Bauer and B. McKercher. New York: The Haworth Press, pp. 29–31.
Selwyn, T. (1995) Landscapes of Liberation and Imprisonment: Towards an Anthropology of the Israeli Landscape, in *The Anthropology of Landscape: Perspectives on Place and Space*, edited by E. Hirsch and M. O'Hanlon Oxford: Clarendon Press, pp. 114–134.
———. (1996) *The Tourist Image: Myths and Myth Making in Tourism*. Chichester: Wiley-Blackwell
———. (2007) The Political Economy of Enchantment: Formations in the Anthropology of Tourism. *Suomen Antropologi: Journal of the Finnish Anthropological Society*, 32 (2): 48–70.

———. (2010) The Tourist as Juggler in a Hall of Mirrors: Looking Through Images at the Self, in *Culture, Heritage and Representation: Perspectives on Visuality and the Past*, edited by E. Waterton and S. Watson. Farnham: Ashgate, pp. 195–214.

———. (2013) The Self in the World and the World in the Self: The SOAS MA in Anthropology of Travel, Tourism, and Pilgrimage. *Journal of Tourism Challenges and Trends*, 6 (2): 95–125.

Seremetakis, C. N. (1996a) Contexts, in *The Senses Still: Perception and Memory as Material Culture in Modernity*, edited by C. N. Seremetakis. Chicago: University of Chicago Press, pp. vii–xi.

———. (1996b) The Memory of the Senses, Part I: Marks of the Transitory, in *The Senses Still: Perception and Memory as Material Culture in Modernity*, edited by C. N. Seremetakis. Chicago: University of Chicago Press, pp. 1–18.

———. (1996c) The Memory of the Senses, Part II: Still Acts, in *The Senses Still: Perception and Memory as Material Culture in Modernity*, edited by C. N. Seremetakis. Chicago: University of Chicago Press, pp. 23–44.

Serres, M. (1995) *Angels: A Modern Myth*, trans. F. Cowper. Paris: Flammarion.

———. (2008) *The Five Senses: A Philosophy of Mingled Bodies*, trans. M. Sankey and P. Cowley. London: Continuum.

Shannon, K. (2009) Evolving Tourist Topographies: The Case of Hue, Vietnam, in *Travel, Space, Architecture*, edited by J. Traganou and M. Mitrašinović. Franham: Ashgate, pp. 230–250.

Sharr, A. (2007) *Heidegger for Architects*. London: Routledge.

Shaw, G. B. (1946) *Saint Joan*. London: Penguin.

Sheffer, G. (2006) *Diaspora Politics: At Home Abroad*. Cambridge: Cambridge University Press.

Sheller, M. and Urry, J. (eds) (2004) *Tourism Mobilities: Places to Play, Places in Play*. London: Routledge.

———. (2006) The New Mobilities Paradigm. *Environment and Planning A*, 38: 207–226.

Shelton, A. (2011) Museums and Anthropologies: Practices and Narratives, in *A Companion to Museum Studies*, edited by S. Macdonald. Chichester: Wiley-Blackwell, pp. 64–80.

Shepherd, R. (2015) Why Heidegger Did Not Travel: Existential Angst, Authenticity, and Tourist Experiences. *Annals of Tourism Research*, 52: 60–71.

Shilling, C. (2003) *The Body and Social Theory*, 2nd ed. London: Sage.

Short, J. R. (1991) *Imagined Country: Environment, Culture and Society*. London: Routledge.

Singh, T. V. (ed) (2012) *Critical Debates in Tourism*. Bristol: Channel View Publications.

Sinha, C., Sinha, V., Zinken, J. and Sampaio, W. (2011) When Time Is Not Space: The Social and Linguistic Construction of Time Intervals and Temporal Event Relations in an Amazonian Culture. *Language and Cognition*, 3 (1): 137–169.

Sinha, V., Sinha, C., Sampaio, W. and Zinken, J. (2012) Even-Based Time Intervals in Amazonian Culture, in *Space and Time in Languages and Cultures: Language, Culture and Cognition*, edited by L. Filipović and K. Jaszczolt. Amsterdam: John Benjamins Publishing, pp. 15–35.

Skinner, J. (2007) Emotional Baggage: The Meaning/Feeling Debate Amongst Tourists, in *The Emotions: A Cultural Reader*, edited by H. Wulff. Oxford: Berg, pp. 339–353.

———. (2016) Walking the Falls: Dark Tourism and the Significance of Movement on the Political Tour of West Belfast. *Tourist Studies*, 16 (1): 23–39.

Skinner, J. and Theodossopoulos, D. (2011) Introduction: The Play of Expectation in Tourism, in *Great Expectations: Imagination and Anticipation in Tourism*, edited by J. Skinner and D. Theodossopoulos. London: Berghahn, pp. 1–26.

Small, J. (2016) The Experience of Time in Long-Term Travel. *Tourism Geographies*, 18 (4): 341–358.

Small, J. and Darcy, S. (2011) Understanding Tourist Experience Through Embodiment, in *Accessible Tourism: Concepts and Issues*, edited by D. Buhalis and S. Darcy. Bristol: Channel View publications, pp. 73–97.

Small, J., Packer, T. and Darcy, S. (2012) The Embodied Tourist Experiences of People With Vision Impairment: Management Implications Beyond the Visual Gaze. *Tourism Management*, 33: 941–950.

Smith, A. (1991) *National Identity*. London: Penguin.

Smith, M. and Kelly, C. (2006) Holistic Tourism: Journeys of the Self? *Tourism Recreation Research*, 31 (1): 15–24.

Solnit, R. (2002) *Wanderlust: A History of Walking*. London: Verso.

Somerset, A. (1997) *Elizabeth 1*. London: Phoenix, Orion Books.

Sommer, A-L. (2010) Nature Choreographed, in *The Humanities in Architectural Design: A Contemporary and Historical Perspective*, edited by J. Lomholt, N. Temple and R. Tobe. Abingdon, Oxon: Routledge, pp. 226–236.

Starkey, D. (1998) *Henry V111*. Channel 4 Television, 29th March.

———. (2001) *Elizabeth: Apprenticeship*. London: Vintage Books.

Stein, R. (2008) *Itineraries in Conflict: Israelis, Palestinians and the Political Lives of Tourism*. Durham, NC: Duke University Press.

Steiner, G. (1989) *Martin Heidegger*, with a new introduction. Chicago: University of Chicago Press.

Steiner, C. J. and Reisinger, Y. (2006a) Understanding Existential Authenticity. *Annals of Tourism Research*, 33 (2): 299–318.

———. (2006b) Ringing the Fourfold: A Philosophical Framework for Thinking About Wellness Tourism. *Tourism Recreation Research*, 31 (1): 5–14.

Stephenson, M. (2004) Tourism, Racism and the UK Afro-Caribbean Diaspora, in *Tourism, Diasporas and Space*, edited by T. Coles and D. J. Timothy. London: Routledge, pp. 62–77.

Stocking, G. (1987) *Victorian Anthropology*. Oxford: Maxwell Macmillan.

Stokes-Rees, E. (2013) Making Sense of a Mélange: Representing Cultural Citizenship in Singapore's Asian Civilisations Museum. *Museum Anthropology*, 36 (1): 33–50.

Stoller, P. (1984) Sound in Songhay Cultural Experience. *American Ethnologist*, 11 (3): 559–570.

———. (1989) *The Taste of Ethnographic Things: The Senses in Anthropology*. Philadelphia: University of Pennsylvania Press.

Strathern, M. (1982) The Village as an Idea: Constructs of Village-Ness in Elmdon, Essex, in *Belonging: Identity and Social Organisation in British Rural Cultures*, edited by A. P. Cohen. Manchester: Manchester University Press, pp. 247–277.

———. (1992) *After Nature: English Kinship in the Late Twentieth Century*. Manchester: Manchester University Press.

Stretch, E. (2014) Floods Stormageddon – An Englishman's Home Is His Castle as Builder Makes a Moat Round £1m Home. *The Mirror* [online], 7th February. Available at: www.mirror.co.uk/news/uk-news/floods-stormageddon – englishmans-home-3123425 [accessed 30th June 2014].

Sykes, N. (1953) *The English Religious Tradition*. London: SCM Press.

Tan, C-B., Cheung, S. and Hui, Y. (eds) (2001) *Tourism, Anthropology and China: Studies in Asian Tourism*, no. 1. Bangkok: White Lotus Press.

Taussig, M. (1990) Violence and Resistance in the Americas: The Legacy of Conquest. *Journal of Historical Sociology*, 3 (3): 209–224.

———. (1992) *The Nervous System*. London: Routledge.

Taylor, P. J. (2001) Which Britain? Which England, Which North? in *British Cultural Identities*, edited by D. Morley and K. Robbins. Oxford: Oxford University Press, pp. 127–144.

Terry, A. (2013) Gender, Canadian Nationhood and 'Keeping House': The Cultural Bureaucratisation of Dundurn Castle in Hamilton, Ontario, 1900–1960s. *Gender & History*, 25 (1): 47–64.

Thomas, J. (1999) *Time, Culture & Identity: An Interpretive Archaeology*. London: Routledge.

Tilley, C. (2009) What Gardens Mean, in *Material Culture and Technology in Everyday Life: Ethnographic Approaches*, edited by P. Vannini. New York: Peter Lang, pp. 171–192.

Tilley, C. and Cameron-Daum, K. (2017) *An Anthropology of Landscape*. London: UCL Press.

Timms, B. and Conway, D. (2012) Slow Tourism at the Caribbean's Geographical Margins. *Tourism Geographies*, 14 (3): 396–418.

Trant, J. (2009) Emerging Convergence? Thoughts on Museums, Archives, Libraries, and Professional Training. *Museum Management and Curatorship*, 24 (4): 369–387.

Tsintjilonis, D. (2006) Monsters and Cariacatures: Spirit Possession in Tana Toraja. *Journal of the Royal Anthropological Institute (NS)*, 12: 551–567.

Tuan, Y-F. (1977) *Space and Place: The Perspective of Experience*. Minneapolis: University of Minnesota Press.

———. (2005) Architecture, Route to Transcendence, in *Architourism*, edited by J. Ockman and S. Frausto. Munich: Prestel Publishing, pp. 118–121.

Tucker, H. (2003) *Living With Tourism: Negotiating Identities in a Turkish Village*. London: Routledge.

Turner, B. S. (1996) *The Body and Society: Explorations in Social Theory*, 2nd ed. London: Sage.

———. (2008) *The Body and Society: Explorations in Social Theory*, 3rd ed. London: Sage.

Turner, V. W. (1974) *Dramas, Fields and Metaphors: Symbolic Action in Human Society*. New York: Cornell University Press.

———. (1978) Encounter With Freud: The Making of a Comparative Symbologist, in *The Making of Psychological Anthropology*, edited by G. D. Spindler. Berkeley: University of California Press, pp. 558–583.

———. (1982) *From Ritual to Theatre: The Human Seriousness of Play*. New York: Performing Arts Journal Publication.

Turner, V. W. and Bruner, E. M. (eds) (1986) *The Anthropology of Experience.* Urbana: University of Illinois Press.

Urban Adventures. (2017) Available at: www.urbanadventures.com/delhi-tour-gandhi-s-delhi [accessed 1st June 2017].

Urry, J. (2000) *Sociology Beyond Societies: Mobilities for the Twenty-First Century.* London: Routledge.

———. (2007) *Mobilities.* Cambridge: Polity Press.

———. (2009) Aeromobilities and the Global, in *Aeromobilities*, edited by S. Cwerner, S. Kesselring and J. Urry. London: Routledge, pp. 25–38.

Vale, L. J. (1992) *Architecture, Power, and National Identity.* New Haven: Yale University Press.

van Uffelen, C. (2012) *Airport Architecture.* Berlin: Braun.

Vannini, P. (2012) *Ferry Tales: Mobility, Place, and Time on Canada's West Coast.* New York: Routledge.

Vannini, P. and Vannini, A. (2016) *Wilderness.* Abingdon, Oxon: Routledge.

Veijola, S. and Jokinen, E. (1994) The Body in Tourism. *Theory, Culture & Society*, 11: 125–151.

Vertovec, S. (2004) Religion and Diaspora, in *New Approaches to the Study of Religion: Volume 2*, edited by P. Antes, A. Geertz and R. Warne. Berlin: Walter de Gruyter, pp. 275–304.

Victoria and Albert Museum. (2016) London. Available at: www.vam.ac.uk/content/exhibitions/disobedient-objects/disobedient-objects-about-the-exhibition/ [accessed 25th May 2016].

Virilio, P. (1994) *Bunker Archaeology*, trans. G. Collins. New York: Princeton Architectural Press.

Visit Berlin. (2017) Available at: www.visitberlin.de/en/checkpoint-charlie [accessed 29th June 2017].

Visit England. (2017) Available at: www.visitengland.com/things-to-do/heritage#south%20east%20england&heritage [accessed 1st June 2017].

Wagner, R. (1981) *The Invention of Culture*, revised and expanded ed. Chicago: University of Chicago Press.

Walsh, K. (1992) *The Representation of the Past: Museums and Heritage in the Post-Modern World.* London: Routledge.

Wang, N. (1999) Rethinking Authenticity in Tourism Experience. *Annals of Tourism Research*, 26 (2): 349–370.

Waterson, R. (1997[1990]) *The Living House: An Anthropology of Architecture in South-East Asia.* London: Thames and Hudson.

Waterton, E. and Watson, S. E. (eds) (2010) *Culture, Heritage and Representation: Perspectives on Visuality and the Past.* Farnham: Ashgate.

Wearing, S., Stevenson, D. and Young, T. (2010) *Tourist Cultures: Identity, Place and the Traveller.* London: Sage.

Weiner, A. (1985) Inalienable Wealth. *American Ethnologist*, 12 (2): 210–227.

Weiner, J. F. (2001) *Tree Leaf Talk: A Heideggerian Anthropology.* Oxford: Berg.

Weir, A. (2002) *Henry VIII: King and Court.* London: Pimlico.

Weiss, E. (2010) Establishing Roots at Israel's Ben Gurion Airport Garden: Landscapes of National Identity. *National Identities*, 12 (2): 199–210.

Wendell, S. (1996) *The Rejected Body: Feminist Philosophical Reflections on Disability.* New York: Routledge.

White, C. J. (2005) *Time and Death: Heidegger's Analysis of Finitude*, edited by M. A. Ralkowski, Forward by H. L. Dreyfus. Aldershot: Ashgate.
Wierzbicka, A. (2008) Why There Are No 'Colour Universals' in Language and Thought. *Journal of the Royal Anthropological Society (N.S.)*, 14 (2): 407–425.
Willerslev, R. (2007) *Soul Hunters: Hunting, Animism, and Personhood Among the Siberian Yukaghirs*. Berkeley: University of California Press.
Willett, F. (1994) Museums: Two Case Studies of Reaction to Colonialism, in *The Politics of the Past*, edited by P. Gathercole and D. Lowenthal. London: Routledge, pp. 172–183.
Winter, T. (2007) *Post-Conflict Heritage, Postcolonial Tourism: Culture, Politics and Development at Angkor*. Abingdon, Oxon: Routledge.
———. (2009) Asian Tourism and the Retreat of Anglo-Western Centrism in Tourism Theory. *Current Issues in Tourism*, 12 (1): 21–31.
Winter, T., Teo, P. and Chang, T. C. (eds) (2008) *Asia on Tour: Exploring the Rise of Asian Tourism*. Abingdon, Oxon: Routledge.
Wittgenstein, L. (1980) *Culture and Value*, 2nd ed, edited by G. H. von Wright, G. and H. Nyman, trans. P. Winch. Oxford: Blackwell.
Wolin, R. (2016[1990]) *The Politics of Being: The Political Thought of Martin Heidegger*. New York: Columbia University Press.
Woodward, I. (2001) Domestic Objects and the Taste Epiphany: A Resource for Consumption Methodology. *Journal of Material Culture*, 6: 115–136.
———. (2009) Material Culture and Narrative: Fusing Myth, Materiality, and Meaning, in *Material Culture and Technology in Everyday Life: Ethnographic Approaches*, edited by P. Vannini. New York: Peter Lang, pp. 59–72.
Wright, P. (1985) *On Living in an Old Country*. London: Verso.
Wright, S., Suchet-Pearson, S., Lloyd, K., Burarrwanga, L. L. and Burarrwanga, D. (2009) 'That Means the Fish Are Fat': Sharing Experiences of Animals Through Indigenous-Owned Tourism. *Current Issues in Tourism*, 12 (5–6): 505–527.
Young, I. M. (1980) Throwing Like a Girl: A Phenomenology of Feminine Body. Comportment Motility and Spatiality. *Human Studies*, 3 (2): 137–156.

Index

Printed in the United States
by Baker & Taylor Publisher Services